STUFF OF SLEEP AND DREAMS

4520

LEON EDEL

Stuff of Sleep and Dreams

EXPERIMENTS
IN LITERARY PSYCHOLOGY

1817

HARPER & ROW, PUBLISHERS, New York
Cambridge, Philadelphia, San Francisco, London
Mexico City, São Paulo, Sydney

Library of Congress Cataloging in Publication Data

Edel, Leon, 1907–
  Stuff of sleep and dreams.
  Includes bibliographical references and index.
  1. English literature—History and criticism. 2. Authors, English—Psychology.
  3. American literature—History and criticism. 4. Authors, American—Psychology. 5. Psychology and literature. I. Title.
PR408.P83E3 1982   820'.9'353   81–47787
ISBN 0–06–014929–9   AACR2

---

82 83 84 85 86 10 9 8 7 6 5 4 3 2 1

For Marjorie

O body swayed to music, O brightening glance,
How can we know the dancer from the dance?

We are such stuff
As dreams are made on . . .
The Tempest

Stuff of sleep and dreams, and yet my Reason
at the Rudder.
COLERIDGE, *Notebooks*

CONTENTS

PART IV

FOREWORD

We know that all literature is a form of disguise, a mask, a fable, a mystery: and behind the mask is the author. The questions I ask in this book—and attempt to answer in various ways—are psychological questions. Some of them may seem a bit frivolous and flighty. Why did Thoreau *really* go to Walden Pond? Why did Tolstoy preach abstinence from tobacco and sex to his peasants and then light a cigarette in his study and go to bed with his wife? Or why did Rex Stout, with his kingly name, create a stout detective who had the name of an emperor? Simple and curious little inquiries can sometimes lead us into complex webs of being, emotional explosions, and fascinating biographical insights. Sherlock Holmes used to solve his crimes by assembling bits of circumstantial evidence: a spot on a suit, some mud on a boot, or a series of strange incidents. There are equally important bits of psychological evidence in the writings of literary folk—the words they use, the slips they make, the images they conjure up—which are quite as important as any circumstantial evidence we might find.

I have written this book at various times during three decades as a series of "experiments" told in various biographical narratives. Some were published in literary and psychological journals and have now been revised, rewritten, and enlarged by commentaries and "afterwords." Others—at least five of these papers—have been written expressly for this book to enlarge my general thesis: that literary study (that is, biography and criticism) can no longer afford to close its eyes and look away from psychological truths in literary works: they are a part of the truths sought in literary criticism and in biography. I have called the application of this new and modern body of information about human nature, personality, character, and motivation "literary psychology," to distinguish it from the other psychologies that are concerned with treating the neuroses and pathological conditions of mental health. In other words, literary psychology is criticism and biography divorced from psychotherapy. We do not "put literature on the couch," as some claim. We can't, in reality, and if we could, we shouldn't.

Readers will notice that the central part of my book deals with art and depression—that melancholy which inspired a great ode by Keats and a vast "anatomy" by Burton. Benjamin Rush, America's original psychiatrist (who also signed the Declaration of Independence), called depression "tristimania"—a term I find useful even if perhaps unscientific. I believe that the various forms of artistic despair, the depressions that nurtured Virginia Woolf's art or someone's as recent as Robert Lowell's, need continuous and careful study on the literary side: their works represent a brilliant triumph over illness.

And then I have thought it useful to include certain memories here: my chance meeting with Yeats, my observations of Joyce in Paris from 1928 to 1932, and, most important of all, the account of my journey to Vienna, where I first discovered psychology when I was a young man and met Alfred Adler. This account, together with my study of James Joyce's "psychopathology" and T. S. Eliot's struggle against inertia of the will, is among my new narratives. Slightly earlier is my discussion of the nature of psychological evidence. I have not included certain papers I contributed to various psychological and psychoanalytical books and journals, since their substance has been transferred into the discussions in these pages. But perhaps I should say that I have used in various places parts of my original essay "Psychoanalysis and the Creative Arts," published in Dr. Judd Marmor's *Modern Psychoanalysis* (1968, pages 626–41);

and my contribution to the late Dr. Silvano Arieti's major compendium, his *American Handbook of Psychiatry,* which constitutes Chapter 47, "Literature and Psychiatry" (pages 1024–33); and my long essay on literature and psychology in the *Encyclopedia of World Literature in the 20th Century* (vol. 3, 1971) and the earlier version of it in *Comparative Literature* (1961). There are sundry other papers, like my study of biography and psychoanalysis published in the *International Journal of Psychoanalysis* (13 [1961], nos. 4–5, pages 458–66), which belong more properly to what I hope will be my collected papers on biography. The present volume can be said to comprise my collected papers in literary psychology, or all that I wish to preserve out of my numerous writings in this field.

I wish in particular to thank the Rockefeller Foundation for a sojourn at its Bellagio Study and Conference Center at Lake Como in Italy, where during the autumn of 1980 I found ideal conditions for the writing of my difficult paper on T. S. Eliot's "abulia" and where I also completed the account of my journey to Vienna and a portion of my paper on Coleridge and Dickens. I am grateful also to Jean Strouse for rereading my paper on Alice James and making some helpful suggestions after publication of her biography of this singular woman. A certain amount of this material has appeared in the *American Scholar,* particularly some of the Joyce memories. My principal sources and the provenance of the various papers is given in the notes at the back.

L.E.

A Mini-Lexicon for This Book

Psychology: That biological science which studies the phenomena of conscious life and behavior, in their origin, development, and manifestations.

Psychiatry: The specialized study of mental and nervous disorders, sometimes including psychopathology and some branches of psychology.

Psychoanalysis: A system of psychology and a method of treatment of emotional problems and mental and nervous disorders, developed originally by Sigmund Freud and since much expanded and modernized. It involves a dynamic view of all aspects of mental life but is profoundly concerned with unconscious as well as conscious experience. An elaborate technique of investigation is employed which attempts constantly to use verbalized memories and "free" association.

Literary Psychology: The adaptation of psychology and psychoanalytic concepts to the study of mankind's ability to create and use myths and symbols, in essence a study—without therapeutic purpose—of what literature *expresses* of the human being who creates it.

I

A Journey to Vienna

Stuff of Sleep and Dreams

The Nature of Psychological Evidence

A JOURNEY TO VIENNA

Half a century ago, in 1930, in the confident world of my youth and the time between wars, I set out on a journey into the big embracing world. One sets out—that much one knows—and the rest is unpredictable. I was a student and lived very much for the moment. With my reddish beard, my bohemian-intellectual nature, my small bundle of clothes, my little bundle of culture—and a few francs—I felt I could travel to the ends of the earth. But I confined myself to a Rhine journey by boat and third-class carriage. I went in quest of—I would be hard put to say what. One was supposed simply to see the world. I was ready to plunge into anything; I was rather ignorant. I wanted to look at scenery, cities, people, museums; and I was hungry for music. I was, in short, a rather aesthetic young man.

Today I would have to say I was a square, brought up to lingering Victorian ways, mind over body. Of the instinctual things, of more intimate relations with men and women, particularly women, the deeper soundings of passion with either sex, I couldn't have known less. I had been brought up like so many of my generation to vague storybook things and the traditional virtues. I was young, vigorous, ambitious, and not without certain residual anxieties of adolescence. Women used to smile at me. I used to smile back. Nothing happened. I did nothing to make something happen. At concerts charming young men used to speak to me, but I recognized none of their signals. I must have been a very disappointing fellow. It was only later that I came to understand the never-never-land of my younger years. They might be summarized as a kind of blundering into life. My little journeys were innocent, lonely, artistic, anxious, and rather mindless. Behind my bohemian air and general alertness, my sophisticated and well-trimmed beard and my accumulated folklore of art, there was still the face of a literate Huck Finn, a boy from the prairies bound to my early provincialities and virginities.

That summer I traveled first on the Rhine steamer and looked at little castles later so inspiring to Disney; I was surprised at their smallness, and they stood in a landscape that seemed tame. They had seemed much more enchanting in storybooks and the book about operas. I then drifted to Munich, where I ate sausage and drank beer, looked at Breughels, and heard *Don Giovanni* for the first time at the municipal opera house. I melted into the music rather than into the life of the streets. In that city, given my dream state, I got no sense that trouble was brewing. I subscribed to Keynes's view that the Treaty of Versailles had been an abomination, without understanding how it had become, in Hitler's hands, a tool for his neo-napoleonic ambitions. I later remembered ominous signs—but I had not been equipped to read them. In a German pension, a few weeks earlier, I sat at table with assorted travelers and listened to a peevish thin-faced man, referred to as the Count, snarl at a florid fat ex-army captain—a Fascist snarling at a Nazi. As their voices rose, I was struck by the agitation of the landlady out of her massive mounds of flesh. She ladled soup swimming with grease and in a rich sad pleading voice said, "Gentlemen, gentlemen, please, no politics, remember, we agreed, no politics at the table." But the debate was too heated to stop and there continued to be spasmodic flare-ups. This should have been a primary lesson in what was to come. It would take time to sink in; indeed, I remember it only through historic hindsight. I had been reared to the world's gentilities, not to horrors.

While I was in Munich I read about the Passion Play at Oberammergau which was being given that year. I bought a ticket and took the train into the Bavarian Alps with a horde of tourists. In the crowded village I was assigned to one of the private houses and slept in a soft down-filled bed amid compulsive German cleanliness and German clichés. My angular big-boned landlady proudly displayed her young son, who had a walk-on part in the play. He autographed a picture postcard of himself as if he were the star. On a day of great summer's beauty, when the air was soft and cool, I sat in the theater under the big girders and the open blue sky as villagers and peasants reincarnated the epochal journey from Bethlehem to the Cross. I experienced moments of strong emotion as well as moments of rustic show biz, for the peasant play was done with simplicity and sincerity and much devotion but contained strange worldly touches. To a brash irreligious outsider like myself, there were moments of silent laughter—not least when during the Crucifixion I became aware that the Christ of Alois Lang was attired in what looked very much like a pair of pink tights. The birds twittered all day high above the theater, and the sun provided natural lighting from its early morning brightness to the stretching shadows of the late afternoon. It was strange to emerge at sundown, having lived through Death and Resurrection, to drink steins of beer in a smoke-filled tavern amid the clacking of wooden shoes and spirited yodeling.

From Oberammergau I started for Vienna, but learning of the Salzburg festival I stopped in that lethargic mountain town to pay homage to Mozart. I found a room in a private house with a stout matron for landlady, who put me into a bedroom filled with heavy furniture suited for large stout people. I felt very small in it, but she was kind and her prices were reasonable. She brought me a cup of chocolate every morning and some heavy rye bread. I wandered among tourists and sat in cafés but made no conversation with strangers. I saw two operas, Gluck's *Iphigénie* conducted by Bruno Walter and a rousing performance of *Rosenkavalier* conducted by Clemens Krauss. I had a heavy evening of Bruckner, and some Beethoven, and I heard

Mozart serenades played by candlelight in the big square before the archiepiscopal palace. I went also to two plays produced by the reigning genius of the theater, Max Reinhardt. I
am struck now, looking back at my twenty-two-year-old self, by
my penchant for transcendant things, for I witnessed that summer not only the unpolished theatricals of the villagers telling
the story of Christ but also the consummate theatricalities of
Reinhardt retelling the story of Everyman in front of the Salzburg cathedral, an eighteenth-century imitation of St. Peter's in
Rome. From watching the ascent of Christ, I was spectator to
the descent of *Jedermann*. Reinhardt staged his play using all
the resources of the long wide square: unearthly voices from
pinnacles and towers, unearthly music from within the church.
The feasters were arrayed before us at the hour of sunset, with
Death in attendance at the feast. The allegories of life and death
were illuminated by the declining August sun. Everyman was
acted by Alexander Moissi, with beautiful intensity: I thrilled to
his voice, the light in his eyes, his fears, his terrors as Death
suddenly rose behind him. But death to me, in my insouciant
youth, was mainly a word, like sex, and I felt much more the
"theater" in the play than its profound humanity. Reinhardt
used a mountain, an entire cathedral, and a broad town square
as setting. By the time it was over and Everyman was stepping
into his grave, accompanied by his Good Deeds, it seemed as if
Max Reinhardt had even commandeered the sun to provide the
final fading of the lights, gilding the towers from which I had
heard earlier the reverberating ghostly summons to *Jedermann*
—to his fate and ultimate separation from the world of men.
Night—dark, unfathomable—swallowed him up.

But the sun rose again brightly the next morning and I traveled on to Vienna, which had once been a city of light but was
now the dying capital of a dismembered empire. Today, if I
were on my way to Vienna, I would know myself bound for the
city of Freud. In 1930, however, the name of Freud did not

cross my mind. I thought instead of the bewhiskered Franz Josef, whose face I had seen on postage stamps as a boy. I thought of Johann Strauss. But there was little music for me to hear in Vienna: the opera was closed; all the musicians were in Salzburg. I visited St. Stephen's and sundry *ratskellers.* I enjoyed lolling in the cafés drinking chocolate or coffee surmounted with *Schlagsahne,* reading the newspapers automatically delivered to me by bulky obsequious waiters while little string ensembles played waltzes. I studied the Viennese women; so many of them seemed like Valkyries in their well-proportioned massiveness and elegance. I admired them as one admires sculptures at a museum.

I had been asked by two English students (brothers, with whom I had lived in London in a flat at the top of Regent's Park) to look up their elder sister. She was studying piano with Artur Schnabel, and I dutifully telephoned her, expecting she would think me an irrelevant intruder. But she was friendly and joined me for a drink and took me to Schoenbrunn, the summer palace of the faded empire. Did we sit at a little table and drink beer in front of formal gardens? Some such image lingers in my memory, during which this sedate Englishwoman listened patiently to my chatter about Salzburg and my account of life in London with her younger brothers. She mentioned, in passing, that she was attending an interesting seminar for foreign students being given by the renowned Dr. Alfred Adler, a disciple of Freud. I was up to date on that; the papers always spoke of Dr. Adler as if he had invented low self-esteem. "Oh," I said, "the inferiority complex!" My companion rejoined, "Yes, if you wish, but he calls it 'individual psychology.' " Then she had an afterthought. "Would you like to meet the old boy? He's really very nice and gentle and doesn't at all mind having visitors." This seemed to me a very sociable idea; a psychological afternoon in Vienna seemed as appropriate as a night at the Viennese opera. How was I to know this would be a prime initiation?

Dr. Adler received me with American informality, but it had

in it a certain European courtliness. He put me at ease among
the group of medical students, psychiatrists, and clinical work-
ers who had come from many countries. He gave the seminar
in English, in a well-lighted room in his apartment. Adler was
chubby and wore a wisp of a mustache, so that I associated him
with Oliver Hardy. He had bright inquiring eyes, but at first
glance I thought of him as the Germanic Herr-Doktor-Profes-
sor. His personality changed from the moment he began to talk;
he spoke with eagerness and enthusiasm and seemed in full
command of all he said. I liked his authority and his vitality. I
have just looked through some old letters, but they are not
enlightening. My memories are better than my flat declaration
on 31 August 1930 (I was twenty-two):

> I went to Adler's seminar in the afternoon and in the evening sat
> with him and his followers at the Café Siller. I learned more in my
> week in Wien about "individual psychology" and Adler's common-
> sense school than I could have learned following a college course for
> four years. His disciples fairly live and breathe "individual psychol-
> ogy."

Those few evenings at the Café Siller in the soft sound-filled
night beside the Danube remain with me as strange overtones
of feeling. I found them rich in the sense of the traditional
professorial *Stammtisch* and its relaxed geniality. We were a
polyglot group. Here Adler, on most evenings of his seminar,
met his students, outside the formality of his teaching. But he
maintained some formalities: that first evening he politely
seated me on his left in my role as guest from another discipline.
He addressed himself in a very professional way to questioning
me. My own inferiority complex made me wonder self-con-
sciously why he bothered. I wasn't a clinician, I wasn't a psychologist; I was just a "literary" man with a Parisian Latin Quarter façade, who had published nothing. He asked what I was
studying at the Sorbonne. I told him I worked in "comparative
literature." Fishing for conversation, I asked him in turn (hav-

ing read nothing on the subject) whether individual psychology might be helpful to someone like myself. He proceeded to explain "applied psychoanalysis" to me; if I wanted to be a biographer or critic I had to look at some of the material clinicians examined. What were a writer's personal relations, his family relations? How did he set about his career?

Alfred Adler was sixty when I met him, and near the end of his active life. He would die in exile seven years later, his life broken by Hitlerian *Anschluss.* He had founded his school of psychology as an offshoot of Freud, on the eve of the first war, and established the first child guidance clinics in the Vienna school system. I met some staff members of these clinics, who explained to me the general basis for Adlerian psychology. I see now that Adler had been less concerned with general theory than his celebrated master and was much more interested in clinical immediacies. His observations led him to significant speculations on how human beings use power. He was interested—no doubt out of deep personal experience—in the universal struggle of men and women to escape from an anonymous world. It takes an intimate closeness to the life process— that is, an awareness of the small round of daily existence—or, at the other extreme, a serene philosophical mind, to accept God's hard existential conditions. Few want to understand the process of Everyman—that is, of living and dying—or our emergence from private worlds into the private worlds of others. We find it unbelievable that some day Death must visit us in the midst of feast or starvation.

So Adler, observing the active drives, compulsions, defenses, the whole great question of "survival," evolved a belief that humans strive for some kind of superiority, some manner of power, some way of self-exaltation; anonymity is a kind of death, whether they live lower- or middle-class lives or have been brutalized by feudal systems. He had started as a botanist, I believe, and one of his assistants explained to me that very early he had been struck by the way some saplings in the center of the forest grow to great heights to reach sunlight, while others are extinguished in the general crush. Adler spoke beyond such simplifications; he talked of the individual carrying the imprint of his society, but he did not accept altogether Freud's insistence that civilization is achieved by repression of our barbarisms and by controls in the ego. In some such way, Adler was led to proclaim his "individual psychology"—trying to understand individual life-styles rather than moldings from universal patterns. The opinions we as individuals hold of ourselves, as well as the society and the world around us, were at the heart of Adlerian psychology.

He paid attention accordingly to such psychic disorders as exist among individuals who feel themselves unequal in the world and esteem themselves lower than others. Low self-esteem breeds anxiety, fear, excessive timidity, and a burden of guilt; it fosters rage and frustration, exaggerated competitiveness, and often concomitant violence. Adler was among the earliest to ask therapists to pay attention to "organ dialect" in an individual—a kind of prophet of biofeedback therapy. He theorized that a single defective organ, a heart or kidney condition or a liver ailment, had its effect on the psyche and made patients feel they were inferior in natural and physical endowment to others. And all these considerations were encapsulated in the human struggle for power, even among the powerless, who feed their days with dreams of glory. Biographers, he told me, need to remind themselves constantly of the nature of the human struggle for some form of human expression and self-assertion. He was particularly illuminating about the struggle between siblings in a given family.

Those evenings at the Café Siller, with our coffee or chocolate and the toppings of whipped cream and Viennese pastries, the atmosphere created by a dignified yet informal fatherly shepherd amid his little flock, the awe in which students and clinicians stood of the pleasant, amiable, sweetly reasonable man, the questions and answers and small talk—I suddenly felt myself in the midst of a high civilization. When I returned to Paris a few days later, the first thing I did was to buy some French translations of various psychological works; in particular, I said to myself that I had to gain some understanding of Freud. It was the beginning of my explorations: I still have a little blue-covered French paperback containing three of Freud's essays on infantile sexuality.

Many years would elapse before the lesson of Vienna—and this little moment with Alfred Adler—would be learned. Other things had to be lived through: a depression, another war, the century's malaise, my own malaise of aging amid personal and societal uncertainties. But bit by bit, as I began to write and publish, I found myself using my ever-increasing knowledge of the psychology we have learned in modern times. After a while I came to believe that we can hardly write a line without informing ourselves of the promptings unveiled for us in the psychoanalytic study of the imagination. They lie close to the heart of all literary creation.

STUFF OF SLEEP
AND DREAMS

The seed had been planted during my youthful journey, and with the passing years (and much personal history) it ultimately took deep root. I was led, by my own searches, into the practice of what I have named "literary psychology": the study of what literature expresses of the human being who creates it. The experiments contained in this volume came into being during the three decades after my return from the second war. Rereading them, I have been struck by the few simple themes they develop. The idea that animates them is that a literary work is never impersonal. It is a profound act of metamorphosis in which writers most often assume masks of the impersonal, very much as in the disguises of sleep we tend to depersonalize many of our dreams and even pretend we are not their authors. T. S. Eliot described this as "the struggle which alone constitutes life for a poet—to transmute his personal and private agonies into something rich and strange, something universal and impersonal."

Yeats's famous and inspired question "How can we know the dancer from the dance?" touches the heart of our problem. In the act of dancing, the dancer and the dance are doubtless one. At least we have an illusion of unity and singleness. But the reality remains that there is both a dancer and a dance—a poet and a poem, a novelist and a novel, a playwright and a play—even a biographer and a biography. Yeats himself, in the line that precedes his question, evokes a body "swayed to music, O brightening glance." The body becomes the dance; the dance

becomes the body; but within the transmutation of veils or
costume and the physical swaying, within the motions and actions and tossings of the head and particular use of limbs when
the dancer, so to speak, throws dust in our eyes, we still retain
a sense of a human entity performing in time and space—as
we hear the poet's voice or the voice of a storyteller within
the poem or story. What is expressed in poetry is not only the
recorded poem or a given text or sound or plasticity but the
intimate message within the text, in which an artist seems to
say, Listen to me, marvel at what I do, it is all magical—as when
Milton's character of Samson in that classic drama proclaims the
darkness of noon and in the memorable line "Dark, dark, dark
. . ." expresses also the fact and the anguish of Milton's own
blindness. Personal emotion drives the seemingly impersonal
statement, and some part of this emotion is conveyed to us. We
may not unravel the mystery of the metamorphosis, but we
recognize that it exists, for in modern times very little art has
sought anonymity. To recognize this is to go beyond creation
into all that is most characteristic and individual in the given
creator.

The first and perhaps greatest literary psychologist in English
literature was Samuel Taylor Coleridge (1772–1834), whose casual exclamation "Stuff of sleep and dreams, and yet my Reason
at the Rudder" I use as epigraph and title for this book. Long
before Coleridge, Leonardo da Vinci had asked, and wondered,
why the eye sees more clearly and vividly in dream than in
imagination. Our dreams and fancies come to us wholly out of
our interior being. We are their sole authors. Coleridge wrote
in a poem, "My eyes make pictures, when they are shut," and
spoke of "excursions in my own mind." Our eyes are closed in
sleep—and yet we see. The body is in repose—and yet we act.
Art begins in the back rooms of concealed memory, old sensations and hidden feelings. But what starts as impalpable motion
is altered by the artist into something material in time and

space—in words, in marble, in pigment, in drama, in song and dance. The literary psychologist steers a course with Coleridge's rudder by a series of significant insights, by pursuing unanswered questions. But we can never describe the integrative action, so complex and so deeply grounded in the filaments of our being. Some poets, like Auden, held that we shouldn't try to grasp those filaments and trace their connections. Coleridge tried, however, long ago, and his example and precedent gives us license (if we need it) to pursue the mysteries even if, in the end, we may find them insoluble. I read *Biographia Literaria* long after my adventure in Vienna and came to understand how the poet, in the sufferings of his illness which led to an opium addiction, was also led to supreme moments of self-awareness. We perhaps know best that we exist when pain—even the pain of emotion—announces possession of our body or our feelings. Out of self-awareness comes selfhood, and Coleridge, a century before Freud, coined the word *psychoanalytical* and even the word *psychosomatic.* He used the words to describe not therapies but what he was seeing in his own unconscious being: he caught only glimpses. He spoke of the "mastercurrents below the surface" and of "flights of lawless speculation" to describe the uncontrolled findings which we arrive at in some remote part of our inner selves. Self-intuition he called a "sacred power," writing that "the fancy is indeed no other than a mode of memory emancipated from the order of time and space" and—capital statement!—the fancy is "blended and modified by choice." (Freud would add that the choice always is made in answer to unconscious and determined promptings.) Coleridge observed that "the fancy must receive all its materials ready-made from the law of association," a priceless insight that Freud would explore in interpreting dreams, or that Proust would pursue in the examination of his own memories. "Choice," "association," the fancy emerging from "mastercurrents" of our being—Freud in the fullness of time came precisely to these matters and went on to inquire into imaginative choice and to study "free" association to our dreams and to our Proustian search for "lost time" that is "involuntary memory." "The richness and variety of Coleridge's notes on sleep and dreaming," writes the eminent Coleridgean scholar Kathleen Coburn, "is a subject in itself for an experienced analyst with the soul of a poet and a wide reading equal to Coleridge's own. No wonder," she adds, "no one has explored it. One can scarcely imagine what it was like to write or think like this about dreams at a time when dreams were treated in the context of prophecy, foreboding, tabus and ghosts." There are in Coleridge's notebooks some three hundred entries dealing with sleep and dreams.

Writers have from far back remembered their dreams and listened to them. Dostoevsky's, re-created for his novels, are particularly vivid, so vivid indeed that we often feel as if we had dreamed them ourselves. In England, Charles Dickens used dreams often in telling his stories—his *Christmas Carol* is a series of story dreams: they do not, however, resemble real ones. Dickens made a particular distinction between dreams that are created to suit the convenience of a story and the genuine dream stuff which distorts reality and touches upon the fabulous. In a letter of 1851 he wrote:

> If I have been perplexed during the day in bringing out the incidents of a story as I wish, I find that I dream at night, never by any chance of the story itself, but perhaps of trying to shut a door that *will* fly open, or to screw something tight that *will* be loose, or to drive a horse on some very important journey, who unaccountably becomes a dog and can't be urged along, or to find my way out of a series of chambers that appears to have no end.

And he added, "I sometimes think that the origin of all fable and allegory, the very first conception of such fictions, may be referable to this class of dreams." Dickens pointed to the fabric of dreams shared by all dreamers:

> We all fall off that Tower, we all skim above the ground at a great pace and can't keep on it, we all say "this must be a dream, because I was in this strange, low-roofed, beam-constructed place once before, and it turned out to be a dream" . . . we all confound the living with the dead, and all frequently have a knowledge or suspicion that we are doing it.

An author with so clear an observation of the phenomenon of dream was capable of certain audacities, and little attention has been paid to Dickens's attempt to turn himself into a healer, using hypnotism quite in the manner of the early Freud. Dickens was attracted to mesmerism when he saw the eminent Dr. John Elliotson hypnotize a patient in 1838. He found he himself could hypnotize most persons without difficulty, and there came a moment when he went beyond the parlor-game amusement of mesmerism to attempt its therapeutic use. Given his powerful charisma, as well as his sense of power, he pushed his experiments further than might be supposed. During his first American tour in 1842 he resorted to hypnotism to arrest his wife's headaches and insomnia. "In six minutes," he wrote, "I magnetized her into hysterics and then into magnetic sleep." He tried again the following night with even greater success.

Three years later, while he was staying near Genoa, Dickens experimented with a more complicated case. He had formed a friendship with a Swiss banker, Emile De la Rue, whose wife was English. In time he learned that Madame De la Rue suffered from terrible hallucinations. Dickens offered to try hypnosis to help her, but before doing this (in anticipation of Freudian and post-Freudian procedures) he took her history in a thorough manner. He made her recite in detail the hallucinations she had experienced. She told him she recurrently found herself on a hillside under a very blue sky, but her feelings were far from being in harmony with the landscape. Unseen people hurled stones at her; she felt that some evil man haunted the place—though she did not see him, for, she said, she was terrified at the thought of looking at him. Dickens noticed that she trembled as she spoke. She was a victim of continuing anxiety and fear. Dickens had remarked in his own dreams that a recurrent dream tended to return so long as he did not tell it to someone. Once told, he seemed rid of it. As he put it, "Secrecy on the part of the dreamer, as to these illusions, has a remarkable tendency to perpetuate them." He was aware also that dream triggers were rarely of significant incidents; a dream went back most often to some minor and even insignificant bit of memory during the previous day. For these reasons he did his best to elicit the details of Madame De la Rue's powerful hallucinatory experiences, both in the daytime and at night. He hoped the telling would by itself be helpful. Then he proceeded to hypnotize her whenever she entered into a state of hallucination. Unfortunately we have very few details, but we know that Dickens became fascinated by the problem; in very short order Madame De la Rue became highly dependent on him; and, in turn, Mrs. Dickens became extremely jealous.

The compulsive nature of Dickens's treatment may be commented upon. On one occasion De la Rue woke Dickens at 1 A.M. and the novelist found the wife "rolled into an apparently insensible ball." In her terror, she had apparently assumed a fetal position, as is sometimes the case. Characterizing this as a "tic on the brain," he was able within half an hour to put her into a deep sleep. However, the therapy fluctuated. Sometimes, when the two families traveled together, Dickens worked on his patient during the journey "under olive trees, sometimes in vineyards, sometimes in the travelling carriage, sometimes at wayside inns during the mid-day halt." Once, Dickens's biographer tells us, his wife awoke to find the novelist "striding up and down the bedroom with all the candles lit. He had just come from struggling with Madame De la Rue's terrors and was still violently agitated with the experience." As may be imagined,

Mrs. Dickens was deeply troubled by the obsessive character of his treatment. Nor did there seem to be any end to it; today we can see that there had been both a "transference" and a "counter-transference"—and besides, Dickens was working in the dark, in a blind belief in hypnotic power. To his wife's jealousy the novelist replied that his effort to achieve a cure was simply "an illustration of the intense pursuit of an idea that took complete possession." And he added this was one of the qualities that made him "different from other men." This did not assuage Mrs. Dickens's jealousy, and ultimately the novelist detached himself from his therapeutic endeavors by teaching De la Rue how to hypnotize his wife at crucial moments. We gather from later correspondence between Dickens and the De la Rues that the effect continued to be only palliative.

Turn where we will among pre-Freudian writers, we find them fascinated by their dreams. Hawthorne described the "topsy-turvy" world of sleep. Thoreau dwelt on dreams as containing the truths of our lives. And Conrad, who of all writers was most deeply aware of his unconscious, told us that "no relation of a dream can convey the dream-sensation, that commingling of absurdity, surprise and bewilderment in a tremor of struggling revolt, that notion of being captured by the incredible which is the very essence of dreams."

Freud would write his classic work *The Interpretation of Dreams* at the turn of the century, and since that time there has been an increasing awareness that the faculties or promptings, the symbols and memories we use in dream belong also to the imaginations that use them in the conscious process of creating literature. Writers are continually transforming memory into symbolic fable; and within this process there is what Henry James called "associational magic," their infallible way of matching like with like and their continual need to metamorphose experience as a way of making it more palatable or understandable to themselves—and to their readers.

Each artist draws upon a personal world of symbols. And the explorer cannot retrace the writer's paths; nor, indeed, can the writer. Memory brings up memory; and within the unfathomable of consciousness the poet or novelist makes choices, selects appropriate images, finds and describes the strange shapes that seem to exist in a netherworld of the mind. The interpretation of literature is perhaps even more difficult than the interpretation of dreams, for the psychoanalyst usually has the dreamer to provide help, where the literary psychologist works with the text alone and can only go where the text leads. How are we to separate fact from fancy? And isn't any "separating out" doomed to fail? One reads at best between the lines—and yet between these lines the character and the personality of the artist speak to us. Only those who have learned to understand their own dream work are qualified to understand the dreams of others in these unending experiments in which we trace the backward roads to genesis. What literary psychology proposes is nothing less than the exploration of man's ways of dreaming, thinking, imagining, behaving—and the exploration is conducted on the terrain of man's imaginative creations. Kenneth Burke has illustrated our quest by observing that "if a man talks of glory but employs the imagery of *desolation,* his true subject is desolation." Linguistic studies, particularly in France, have plunged into the psychological examination of *words* used in literature. But literary psychology must go beyond the divagations of men like Lacan into the very fabric: the kind of story told, the choices made by the author, and the search, as proposed by Burke, for the true or inner subject that resides within the poem and story.

Above all, we recognize that the intellect alone does not serve us sufficiently in this kind of work. Writing is not only thinking, it is feeling; and unless we are prepared to look objectively into feeling (and can keep our own emotions from becoming confused with emotions contained in the words of the text), we run the risk of reading ourselves into the work of another, as Dickens's obsessions became tangled with the hallucinations of Madame De la Rue. Too many critics have turned the printed page into mirrors for themselves.

Once we seek the "why" of a story or poem, and remain aware of self-delusion and rationalization, we find ourselves facing propositions like those of the Zen masters or the old Talmudists. But not quite—we do not ask how many angels dance on the point of a needle, although it is a good question. We inquire first why this question is asked, and what premises of belief it contains. Thoreau tells us he went to Walden Pond to suck the marrow out of life—but why did he *really* go to Walden Pond? One doesn't need to live by a pond to suck the marrow of life. A dedication of a book, properly pursued, may reveal unsounded areas of feeling and a fascinating relationship. We explore choices and associations, motives and behavior, moving about among characters in poetry and fiction by remembering always that they are but figments of a creative imagination and that it is in that imagination that the real encounter occurs.

In doing this we boldly must attempt to tell the dancer from the dance, even though we have been charmed and even bewitched by the dance itself. Henry James's way of expressing Yeats's question was to assert that "the artist is present in every page of every book from which he sought so assiduously to eliminate himself." If we consult the author's presence, we uncover many new wonders and pursue a truly engaging and lively shadow dance within the critical and associative imagination.

This book which you hold in your hand is a book of mysteries. Literary psychology is the art of discovering the unseen through the seen; it is the art of defining a shape when we see a shadow. I hold that to seek the dancer in the dance or the author in the book is a legitimate object of artistic, critical, and scientific inquiry. If this inquiry takes us into the troubles and torments of human existence, it leads us at the same time to mankind's most characteristic way of transcending our existential state; by metamorphosis and transfiguration we find ourselves in the midst of the glories of the human fancy—and attempt to find an answer to Shakespeare's question:

> Tell me where is Fancy bred,
> Or in the heart or in the head?

THE NATURE OF
PSYCHOLOGICAL EVIDENCE

"Tell me where is Fancy bred/Or in the heart or in the head?"
Shakespeare's precise and lightly phrased question in the *Merchant of Venice* almost carries its own answer. A modern and
less poetic reply would be that we produce our fancies in our
unconscious out of our body's history, and the intellect, or
"head," ultimately goes to work to give them shape and reason.
Heart in Shakespeare's time was about as good a way of expressing the unfathomable of the unconscious as any word we possess
today. And since we deal with the unfathomable, we are reduced always to dealing with its signs or signals. These, as T. S.
Eliot told us long ago, are the objective correlatives of what is
hidden from us.

I

Psychological evidence, it follows, is composed in part of
dreams, imaginings, and observed human actions. It is our task
to examine this kind of evidence and to study it, using all the
scholarly and judicial methods known to us. It helps when we
encounter the words "psychological evidence" in Henry
James's curious novel *The Sacred Fount.* We are given an opportunity to see what that master of fictional psychology believed
such evidence to be. This minor work of 1900 deals with a
narrator consumed by curiosity of a very natural kind: at a
gossipy weekend party he wants to discover who is sleeping
with whom, and what effect the various involved persons are
having on one another. Since he is a gentleman—that is, a

voyeur with codes and rules—and has a puritan conscience, he begins, after a while, to ask himself whether he should, as he puts it, "nose about for a relation that a lady has her reasons for keeping secret." He makes this remark to a painter, who offers the wisdom of his art. "Nosing about," the painter says, is harmless so long as one sticks to "psychological evidence." He adds, "Resting on psychologic signs alone it's a high application of the intelligence. What's ignoble is the detective and the keyhole."

We may ask what Henry James meant by "psychologic signs." I believe he meant those signs we can observe empirically if we are watchful. Faces speak to us; so do actions. Our job is to discover what meanings these possess. An early Jamesian example is to be found in a letter he wrote to Grace Norton about life in Boston: "Mr J. T. Fields lectured here on Cheerfulness lately (as who should say: I know I'm a humbug and a fountain of depression, but grin and bear it)." This could be called a therapeutic observation. James recognizes that beneath Fields's exuberance there lies a chronic state of depression; indeed, he calls it a "fountain" of melancholy. James noticed this without benefit of Freud. If we were to allow ourselves to sit on the sidelines at almost any party, we would see how certain kinds of wit are substituted for aggression, how a hostile gesture can accompany an expression of affection, or how a slip of the tongue reveals what the speaker really feels. Slips of the tongue are best studied, I might add, during election time. When former President Nixon once tried to say that he would get rid of certain farm problems, his tongue slipped and what emerged was that he would abolish the farmers. He would have heartily liked, I'm convinced, to abolish them at that particular moment. His tongue, as we say, ran away with him, and he told us what was really in his mind. When the late Pope John Paul I announced that he did not want to be crowned with the supreme symbol of the papacy, the magnificent crown which most of his predecessors had worn before him, he gave us a "psychologic sign." We might say it expressed meekness and humility; perhaps a more accurate interpretation might suggest that he was saying he did not really want to be pope. And his month's apostolate again and again illustrated his ambivalence about the power conferred upon him. If I were writing his life, I would start by trying to find answers to this great psychological drama enacted in the Vatican before the entire world.

Let us look at another passage in Henry James which shows us that he knew very clearly what he meant by "psychologic signs." Madame Merle asks Isabel Archer in *The Portrait of a Lady,* "What shall we call 'self'? Where does it begin? Where does it end?" She provides her own answer. The self, she says, "overflows into everything that belongs to us—and then it flows back again. I know a large part of myself is in the clothes I choose to wear. One's self—for other people—is one's expression of one's self; and one's house, one's furniture, one's garment, the book one reads, the company one keeps—these things are all expressive." Madame Merle thus also talks of "psychologic signs," and Freud or any of his followers listening to her might have added, "Yes, and one's dreams, the poems one writes, the stories one invents, the jokes one tells—all these are also a part of the self."

I am not trying to suggest that the study of such signs or hints in a literary work is the whole of literary psychology. Within the practice of criticism—as we practice it—and within the writing of biography or history, we should learn how to read "psychologic signs": in documents, in text, in what we know about a writer and what the writer makes us know about private myth through chosen symbols and the metamorphoses of image. All this is perhaps even more than "a high application of the intelligence," as Henry James said. It is the very secret of method; it takes some of us closer to scientific literary truth than any method we have found so far. The primary psychological fact resides in choices, and these have *unconscious* promptings. In literary psychology we are involved in a choice—a choice of words, of names, of images, the forms a writer creates, even the punctuation marks—everything in the work which expresses the writer belongs to the formed nature of the writer's imaginings. Notice Madame Merle said that "a large part of myself is in the clothes I *choose* to wear." In the ensuing passage Isabel Archer denies the idea of choice. She argues that her clothes express her dressmaker, not herself. Madame Merle looks beyond such a simplification. Somewhere within, we assent or dissent from the actions of the dressmaker or the tailor, even when we allow ourselves to be persuaded by them. Behind what these personages *technically* do, we make the choices. In the end we clothe ourselves. Once we are clothed, the clothes express us. The ultimate choice is ours.

I I

Some years ago I lectured in Boston on the writing of biography. Afterwards a young professor of English at one of the local colleges told me that he was about to become the Boswell of Rex Stout, the detective-story writer, then a very old man. How, asked my excited questioner, should he go about becoming a biographer? This was a large question. Yet, to my own surprise, an instant reply arose from my unconscious. I had, in my younger days, read a great many of Stout's Nero Wolfe mysteries, and I heard myself say, "You might inquire why Rex, being a king, chose to make his detective, Nero, an emperor. Also, why he chose a wicked emperor." Then I heard myself adding that I knew Rex Stout as a tall thin man. He made Nero Wolfe very stout indeed, 260 pounds, thereby reversing the saying that in every stout man a thin man struggles to be freed. In Rex Stout, apparently, a fat man resided somewhere within his fine spare athletic figure.

We had, I observed, an engaging mystery. A detective in fiction is nearly always some form of the creator's *persona*. Nero Wolfe is the opposite of all we superficially know about Rex Stout. Rex was a fighter for causes and a man with considerable bite to him; Nero Wolfe is quiet and retiring and stays home.

Unlike the Nero of history, who was gross and fiddled while Rome burned, Nero Wolfe is a man of delicacy. Nero the emperor was violent. Nero the detective—whose surname Wolfe seems to contradict his fatness and outward passivity—dissociates violence from himself and hires a legman, named Archie Goodwin, to do the rough stuff of modern detective work, the spying and slugging and getting slugged. Archie often gets roughed up. Nero meanwhile fiddles with his orchids and gourmet recipes and puts his ratiocinative mind to work on the evil that must not go unpunished.

I told the young biographer that Rex Stout's nomenclature, personal and fictive, gave me the impression that the real-life author was converting certain powerful feelings, probably aggressive and violent, into his particularly clever art. In a highly creative and imaginative way, he was writing out little dramas of good and evil derived from his own problems. We notice that Archie Goodwin is a winner of the good. Nero Wolfe achieves the good by physical inertia and sheer force of intellect. I said that this probably pointed to ways in which Rex Stout was handling certain anxieties with which most humans have to cope. Stout dissociates violence from himself by choosing the name of violence; yet he makes the bearer of the name benign. Also, the lupine in Nero's name speaks for a ravenous ferocity, yet this is converted into the gourmet side of the fat detective.

Some weeks later, still intrigued by the name game I had begun to play in Boston, I told myself I had not accounted for the Wolfe in Nero Wolfe. The answer wasn't difficult to find. Rex Stout's middle name was Todhunter, his mother's family name. A *tod* is Scots for fox; so he came of a family of fox hunters on his mother's side. To summarize, the king was transformed into emperor, the Stout was literally turned into fatness, and the Todhunter was turned from fox into wolf. Good enough. These observations received a surprising validation: I came on the fact that Stout invented another detective before Nero Wolfe who proved to have little appeal. His name, however, was molded in the same pattern. He was called Tecumseh Fox. This shows how insistent fancy can be, how the unconscious imagination dictates choices which seem to most people simply accidental. Tecumseh was a Shawnee. He lived a great wishful dream of an Indian empire across North America. So *imperium* and the mother's fox family were united in Rex Stout's imagination long before he created Nero Wolfe.

Once one becomes involved in this kind of evidence, the inquiring imagination working on psychological signs and signals refuses to stop. I found myself pondering the relation between Archie Goodwin and Nero Wolfe, for Archie too is a creation of Stout's mind. Putting Archie and Stout side by side we can see, if we inform ourselves, that Archie, the winner of the good, is the pragmatic, compulsive, practical author himself; anyone who knew Rex Stout knew him as a man of goodwill, active, practical, and down-to-earth, agile both mentally and physically. He made a fortune in banking before he made his fortune in writing. His choice of names represented an interesting splitting apart of the man and his myth—Rex Stout as he appeared to the world, and the unconscious mythic Stout who emerged as stout Nero Wolfe. In my theorizing about biography, I have always argued that if a biographer can tap the unconscious myth of a subject, the battle is more than half won; we have a key to the material that is illustrative and relevant and can then know what is routine and irrelevant. The self myth is the truest part of an individual: by that myth we always seek to live; it is what gives us force, direction, and sustenance. The personality the world sees is usually much less interesting. Who does not remember Thurber's story of Walter Mitty? The hidden myth of Rex Stout was a dream of himself as a big man, a heavy man, an emperor. Indeed, for two decades and more he was king-emperor of the American Authors' Guild. He argued copyright with senators; he had access to the White House during the FDR era; he knew most of the public American figures of his time—in short, he acted out both the fox-self and the wolf-self, the king-self and the emperor-self. In his detective stories he embodied problems of crime and punishment, guilt, rivalry, competition, aggression—and his own large and on the whole benign and constructive drive to power.

Some time after I set down my observation of the curious use of opposites in the imagination of Rex Stout—passive-violent fat-thin, good-evil—I learned that he himself used to say he invented Nero Wolfe by making him the opposite of Sherlock Holmes. The data were given me by someone who had talked with Stout. "He told us," this witness said, "that when he began to write detective stories he realized that Doyle was king." Notice Rex using kingship in this remark. "He, Stout, told us that Holmes was of the utmost importance, and so he decided that his detective would be the opposite of Holmes in appearance and personality and would perhaps arrive at a state of importance also. For example: Holmes was tall and thin, Wolfe would be short and fat. Holmes played the violin, Wolfe raised orchids. Holmes took dope, Wolfe drank beer. Holmes would go anywhere to solve a case, Wolfe would not leave the house." If we carry this further we also see that it applies to Archie Goodwin, bright as a penny, the opposite to the dull, stolid, Victorian Dr. Watson.

We now see that Stout was engaged in a double process: he not only created the opposite of himself in Nero Wolfe, but the opposite of a detective out of literature, with whom he seems to have identified himself—so much so that he wanted to make him over into his own mythic imperial image. On the surface Rex Stout and Conan Doyle seem dissimilar in all their externals. Conan Doyle was a doctor, a distinctive Victorian; Stout was an American. Conan Doyle had a strong romantic streak in him; he liked adventure, travel, sport, and romantic storytelling. He traveled on a whaling ship; he took a cargo steamer to Africa. He organized sports clubs. But if we look beyond the externals we see that in everything the two did, they resembled each other remarkably. Both had king complexes. They sought power, each in his own way. Their desire for rule, for eminence, for the heady feeling of domination—this was common to both, and both found their power in what they created. Given their personal myth, it is less of a coincidence that their creations are allied—that Stout should attach his *persona* to Doyle's and alter it as an outcome of his own psychic needs. They were born leaders—or, at the least, passionate would-be leaders.

We may ask, then, why did Doyle choose the name Sherlock Holmes? The detective was named for Oliver Wendell Holmes, the American medical autocrat of the breakfast table, who was an uncommon sleuth in his laboratory and combined, like Doyle, medicine and literature. Here too we see a case of identification: Doyle, the writing British doctor, identifies with a famous writing American doctor. What a strange thought, that the man from Baker Street should have a Boston ancestor! The name-choosing, about which a great deal more might be said, provides symptoms of the similar life myths of the two writers. Sherlock Holmes admittedly is the more original of the two detectives, simpler, less subtle, less elusive than the complex Nero Wolfe. He is also more visible publicly, partly because he is physically more active. And Doyle is Dr. Watson—as Archie is Rex Stout. Doyle in his public life was as respectable, as dull, as mediocre as Sherlock's companion, sound, hearty, very much the roast-beef-and-Yorkshire-pudding type: wholly addicted to the superficial and the external. The two man-on-the-street minds of these sleuthing stories, Watson and Goodwin, become also the audience which reads them and identifies with them. The readers are enabled to look at genius and ratiocinative skill through their own dreams of adventure and power.

Put in another way, Sherlock Holmes is that part of Dr. Watson—or of Conan Doyle—which could not permit itself to be seen by the Victorians save in disguise. Doyle-Watson remains eminently respectable and full of placid common sense; Sherlock Holmes is the myth, Doyle's liberated and liberating unconscious self cutting loose from Victorian moral bondage, taking great flights, always avoiding the commonplace, ready to plunge into iniquitous dens and to reach for the needle where Drs. Watson and Doyle wouldn't have dreamed of doing so themselves, least of all playing a moody fiddle. By the same token, Nero Wolfe was what Rex Stout, through probable feelings of guilt, could allow himself to be only in his imagination: evil stoutness metamorphosed into benignity.

Doyle sought a similar kind of *imperium* but in a different frame, for he lived in Queen Victoria's Empire. He did fight for better divorce laws; he ran (unsuccessfully) for Parliament; he crusaded against the paintings of the Post-Impressionists, whose art the Dr. Watson in him could not comprehend; and finally, world famous, he became a leader of the Spiritualists. One point of striking resemblance between the two may be noted: Doyle was a hawk during the Boer War and was knighted by Victoria for his propaganda on its behalf; Stout, in his youth a founder of the *New Masses,* was a Vietnam hawk.

This duality of the common self and the imagined self—what is this duality but the creative and imaginative writer in bondage to the usual and the routine, the bondage of society and conditioning? Doyle or Stout rescues himself by putting his literal and prosaic self into print as Dr. Watson or Archie Goodwin and allowing the imaginative other self to achieve all freedoms beyond common reach—and all the power that can prove Scotland Yard stupid and Manhattan police inspectors mediocre.

While I was indulging in my name game about Rex Stout, his publishers sent me the proof copy of his newest Nero Wolfe mystery, written at the ripe age of eighty-five. I was interested to see how the old man was performing, with the sense I had that he could not live to write many more such books. The manifest evidence was there, as in all the other mysteries, although this work showed an inevitable slowing-down, a lack of the old force and rhythm. The latent content was surprising and saddening. For what Stout announced in this story—without, I am sure, realizing it—was that he was about to die. I made this assumption from the nature of his fantasy. For the first and only time in the more than forty Nero Wolfe mysteries, the murder occurs in Wolfe's own home, in his guest room. The plot revolves around his personal responsibility, since he himself is one of the suspects. In an earlier thriller, *The Red Box,* there are murders in Nero Wolfe's office; the significant statement of this novel is that death has finally entered Nero Wolfe's home. He solves the crime under a cloud; the fat orchid grower is in deep depression. Will he be able to solve the next crime? Or is he his own last case? It is interesting that quite independently Agatha Christie was concerned about her last case in a similar way. Stout died a few weeks after publishing *A Family Affair.*

III

I hope I have demonstrated how much the committed literary psychologist resembles the psychoanalyst. And yet we must remind ourselves of certain important—indeed, highly significant—differences. Dr. Phyllis Greenacre, in her study of Charles Darwin entitled *The Quest for the Father,* draws a valuable distinction which we may apply here. The distinction she makes is between a psychoanalytic writer who wishes to write a biography and the psychoanalyst engaged in therapy. It is apparent, she writes,

> that the psychoanalytic biographer approaches the study of his subject from vantage points precisely the opposite of those of the psychoanalytic therapist. The latter works largely through the medium of his gradually developing and concentrating relationship with the patient who is seeking help and accepts the relationship for this purpose. The personal involvement and neutrality of the therapist permit the patient to be drawn almost irresistibly into reproducing toward the analyst, in only slightly modified forms, the attitudes (and even their specific content) which have given rise to his difficulties.

In this setting, the analyst can help the patient to become feelingly aware of the nature of his difficulties and to achieve a realignment of the conflict-driven forces within him. Psychoanalysis as a *technique* is distinctly for therapeutic purposes and is not generally useful for investigating the personality structure of the individual who is in a good state of balance.

This is the very distinction I wish to emphasize. What is the precise difference between the therapeutic analyst working with a living patient and the analytical writer who, so to speak, has to work in a cemetery? Dr. Greenacre admirably sums up the kind of work the analytical writer has to do:

> He has no direct contact with his subject, and there is no therapeutic aim. He amasses as much material from as many different sources as possible. Lacking the opportunity to study the subject's reactions through the transference neurosis, he must scrupulously scrutinize the situations from which the source material is drawn, and assess the personal interactions involved in it. Further, the study is made for the purpose of extending analytic knowledge and is not sought by the subject.

If we accept and learn to understand what "literary psychology" is, we can inject a great deal of clarity in a situation muddled by history—muddled by the term still sometimes used, that of "applied psychoanalysis." The original belief was that psychoanalysis could be *applied* to literature; but it patently can't, for its sole mission is to be applied to a patient, and I had not heard that literature, at its best, was ailing. Out of these early confusions, wholly understandable when we read the history of the psychoanalytic movement, we discern a logical fallacy. Applied psychoanalysis, reduced to its absolute meaning, is a structured paradox. Psychoanalysis can only be applied to a patient; applied elsewhere it would have to be called nontherapeutic therapy, which is absurd! There was, in my opinion, a wrong turning point at that moment; let me recapitulate. The two essential ingredients of psychoanalysis are the therapist and the patient. But in literary studies we have no patients. We have a unique work by a unique individual. Ergo, even if literary folk were qualified, they would be unable to practice psychoanalysis —for there is no psychoanalysis to be practiced. What needs to be more fully recognized is that in these changed conditions Freud's therapeutic discoveries have little relevance. And what is of paramount importance is that we take from Freud perhaps the richest part of his work, his insights into man's ways of thinking, dreaming, imagining—those elements which have also an influence on motivations and behavior. It was the good fortune of the world that Sigmund Freud, whose entire focus was on healing, happened to be a great humanist as well. Let us understand then that literature cannot be psychoanalyzed. But it can be analyzed—and this process of analysis I call literary psychology.

Literary psychology takes three postulates from psychoanalysis. First is the existence of the unconscious in human motivation and behavior, in dreams, imaginings, thoughts; second, that within the unconscious there exist certain suppressed feelings and states of being which sometimes emerge into awareness in the consciously created forms of literature. When in the form of a dream, these feelings are transformed and disguised material, raw data thrown up by the unconscious, most often in mythic and symbolic shape; when in the form of story, poem, play, the same kinds of data have been converted by a literary sensibility and temperament, using a vast literary tradition, into a conscious work of art. Third, by the process of induction—that is, by examining the mental representation in words of things not present to the senses—we can detect deeper intentions and meanings, valuable both to the biographer and the critic. We thus become tentative geographers of the mysterious psyche, where fancy is bred. What an enormously difficult task this can prove! Yet how fascinating, mysterious, and challenging.

There is a striking passage in Robertson Davies's Deptford trilogy dealing with magic and wonder. It is to be found in the third volume, *World of Wonders.* In it a gypsy fortune-teller instructs a young man she befriends how to be observant. The passage offers an admirable illustration of the kind of inductive psychological evidence gypsies and other crystal-ball gazers often use to meet the needs of their clientele.

You have to learn to look at people. Hardly anybody does that. They stare into people's faces, but you have to look at the whole person. Fat or thin? Where is the fat? What about the feet? Do the feet show vanity or trouble? Does she stick out her breast or curl her shoulders to hide it? Does he stick out his chest or his stomach? Does he lean forward and peer, or backward and sneer? Hardly anybody stands straight. Knees bent, or shoved back? The bum tight or drooping? In men, look at the lump in the crotch; big or small? How tall is he when he sits down? Don't miss hands. The face comes last. Happy? Probably not. What kind of unhappy? Worry? Failure? Where are the wrinkles? You have to look good, and quick. And you have to let them see that you're looking. Most people aren't used to being looked at except by the doctor, and he's looking for something special.

You take their hand. Hot or cold? Dry or wet? What rings? Has a woman taken off her wedding-ring before she came in? That's always a sign she's worried about a man, probably not the husband. A man—big Masonic or K. of C. ring? Take your time. Tell them pretty soon that they're worried. Of course they're worried; why else would they come to a mitt-camp at a fair? Feel around, and give them chances to talk; you know as soon as you touch the sore spot. Tell them you have to feel around because you're trying to find the way into their lives, but they're not ordinary and so it takes time.

Robertson Davies's fictional gypsy is describing the kind of psychological evidence Freud used when he explained how the ego is composed of unconscious promptings and defenses as well as a societal veneer, which the gypsy penetrates by looking for telltale signs, in the manner of Sherlock Holmes, or of Henry James at a country house during a weekend party. She sees beyond the bit of mud stuck to the boot or the obvious missing button. She is using distinct "psychologic signs"—body posture, facial expression—and also palpable signs, those signs a good doctor observes in a patient during an illness. Signs and symbols of the unconscious are more numerous than most persons believe, and they have many ways of validating one another.

No direct ways of proving the existence of the unconscious have been found. This often makes the test-tube people very tiresome, because they insist on knowing only what their eye can see. To the artist, indirect proofs are abundant and Freud long ago showed them to us; before Freud, most of our great poets. Our dreams, our slips of the pen and of the tongue, our whole imagination of being—all give tangible form to things hidden from ourselves. "The artist," said Balzac, that most concrete of novelists, "does not know the secrets of his own mind. . . . He does not belong to himself. . . . On some days he does not write a line, and if he attempts to, it is not he who holds the pen but his double, his other self. . . . And then one evening when he is walking down the street, or one morning when he is getting up, a glowing ember lights his brain." Byron cut through to the essence of Freud's demonstration of self-delusion. "I feel," said Byron, "that one lies more to one's self than anyone else." Yeats described our reservoirs of drive and conditioning as "an energy as yet uninfluenced by thought, emotion, or action." I like in particular, and have quoted many times, Thoreau's observation that "in dreams we never deceive ourselves, nor are deceived . . . in dreams we act a part which we must have learned and rehearsed in our waking hours. . . . Our truest life is when we are in the dreams awake."

We must not confuse dream magic with what Freud called our "preconscious" thought, of which we get abundant proof by our ability to recall, although with some effort, things out of the past. Proust's "involuntary memory"—the madeleine and his cup of lime-flower tea—was an experience of the preconscious. Out of the trigger of taste, he released a chain of remembrances which has been the delight of us all; but behind this remembering there remained Proust's unconscious, living its own life and driving him (for reasons literary psychology must explore) to shut himself in his room as if into the womb of night to spin his long novel. No criticism or biography of a writer can ever hope to unravel all the marvels of such creative imaginations; all we can hope is to be given a few extraordinary glimpses. And Freud's remark that "before the problems of the creative artist, analysis must, alas, lay down its arms" may be challenged by literary psychology: before those problems I would say *literary* psychology—in its proper field of the written and spoken word —picks up its arms. Let me again attempt to demonstrate how.

I V

I will now apply literary psychology to the manifest and latent content of a story in a different department of literature. I am reminded by Rex Stout's probably unconscious announcement of impending death in *A Family Affair* of Edith Wharton's tale called "All Souls," one of her most chilling stories of the supernatural. Her heroine is an elderly woman named Mrs. Clayburn, who lives with many servants in a big house in Connecticut. She seems a composed and rational being who belongs to a quite ordered world of privilege and comfort, far removed from any emanations of the occult. Early in the story she has an awkward accident: she twists her ankle and is put to bed by her servants. She is to have X-rays the next day. She spends an uncomfortable night waiting for the dawn, when her maid will come with breakfast at the usual hour. The maid does not come. She rings. No one answers. She remains alone, unaided, unfed. Bit by bit she discovers that the usually responsive world is not responding. The house is still. It is a kind of bad dream, yet she knows she is not dreaming. The exquisite order of her universe is gone. Neither the bell nor the phone establishes communication for her. Where are the servants? Why has life come to a standstill within her own little kingdom? Weak with pain, she finally spends a day and night of terror and loneliness. What has occurred to bring about such strange disconnection? And, as it happens, on All Souls' Eve? The horror resides in these questions. The tale turns in the end into mere anecdote, as if written by Defoe. The next day all is normal; the servants act as if they had never been away. There is no explanation. Comfort is restored. Only the memory of horror remains. It is hinted that the servants may have been attending some witches' coven in the Connecticut hills.

I have given a bare account of a spooky tale. The spookiness resides in the masterly order of the narrative. We can link the tale to Hawthorne, to Henry James, to Sheridan Le Fanu; the ghostly tradition is an old tradition—a strange happening unaccounted for, and therefore mysterious and eerie, with its hint here of eroticism in the witches' sabbath. The literary psychologist learns from the beginning that what is important in a story is not only the power of intellect or the tradition or narrative skill; literature has, above all, its wellsprings of feeling, and the feelings in this tale are present in the terrible isolation and loneliness of Mrs. Clayburn, her terror of being abruptly cut off from the normal ease of her existence. This is like the feeling we sometimes experience in severe illness, of suddenly being narrowed to a bed when the whole world is normally available to us. It is probably a feeling akin to impending death, which is the ultimate cutting off, the ultimate loneliness, the ultimate termination. We may therefore ask—and it is, I think, a good psychological question—what overriding anxiety, what deep emotion, found its correlative in a story by Mrs. Wharton of desertion by servants hired to attend (and at a moment of physical crisis), with resulting bewilderment and panic? Of course, on All Souls' Eve eerie things are supposed to happen; but the happening here is told by the victim as if applicable to any night. Critics cannot dissociate their intelligence and knowledge from their reading, and most students of American literature can at once make biographical connections. We know that

Edith Wharton was perhaps the most servanted writer in our literary annals: the chauffeur, the maid, the old retainers, the gardeners, the cook, and her white-collar staff—the secretary who typed the manuscripts written in that bold, firm hand in bed every morning, the agent who took care of her literary market. Edith Wharton always moved in a world in which she was attended, not only by servants but also by friends, for in her prime she had a salon wherever she went. Cushioned, cosseted against loneliness, "facilitated," as her friend Henry James put it, she never knew what it meant to fend for one's self.

In this light (and our discussion of "All Souls" would be impoverished without it) the literary psychologist cannot avoid asking, Why did Mrs. Wharton have this strange fantasy, that of a woman so facilitated who finds herself suddenly helpless, and without warning? If the servants had gone on strike, or left in rebellion, she would have had sufficient warning. But their silent nonappearance, their total and sudden absence, shows a powerful panic within the controlled and creeping terror of the narrative. No one who has done life's little duties for one's self would have quite the same kind of terror, no one who has lived alone would feel the kind of isolation or have this kind of fantasy; people who have fended for themselves might have feelings of terror and isolation and disturbing fantasies, but these would take other forms, we may be sure. And so we must explore further and ask where this tale belongs in Mrs. Wharton's life, what place it has among her writings. Any literary student would ask this, at some point, in the need to discover the context of life or of art. Even if the story were a trifling potboiler (and the rich Mrs. Wharton did write potboilers to feed her many charities), the panic and terror would still have to have their meaning. And as with Rex Stout, the revelation in itself offers a special chill. "All Souls" was written by Mrs. Wharton, we learn, in February of 1937. It was her last completed tale. She died in August of that year.

What does this story really say? Mrs. Wharton had suffered from a heart condition for some years, but to face this directly would be to accept death; a twisted ankle mutes the hard fact, a simple kind of helplessness expresses the more startling helplessness Mrs. Wharton feels, at the last, in her peopled world. She is face to face with the ultimate loneliness, the ultimate separation; and the tale, in its lively imaginative way, makes light of the terror in Mrs. Wharton's soul, which she cannot altogether bring into full consciousness. She expresses also a wish that the feeling of doom will disappear, for in her fantasy the servants are in their usual places the next day, as if nothing has happened; as if it has all been a bad dream. Such is the beauty of the creative imagination, a delightful form of self-deception. Suddenly our eye lights on the woman's name: Mrs. Clayburn. A note of the supernatural is in it, and I would guess it was not consciously intended by the author. The name expresses what Mrs. Wharton tells herself in the disguises and masks of her tale: earth and fire—there is to be a merging with the elements.

Certain critics make light of "psychologic signs"; they describe them as "reductive"; they say that "psychologizing" reduces a work of the literary imagination to a diagnosis or a label; it is made to seem a function of the writer's disturbed feelings or neurosis. "Reductive" criticism occurs usually in the work of amateurs who are toying irresponsibly with psychoanalytical concepts; their prose is usually laden with technical terms. It would have been easy for me to talk of Rex Stout as a "passive-aggressive" writer instead of describing, in language proper to literary study, how he controlled and reimagined his anger and his conscious distaste for violence. We are not "reductive" when we seek out motivations and origins to show an artist surmounting difficulties by large acts of the imagination and the primacy of craft. Through literary psychology we can discover newer and fresher meanings which traditional study rarely attempts. (In all this I again caution critics and biographers to be certain of their context and the relevance of their observations; to be vigilant always that they are not employing their *own* imaginings.) I can, for example, supply a further reading of the text of "All Souls" and say to myself that perhaps Edith Wharton's story about her disappearing servants goes back to her early childhood when she was more aware—as a lonely child—of servants than of parents, in that large mansion on Fifth Avenue in which she grew up. Her final fantasy may contain remote as well as immediate personal data. Yet the evidence of childhood, if we examine it, only adds richness to the final evidence: for the last fantasy is based on an indisputable scientific fact, that of Mrs. Wharton's impending death, which provides the acute and eerie sense of absence, separation, desertion, panic, not necessarily present in childhood. My remarks about Mrs. Wharton's tale would be "reductive" only if I employed a diagnostic label or used medical jargon, as if she had a case of the measles or some other disease. Psychological signs provide the logic of inductive and deductive reasoning that culminates not in a theorem or a label but in a demonstration of the imagination at its work. I remember one day, when I went to lunch at the Pavillon Colombe, Mrs. Wharton's telling me her doctors were allowing her to climb her stairs only twice a day "and I'm going to use up one of these times right now to change my frock before we have lunch." We had been walking in her garden. This was a year before her death. The cheerful words, the laughter in her eyes, the desire to wear a fresh frock at lunch made light of the limitations imposed in behalf of her weak heart by her doctors. Here too we have a bit of psychological data which illuminates the humorous acceptance and laughter at silly doctors and their prohibitions. This was a part of her fun of life, but also a part of the way in which she defended herself against the grim evidence of waning activity and curtailed freedom—for in her healthy days she was the kind of woman who might have mounted those stairs hourly to change her frock.

V

I have sought to demonstrate that a grasp of the nature of psychological evidence can alter our conceptions of literary study. Perhaps that is why so many scholars find Freud irritating —like T. S. Eliot he is constantly saying to us, "That is not what I meant at all, that is not it at all." For what we see as reality ends up often, in the analytic process, as a concealment of reality. We have made considerable advances in our understanding of man's symbolic and mythic imagination; what we need is to understand the delicate ways in which metamorphosis takes place in our unconscious. We are constantly engaged in this kind of creation, and all literature is a fabled mythology, a land in which great artists, using tradition, dream their fabled dreams and redream those of others, in a kind of universal protean play of emotion and mind. We must therefore not resist psychology. Freud and his successors can be our teachers quite as much as the great masters of literary criticism and biography.

Psychology is the study of emotion, behavior, motivation. The resistances to psychology on the part of literary scholars reside in our failure to see that Freud's quest was for data in man's unconscious where we tend—partly because we lack expertise —to look only at conscious, manifest evidence. The unconscious, being invisible, inaudible, and untouchable, is more than slippery; it is elusive, leaving only a trail of telltale signs—as if we were looking at vague and blurred shadows without knowing what casts those shadows.

Literary study will have to reconcile itself to the "stuff of sleep and dreams." How can we truly understand a literary text if we do not understand where fancy is bred: man's ways of thinking, imagining, feeling? The difference between what literary study has done in the past and what it must learn to do now is the difference between saying *Cogito ergo sum* and *Sentio ergo sum*. We have been saying *Sentio* ever since the Romantic revival, but dealing with emotion as if it were wholly rational and measurable, as if literary creation were an act of carpentry. Any issue of *PMLA* testifies to this. To study the influence of this or that book or writer on an act of creation is to overlook the entire operative consciousness of the artist. To write biographies in the belief that all the minutiae of a life explain the work is nonsense. It is the selective detail, the "psychologic signs," that we must study. Psychology has directed us to look at the myths we create, the emotions that prompt us to do so, and the ways in which our feelings for tradition shape our use of tradition. If we neglect the truest province of literature, the emotions, we work in a twilight of irrelevancy. What I propose is a crossing-over from the territory of the palpable to the impalpable, the scrutinizing of delicate fantasies and thoughts, the exploration of motives and imagined acts.

I will scrape the surface of the extremely complex subject I have treated by trying to set down a bald statement of "doctrine." Even as I read it, I realize that it predicates a larger body of knowledge than is available in the traditional disciplines of literary study:

1. Literary psychology seeks the emotions and the *persona* within the work as distinct from the person of the artist. It is an attempt to study the metamorphoses of the unconscious materials of literary art into conscious image and symbol; and the metamorphoses of fancy into the finished work shaped by language and tradition.

2. The process of literary psychology is thus a study of the artist's emotions and personal myth of existence *as expressed in the work* and in the light of what we know of the unconscious and integrative functions of human activity.

3. The integrity of the literary work as a creative outcome of a personality must be recognized as distinct from the visible life of the creator. When both are studied, we arrive at certain

significant glimpses into "That dolphin-torn, that gong-tormented sea" of creation in which, as Yeats said, "images fresh images beget." The genetic exploration informs criticism as well as biography.

4. Therapeutic systems and models are irrelevant in literary psychology.

The new ways of reading the emotions expressed in human imaginings, fantasies, thoughts, and overpowering conflicts and aggressions, the entire body of psychological knowledge that this century has richly proffered, make it necessary for us to reexamine the nature of literary study. The historian Frank Manuel has said that "a historian can scarcely compose a narrative line without committing himself, implicitly or explicitly, to some theory of personality and motivation." This applies to the literary critic as well as the literary historian. Many of our old disciplines have been validated by psychology. We now use psychological concepts in many more ways than we know; artists have absorbed these into the works we read and teach and study. I am repeating in effect what Freud uncompromisingly said of psychoanalysis: Only those who have had the experience of examining and feeling their own dreams, and have learned what exists in their emotional inwardness—within their personal abysses—can *objectively* attempt to look at what issues from the inwardness of others.

II

THE MYSTERY
OF WALDEN POND

The "mystery" of Walden Pond. What mystery was there? It is a fine New England pond just beyond Concord. The town has crept around it and its old quiet is gone, for the tourists penetrate its solitude. There are hundreds of such ponds in New England and on the Cape; this one's only claim to attention is that it has been touched by literary history: literary memory has built invisible dreams around it. In its natural days it was the site of Henry David Thoreau's hut. He built it—so he told us—to escape from establishments and systems, to loaf and invite his soul (before Whitman uttered these words). He lived beside the pond for a while and ultimately wrote an inspired book called *Walden*.

Why did he do this? He told us why. He said he "wished to live deliberately, to front only the essential facts of life, and see if I could not learn what it had to teach, and not, when I came to die, discover that I had not lived." He spoke of wanting to suck the marrow of life, to live sturdily and Spartan-like, to cut a broad swath and also shave close, and see what life could be like on "its lowest terms." These were noble and important aims. And Thoreau's book poetically describes the pond in all its seasons, the fishing, the cutting of ice, the animals who visited him, and a thousand and one things out of the lore of nature. Each chapter begins with a poetic description; nature and the self merge. Each chapter has its passages of exhortation; Thoreau can scold vigorously. He can also crow about himself, as he said, like a rooster.

Often he tries to take the stance of a Hindu of Concord, for he read the Upanishads, and the Bhagavad-Gita, and the Vedas. Indeed, Robert Louis Stevenson said, "It was his ambition to be an Oriental philosopher; but he was always a very Yankee sort of Oriental." He did not know—for Japan had not yet been opened to the West—that there existed in Japanese the account of a similar residence in a shanty in the woods. Kamo-No Chō-mei's *Hojoki,* almost seven centuries before, described how he lived in a ten-foot-square hut, the dimensions of Thoreau's; but the Japanese sage lived there for thirty years and, in the time-less ways of the East, found answers within himself and his religion. Thoreau did not regard his cabin as his permanent home. The *Hojoki* tells of a way of life; *Walden* was a gesture.

I

It was a gesture, and one that posterity has transformed into a large myth. Who does not say at some moment, "I want to get away from it all"? And usually Thoreau is remembered. "Why don't I go and live in the woods, by a pond, like Thoreau?" Thoreau made much of his frugal economy. He was pleased that he paid no rent. He lived by the work of his hands; that is, by cultivating beans. He caught fish. And by not eating beef and abstaining from coffee, he got along with very little money. Thoreau is never more paradoxical than when he gives us his accounting of his cost of living. He totals it to within half a cent —perhaps tongue in cheek. It is a great show of accuracy; it is his way of demonstrating how finely he has pared things down. Thoreau said most men led lives of "quiet desperation"; and they had mortgages to pay. Of course it was convenient to be a bachelor, which Thoreau was. That is the fascinating outline of *Walden.* It is like Robinson Crusoe—except that Thoreau wasn't on a desert island. Concord was at hand; if he needed help he could get it.

Where, then, is the mystery in all this? Questions, however, do arise, things we do not know, and when one practices literary psychology, stubborn facts intrude. For example, Thoreau got "away from it all," we say. Then we discover that Concord was about two miles from Walden and Thoreau's family house just about one mile away. In fact, as we pursue our searches, we come upon curious information: the diary of the Boston hostess Mrs. J. T. Fields, for example. Thoreau, she records, was a good son; he loved his mother and, she adds, "even when living in his retirement at Walden Pond, he would come home every day." We find confirmation in the first important biography of Thoreau, written by his fellow townsman, the abolitionist and educator Frank B. Sanborn, in 1882. He says Thoreau "bivouacked" at Walden, adding that "he really lived at home, where he went every day."

How different is this from the legend of a solitary Thoreau in the wild woods. One finds echoes of his legend everywhere: recently the *Honolulu Advertiser* reported that the Pacific and Asian Affairs Council of the island of Hawaii, at one with the idea of the "noble savage," spent a beautiful Saturday in the Waipio Valley discussing Walden and hiked into the valley on the Hamakua coast "in order to appreciate Thoreau's life." The newspaper added that Thoreau "spent years living alone in the wilderness of Walden Pond, a day's walk from Boston, Mass"— but, it forgot to say, only twenty minutes' walk from Concord.

One has only to look in the biographies to see the legend at work. Here, for instance, is what the latest and probably most saturated Thoreau biographer, Walter Harding, writes (*The Days of Henry Thoreau*, 1966). Walden Pond, he tells us,

> was not a lonely spot. The well-traveled Concord-Lincoln road was within sight across the field. The Fitchburg Railroad steamed regularly past the opposite end of the pond. Concord village was less than two miles away, and the Texas house [the Thoreau family house] was less than that along the railroad right-of-way . . . Ellery Channing . . . visited the cabin often. . . . It is true that his mother and sisters made a special trip out to the pond every Saturday, carrying with them each time some delicacy of cookery which he gladly accepted.

And it is equally true that he raided the family cookie jar on his frequent visits home. . . . The Emersons, too, frequently invited him to dinner, as did the Alcotts and the Hosmers. They had all done so before he went to Walden Pond and continued the custom after he left. Rumor had it that every time Mrs. Emerson rang her dinner bell, Thoreau came bounding through the woods and over the fences to be first in line.

Thoreau's recent biographer points out that it was doubtful whether he could hear the dinner bell at such a distance; the joke can be taken as symptomatic of something the town knew —that at Walden Pond, Thoreau's ear was cocked to the sounds of Concord. He led neither the solitary nor the Spartan life his book described. His mention in *Walden* of his dinings out suggests that he did not allow his "experiment" to change his customary social habits. "To meet the objections of some inveterate cavillers," he writes, "I may as well state, that if I dined out occasionally, as I always had done, and I trust shall have opportunities to again, it was frequently to the detriment of my domestic arrangements. But the dining out, being, as I have stated, a constant element, does not in the least affect a comparative statement like this." The "comparative statement" included the sentence, "It was fit that I should live on rice, mainly, who loved so well the philosophy of India."

"Hardly a day went by," Harding comments, "that Thoreau did not visit the village or was not visited at the Pond. . . . Emerson was, of course, a frequent visitor at the cabin. . . . On pleasant summer days Thoreau would often join the Emerson family on a picnic or a blueberrying pary. . . . The Alcotts often took their friends out to the pond to see Thoreau. . . . The children of Concord were always happy to go out to Walden Pond and Thoreau was equally happy to have them."

Harding goes on:

Occasionally whole groups of Thoreau's friends came out together to the pond and swarmed into his little cabin. It became quite the fashion to hold picnics on his front doorstep. When it rained, his visitors took refuge inside. He had as many as twenty-five or thirty people inside the tiny cabin at one time. On August 1, 1846, the antislavery women of Concord held their annual commemoration of the freeing of the West Indian slaves on his doorstep, and Emerson, W. H. Channing, and Rev. Caleb Stetson spoke to the assembled group. Afterward a picnic lunch was served to all the guests.

There was also a Walden Pond Society. This "consisted of those who spent their Sunday mornings out walking around Walden Pond enjoying the beauties of nature. Thoreau was unquestionably the high priest of that sect."

"Despite all the visitors," Thoreau's biographer concludes, "despite all his visits to Concord village and to his parents' home, despite his surveying and fence-building and carpentry, and despite the hours devoted to writing, it must not be forgotten that the experiment at Walden was primarily a period of solitude and of communion with nature for Thoreau." We can only ask, What kind of "experiment" was this? What kind of "solitude"? By no definition of the word—and certainly not in terms of the traditional isolation and contemplation practiced by philosophers and visionaries throughout history—can Thoreau be said to have lived a solitary or even contemplative life at Walden. He was a sojourner in civilized life; he was an observant suburbanite; he was simply a man who had at last acquired a room of his own, and in a way which attracted the town's attention. Young girls found excuses for knocking on his door and asking him for a drink of water; and if he pretended to be indifferent and casually handed them a dipper to drink from the unpolluted pond, nothing could have been more satisfying.

Thoreau is distinctly ambivalent in his chapter on solitude. "I find it wholesome to be alone the greater part of the time. To be in company, even with the best, is soon wearisome and dissipating. I love to be alone." Yet he begins the very next chapter in *Walden*—which is called "Visitors"—by saying, "I think that I love society as much as most, and am ready enough to fasten myself like a bloodsucker for the time to any full-blooded man that comes in my way." By invoking his solitude at Walden, Thoreau cultivated an illusion. To be sure, he spent many hours alone and wandered far afield on rambles, but no more alone than many an individual in daily life. The real solitude of Thoreau's time was that of the men and women who traveled in covered wagons to America's heartland and who were totally cut off from society and thrown upon their own resources. They faced danger; they learned the meaning of fear. Thoreau's experiment at no time posed for him any question of true aloneness or of the terrors of the wilderness.

Thoreau, then, lived one kind of life and fancied he lived another; his fancy may have ruled him so completely that he believed he was really a solitary in his little hut showplace. Let us say that he led two lives. There was the life of Walden, which was an experiment to prove something in his fancy; and the life of Concord, which he really wanted to live because he wanted to cut a figure in the world and defy his enemies in the town who did not like eccentricity or individualism. These two lives, we might say, noting his self-preoccupation, were the lives of an individual who perhaps without knowing it was cultivating the myth of Narcissus. Another way of describing the lives of Thoreau is to say he was having his cake and eating it. We may inquire, therefore: What imperious demand of Thoreau's imagination and his inner being was he following? We know today that such behavior does not occur out of the blue. All behavior has a history. If I first asked, Why did Thoreau go to Walden Pond? I will now ask, Why *really* did Thoreau go to Walden Pond?

I I

Such questions are not easily answered. The scientific method would be to seek out all available information about the life of Thoreau that led to his decision in 1845 to build his hut and withdraw from Concord. And we must do this in the light of Thoreau's character and personality.

There are many negative aspects in Thoreau's way of dealing with his neighbors; few spoke well of him. And we can see how the unpleasant and cantankerous side of the author of *Walden* tended to conceal his remarkable gifts. His neighbors were not literary (except for the handful of intellectuals and artists who made Concord the very center of culture and civilization in New England). The farmers of Concord did not read Thoreau, nor could they accept the belligerence of his nonconformity.

Let us see him then in his family setting. There is the big talkative mother. She puts on grand airs in the town. There is Thoreau's mousy father, the pencil maker, living on the periphery of Concord in genteel poverty. What we discover in Thoreau's book is one capital statement. Walden, he says, was "the fabulous landscape of my infant dreams." His mother had taken him there very early: to this body of water that looked so large to a child, to the woods, and to Fair Haven Hill, where the huckleberries were delicious to the childish taste. Is it any wonder that Thoreau even in maturity led the children of Concord on huckleberry parties to Fair Haven like some Pied Piper? Emerson, in his eulogy of Thoreau, said the author of *Walden* was gifted enough to have engineered for a nation, but chose instead to be the captain of a huckleberry party. In this way he underlined Thoreau's want of ambition. "The fabulous landscape of my infant dreams": such landscapes revisit the dreams of our lives, and when they have been associated with some all-enveloping figure, the landscape itself can become a mother; and nature, as we know, is Mother Nature to us all. Nature, Thoreau once remarked, "is my mother at the same time that she is my sister." Perhaps this was why Thoreau could not bear to leave Concord. He was as rooted there as if he were one of its trees. He attended Harvard, for if Walden was but a couple of miles from Concord, Cambridge was but fourteen miles from

Walden, and in those days when people walked, Thoreau was a great walker. Later he visited a few places: Cape Cod; Staten Island, where he lived briefly; the Maine Woods; Minnesota— but the essential fact is he was born in Concord, lived in Concord (and at Walden), and died in Concord.

It is recorded that when he was about to graduate from Harvard he asked his mother what career he might follow. She replied, "You can buckle on your knapsack and roam around abroad to seek your fortune." In early America, with the frontier near at hand, the remark seemed natural enough. Yet Thoreau had a sudden fit of weeping. He read his mother's remark as if she were sending him away from her. His older sister came to his rescue. "No, Henry, you shall not go; you shall stay at home and live with us." Sometime later he said, "Methinks I should be content to sit at the back door in Concord, under the poplar tree henceforth, forever." And this was, in effect, what he did—for life. In his writings he would make a virtue of this embeddedness. He read the great legends and adventures of man into Concord, as James Joyce later read the *Odyssey* into Dublin. One could, with the aid of books, possess an imaginary world in a cabin by a New England pond. "My cottage becomes the universe," said the Japanese Chōmei.

Thoreau clung to Concord; he clung to his mother. When he finally moved from home, after a spell of schoolteaching, it was into Mr. Emerson's house, at the other end of town, to be his handyman. We know Thoreau heard Emerson deliver his lecture on "Nature" at Harvard, and from then on he enrolled himself in the ranks of the transcendentalists—that philosophy which echoed Rousseau and Coleridge and Goethe and flowered as American romanticism. There was much talk in those days—how familiar it seems—of "spontaneity," the right and duty of acting oneself out and "following one's genius wherever it might lead." The established citizenry said this doctrine unfitted the young for society "without making them fit for anything else." But the transcendental idea was a lifetime philosophy for

Thoreau, and Emerson began by being his hero. As early as 1838, James Russell Lowell, after meeting Thoreau, remarked, "It is exquisitely amusing to see how he imitated Emerson's tone and manner. With my eyes shut I shouldn't know them apart." Seventeen years later it seems to have been the same: Sanborn wrote that in Thoreau's tones and gestures "he seemed to me to imitate Emerson."

Thoreau settled into Emerson's house. And with time one glimpses in Emerson's journals a certain kind of disenchantment. The young man's talk, Emerson writes, is "a continual twining of the present moment into a sentence and offering it to me." Why is he never frank? Emerson asks, and again, "I have no social pleasure with Henry, though more than once the best conversation." After two years, Emerson suggested that Thoreau ought to go out into the world and try to do better than be a handyman. He got him a job on Staten Island—that wooded and lovely island, as it was then, across the bay from Manhattan—tutoring the children of a relative. He gave him letters of introduction to literary folk in New York. If Emerson was really sincerely trying to push Thoreau into a little more action, he may also have been using this way of uprooting his too-settled, emotionally passive handyman.

Thoreau, as may be imagined, was not happy in New York. He had difficulty relating to people, and he missed Concord and its woodlands. We must remember there was also much nature and wilderness then around New York. Walt Whitman found it and celebrated it. Thoreau's longing nevertheless was for his familiar place and for Fair Haven Hill. We get a glimpse of the impression he made on a shrewd individual when in Washington Place off the Square he called on old Henry James, father of the novelist who bore his name and of the pragmatist William James. Henry, Sr., was skillful at describing his fellow humans. One remembers his sketching Carlyle as "the same old sausage sputtering and fizzling in his own grease." So his verdict on Thoreau was that he was "the most child-like, unconscious, and unblushing egotist it has ever been my fortune to encounter in the ranks of mankind." He also described him as having "a sheer and mountainous inward self-esteem." Thoreau didn't stay away long from home. After a few months he was back in Concord. But he was not invited to resume his job at Emerson's.

There he was, at twenty-seven, in the paternal house in his own room with his botanical specimens, his journals, his books —the room that had always been his. For a little while he tried to help his father with the pencil making. Ever resourceful, he simply read up in the encyclopedia how the Germans handled their graphite for the excellent pencils they exported to America. With little effort he improved his father's product, enabling the elder Thoreau to go into the more profitable business of supplying graphite wholesale to other pencil makers. This done, Thoreau resumed his outdoor life as an "inspector" (as he put it) of rainstorms and snowstorms. His life with the Emersons had been an extension of his life at home; he had left home but moved only as far as the home of a neighbor. He had tried to leave Concord, but discovered he was too much out of harmony with the wider world.

III

At this moment there occurred an incident which all the biographers have told without asking themselves its significance. Thoreau went fishing with a friend at Fair Haven Bay. They got a good catch—the fish seemed to like Thoreau quite as much as the birds and the squirrels. The season had been dry, and with singular unwoodsmanly carelessness Thoreau lit a fire in a tree stump to cook his fish. He was the one man in Concord who should have known better; in a few minutes the brush was in flames. There was no stopping the fire. Thoreau ran two miles to sound the alarm; he returned to half a mile of flame roaring in the beloved woods of his hilltop and across the farmland. While help was coming, he climbed to the highest rock of Fair Haven Cliff. "It was a glorious spectacle," the excited fisherman wrote in his journal much later, "and I was the only one there to enjoy it." When the farmers came, Thoreau climbed down and joined in the work. Three hundred acres of woodland were consumed before the fire was brought under control. The local newspaper spoke of "the thoughtlessness of two of our citizens." All Concord knew who the two were. The townsfolk had always considered Thoreau eccentric; now they spoke of him as "that damned rascal." He was not only an idler, who could work but didn't, but a polluter, a "woods-burner." The town could not forgive a lapse that threatened life and property. And then for weeks the women complained that their washing was covered with soot. The memory of small towns is long. The women remembered the soot long after Thoreau was dead.

So in the year of Thoreau's retreat to Walden we discover that his reputation in Concord had reached its lowest point. He was *persona non grata* to his fellow citizens. His journal offers us no details. Six years later, however, there is a series of entries that show how the epithet "damned rascal" troubled him.

"Who are these men who are said to be the owners of these woods, and how am I related to them? I have set fire to the forest, but I have done no wrong therein, and now it is as if the lightning had done it. These flames are but consuming their natural food."

And he also wrote, "It has never troubled me from that day to this more than if the lightning had done it. The trivial fishing was all that disturbed me and disturbs me still." Only a deeply troubled man would write in this way so long afterward, to convince himself that he wasn't troubled. "I at once ceased to regard the owners' and my fault—if fault there was in the matter—and attended to the phenomenon before me, determined to make the most of it. To be sure I felt a little ashamed when I reflected on what a trivial occasion this had happened, that at the time I was no better employed than my townsmen."

Thoreau's decision to move to Walden Pond seems to have been, on one level then, a way of withdrawing from a Concord hostile to him, while at the same time remaining very close to it; a way also of asserting himself as an active "employed" man by embracing the career of writer and philosopher: an act of defiance which would demonstrate that his was a better way of life than that practiced by his fellows. Deeper still may have been the petulance of the child saying, in effect, to the town and to Emerson, See how homeless I am; you have forced me to live in a shanty away from all of you. He would arouse pity; he would also arouse interest. Some such jumble of motives lay behind his decision to give an impression of "hermiting" while not being a hermit. The epigraph he chose for *Walden* directly addresses the townspeople. It is a quotation from the book itself: "I do not propose to write an ode to dejection, but to brag as lustily as chanticleer in the morning, standing on his roost, if only to wake my neighbors up." On a subjective level, *Walden* reflects Thoreau's profound dejection: in the depths of the epigraph one hears the cry of a man who must vent his rage—and be heard by the entire town! That he was full of spleen during the spring of 1845, just before he built his cabin, may be seen in a letter written to him from New York by the younger William Ellery Channing, who seems to have provided the impulse for Thoreau's principal act: "I see nothing for you in this earth but that field which I once christened 'Briars'; go out upon that, build yourself a hut, and there begin the grand process of devouring yourself alive. I see no alternative, no other hope for you. Eat yourself up; you will eat nobody else, nor anything else." There is a fund of psychological truth in Channing's answer to Thoreau's rage. Thoreau had long been devouring himself; he had said as much in a poem: "Here I bloom for a short hour unseen,/Drinking my juices up."

Briars consisted of a dozen acres beside Walden. They belonged to Emerson, who readily permitted his former handyman to place his hut there. Thoreau therefore paid no rent. He did not build the hut in the way Americans built log cabins. He bought a hut from a shanty Irishman, took it apart—being an expert carpenter—and reassembled it: in other words, a prefab of a sort. For a few dollars, and on property for which Emerson paid the taxes, Thoreau could live and boast that he was free. He was, moreover, as we noted, a bachelor. There was no wife to dress, there were no hungry children to feed. Here he lived not for years, like Chōmei, but for twenty-six months by his tally, though I would deduct two or three months, including one he spent at home while the plaster in his hut was drying. He plastered and shingled it in the fall of 1845 when he found the hut was too cold for comfort. He combed neighborly attics to furnish his dwelling. And then he didn't emulate Robinson Crusoe. For instance, he took his shoes to the Concord cobbler; he baked bread using purchased rye and Indian meal; he slept not in rough blankets but between sheets. He gave himself creature comforts few Americans in the log cabins of the West enjoyed.

Lowell, in a celebrated essay, mercilessly denounced Thoreau's pretensions. The "experiment" presupposes, he wrote, "all that complicated civilization which it theoretically abjured. He squatted on another man's land; he borrows an ax; his boards, his nails, his bricks, his mortar, his books, his lamp, his fishhooks, his plough, his hoe, all turn state's evidence against him as an accomplice in the sin of that artificial civilization which rendered it possible that such a person as Henry D. Thoreau should exist at all." But the author of *Walden* discovered that his whim of living in the woods caught the fancy of audiences to whom he lectured. Men and women were willing to listen to the fiction of his rude economy as if he were Robinson Crusoe. It is perhaps to Daniel Defoe that we may turn for a significant literary predecessor. The writer who invented a story of a man confronting the loneliness of life on a desert island may be regarded as the forefather of Thoreau's book. Thoreau blended his wide reading and his purposeful observations to the need of a thesis: in his mind he had proved his "experiment" long before he began it.

IV

Writers create worlds for themselves in their books; they tell parables; they offer allegories of the self. When they express these in the form of fiction or poetry or drama we have the work of a transfiguring imagination which uses symbolic statement and myth to disguise autobiography. But when a writer like Thoreau pretends to give us actuality, we are justified in examining how actual it was. This does not alter the beauty of the feeling he may have set down, or the charm of expression, or the general easy sense of *Walden*—the sense of shedding responsibility at the expense of others and making oneself accountable to the self. The deepest picaresque of *Walden* is the way in which its author, building out of his own insecurity and aggression, trying heroically to make himself powerful and secure, implies that hoeing beans and eating them can be a large sufficiency (even when the menu is supported by the maternal cookie jar and Mrs. Emerson's meals).

Within *Walden* there is also parable and mythic statement and paradox and humor. One singular parable haunts the reader. It is foreshadowed in Thoreau's earlier book, *A Week on the Concord and Merrimack Rivers*. In that book he quotes from the Chinese Meng-tsu, "If one loses a fowl or a dog, he knows well how to seek them again; if one loses the sentiments of his heart, he does not know how to seek them again. . . . The duties of practical philosophy consist only in seeking after those sentiments of the heart which we have lost; that is all." In *Walden* this is translated into a personal fable, dropped almost irrelevantly into the book with the remark that the reader must pardon some obscurities, "for there are more secrets in my trade than in most men's." Many have been puzzled by its enigma: "I long ago lost a hound, a bay horse, and a turtledove, and am still on their trail. Many are the travellers I have spoken concerning them, describing their tracks and what calls they answered to. I have met one or two who had heard the hound, and the tramp of the horse, and even seen the dove disappear behind a cloud, and they seemed as anxious to recover them as if they had lost them themselves."

A hound, a bay horse, a turtledove. Thoreau names three members of the animal kingdom close to all mankind. The faithful hound, guide, protector, loyal, lovable. Who does not know the bonds between a man and his dog? And the horse, in older times, in Thoreau's time, plower of fields, the embodiment of strength and thrust and support; animal of sport and chivalry, spirited creature, symbol of our instincts and sexual drives. Who does not know, even today, when the combustion engine has replaced the horse, how many bonds are established between a man and his horse? And finally the turtledove— whose soft cooing and swiftness as messenger, symbol of love and of the Holy Ghost, embodies so much of man's association with the creatures of the air and the mysteries of religion. "Oh that I had wings like a dove! for then would I fly away, and be at rest." The psalm speaks also of getting away from the world's cares, thus a flight to some Walden of the mind.

A hound, a bay, a turtledove. Thoreau had lost them, and in his parable he announced that he always searched for them. Is he not proclaiming the loss of things belonging to the deepest part of himself? Without guide, without support, shorn of drive, there could be no peace, no strength of the spirit, no love. His life was indeed a quest for these lost emotions and the instinctual life. And if he found other men similarly bereft, this was because Thoreau could not recognize that his very condition of life deprived him of human friendship. A man who decides to be a loner must accept the consequences of that decision. Translating into another language, we might say that Thoreau's quest for the lost things of his spirit was a quest for the mature experiences of this world: he could not rise above the contemplation of his own visage. He was, to put it in mythic terms, a fragile Narcissus embodied in a rough New Englander. He talked only of himself; in fact, he announces this in the opening of *Walden:* "I should not talk so much about myself if there were anyone else whom I knew as well." At that rate we should all talk about ourselves. And he wrote a journal which was the mirror of himself—he wrote in it daily. It fills many volumes. He said that even the echoes of his voice were the only "kindred voices" that he heard. A man who listens only to himself will, of course, never discover other voices.

What does man do when he creates a myth? Often he makes everything into opposites. If he is puny he thinks himself a giant. Little Tom Thumb killed ogres and rescued his family, and he was as small as a pea. David symbolized the myth of brain over brawn. Samson was all brawn only so long as his hair was uncut. Shorn, he lost his prowess. Thoreau, shut up in his childhood, could not leave home. He created a myth of how he got away from the world in a supposed wilderness. In the first paragraph of *Walden,* Thoreau remarks that, having stayed in his hut, he is once again a sojourner in civilized society. Had he ever left it? Yes, in the realms of his fancy. He was dependent, insecure, mother-attached, full of longing to be free. He made a myth of self-reliance. But he was a very dependent and cling-ing individual. His spiritual helplessness engendered anger and rage; one is conscious of subdued violence in him, for no man wants to think of himself as helpless. And so he vented his rage on his neighbors and looked down on the hard-working farmers. Thoreau was no saint. He preached what he pretended to prac-tice; he preached only what he imagined—he pursued an ideal, a noble, beautiful, and unreal dream. His spiritual immaturity was nowhere more revealed than in his horror of sex. And this in a lover of nature was strange indeed. All his life was a search for a utopia which many of the impoverished farmers he de-spised had in effect by their own hearth: the warmth of human love, the tenderness and companionship of women and chil-dren, that love which Thoreau in his deepest anguish lavished on animals and plants with whom he could commune in his alienation from his fellows. His neighbors knew this well; otherwise we would not have the anecdote Emerson quoted over Thoreau's grave, about the individual who said, "I love Henry but I cannot like him; and as for taking his arm, I should as soon think of taking the arm of an elm-tree."

Out of his rage Thoreau could proclaim an ideal of civil disobedience—he gave us that formulation—and in a romantic way went to jail for a night because he hadn't paid his tax—a gesture like his residence at Walden. Gestures, however, can fire men's minds; they can lead to unreason and anarchy. Thoreau never thought through to the end the meaning of personal freedom when it is gained at the expense of others.

Man lives by myths. In an age of technology there is a danger that we may discard too many of them; they can, when they are not malevolent and destructive—as Hitler's myth of the master race was—make for order and substitute civilization for barbarism. Thoreau gave us an exquisite myth, a myth of some idyllic retreat—Walden, a desert island, some refuge, some "great good place" of the mind that in a crowded world has a potent appeal. But it is also a flawed myth. In preaching self-reliance he forgot society, he forgot companionship, he did not understand love. He wanted to be Spartan and Athenian at the same time; he managed a mild simulation of the Spartan but could not allow himself Athens. He would have been a tolerably good medieval monk; even then he would find his cell not sufficient. He would leave the order, build his own cell, make his own rules—of course within easy distance of the brotherhood, say a mile or so down the way from the monastery. And then he might waver in his faith. Two years at Walden sufficed. He said he "left the woods for as good a reason as I went there." He added, "Perhaps it seemed to me that I had several more lives to live, and could not spare any more time for that one." So Walden was a mood, a fancy, a fleeting dream. Someone who

looks for the unattainable must keep on looking as Thoreau did
—the hound, the bay horse, the turtledove always eluded him.
There are no utopias in the real world.

Thoreau once said, in a moment of beautiful insight, that
poetry "is a piece of very private history, which unostenta-
tiously lets us into the mystery of a man's life." Instead of accepting Thoreau's own rationalizations, as most biographers
have done, we have sought our way to the mystery of Walden
Pond by a sequence analysis of our data and on the principle of
literary psychology that there is nothing accidental in human
behavior, whether it be the setting down of a poem or the
building of a hut in the woods. The idea is uncongenial and even
repugnant to many; it uncompromisingly says we are determined creatures, and certainly there are more things in our
genes than we at present dream on. It won't do to answer, when
I ask, Why did Thoreau *really* go to Walden Pond?, "Oh, it was
an impulse," or "He went because he wanted to," or "He said
he wanted to suck the marrow out of life." Nothing is just an
impulse. The question is, What prompts it? "As he thinketh in
his heart," says Proverbs, "so is he." The ancients knew this very
well. We may not always understand why certain things are, or
what motivated certain kinds of behavior, but we may be sure
that behavior is related to our constituted educated selves; it is
consistent with the education in our nerve ends and our brain.
Thoreau had many choices. He could have continued to live in
the family house. He could have stayed on in New York. He
could have gone West in a covered wagon. He did none of these
things. He moved instead into his hut on a certain day—it coincided with a national holiday, the Fourth of July 1845. And in
this he did certain characteristic things. He was roughing it, and
he wore a beard, but he took a three-by-three-inch mirror with
him into the hut. We can pause and speculate about that mirror
and what need it fulfilled beside the larger one of the pond
itself, nature's mirror. Why he needed to carry out what he

called his "experiment" is in itself a question. And his experiment took a very special form. We must probe unconscious as well as conscious promptings, recognizing the risks we take and that much of our work is inductive.

But out of all the little things we observe, Thoreau built the myth of himself. Out of his small irritations and cantankerous opinion, he wrote a book for the world. *Walden,* then, is the myth of Thoreau; it *is* Thoreau. We return to it for its exquisite moments of emotion, for its sense of nature, for its poetic moods, for its literary feeling.

We must discount some of Thoreau's irritableness and self-righteousness; there are indeed moments when the rooster crows out of tune. *Walden's* half-truths seem superficial and ill-natured; yet it became, as I said, an impermeable myth. It seems to fit all the stages of our national growth, all the rapacity of our creation; and it becomes more powerful with every foot of cement that covers our soil and every skyscraper that blots out the blue. For a biographer who seeks all the little facts and tries to establish all the tidy little truths, it holds a high cautionary lesson. A legend can be more powerful than the truth—indeed, in the end it can become the truth.

JAMES JOYCE

At the Opera

I saw James Joyce for the first time at the Paris opera in 1929. I went to the opera because I knew he would be there and I wanted to have a good look at him. From my eighteenth year, when I had obtained a copy of the banned *Ulysses,* he had been my personal culture hero, as he was for an entire generation of literary people, many of whom traveled to Paris and walked away from Shakespeare & Company in the rue de l'Odéon clutching their precious copy of the censored book in its sea-blue covers—the blue, we were assured, of the Greek flag. Joyce from the first had a way of putting as many meanings into a color or a word as possible; his portmanteau of language was always tightly packed.

I have to put myself back into my twenty-two-year-old self, wearing my beret and wandering on the fringes of the so-called "lost generation." I certainly didn't feel lost. I wanted to set eyes on Joyce, and every time I went to Sylvia Beach's shop I looked around for the guiding genius of the place. I remember seeing a great many celebrities at Shakespeare & Company, but during my first year in Paris I never had a glimpse of James Joyce. Miss Beach sheltered him; he was mysterious, he was legendary, he was invisible. Exile, toil, persecution, poverty, cunning—he seemed himself the reincarnation of Odysseus. What writer would have had the audacity to put a single day— a Dublin day, at that—into one book, to clutch at one moment in time out of eternity and a timeless world—and to do it with words alone? This was the excuse for my youthful idolatry.

My reason for going to the opera, aside from curiosity about Joyce himself, was to respond to a call he had issued through Miss Beach. Odysseus wanted all hands on deck to applaud an Irish tenor named John Sullivan who had been engaged by the Paris opera to sing *Guillaume Tell* and *Les Huguenots* but was being given few opportunities to do so. Joyce believed it was rank discrimination: the opera people were playing favorites, and poor Sullivan needed money and recognition for his virtuosity. "Sullivan sings 45 G's, 93 A flats, 92 A's, 54 B flats, 15 B's, 19 C's, and 2 C sharps"—the statistical Joyce talked very much like his Leopold Bloom. He added, "Nobody else can do it." This idea of the unique performer, the unique performance sounded like Joyce himself. Who else would count every sharp and flat? He had identified himself wholly with his compatriot. He began to think of Sullivan as a "banned singer," like himself, the "banned writer." And he would write "From a Banned Writer to a Banned Singer" in the language of *Finnegans Wake.* But I had to recognize, when I informed myself, that *Les Huguenots* and *Guillaume Tell* were not the most popular revivals of the season. And doubtless the administration of the Place de l'Opéra had to give other singers their turn; a singer named Lauri-Volpi, a lyrical tenor, seemed to be favored. Giacomo Lauri-Volpi appears in the "Banned Singer" as "luring volupy," characterized as fit only to intone love songs.

At any rate Joyce was organizing an informal claque, and I made myself a member of it. We paid for our own tickets. I remember I went to the box office the morning the seat sale opened and waited a couple of hours in line to obtain a good cheap seat. My student's purse contained only a few francs, but we were not to clap for our supper. Such are the loyalties of hero worship. Instead of buying an eight- or ten-franc seat (about 35 cents) in the front row of the top balcony, as I invariably did, I invested a dollar in a second-tier front seat. I would command a view of the entire opera from the middle right side of the horseshoe. After all, I was to have not only the singing of

Sullivan (who had to be good, if Joyce said so) but a glimpse of the Great Man himself. It was well worth the price of a couple of Latin Quarter meals.

I arrived early and watched from my advantageous position. The stalls were very well dressed, and the cheaper seats were soon filled. I scanned the operagoers for a sight of Joyce, but there was no sign of him in the great russet acoustical chamber, with its celebrated chandelier from which Lon Chaney had swung. What a busy place! An air of anticipation and excitement, and the usual lines struggling to get seated while the black-dressed *ouvreuses* pocketed their tips with that mixture of motherliness and avarice for which they are famous. The fiddles were tuning up. I swept my little opera glass across the seats on the theory that the leader of our claque was already in his place. I was sure I'd find him. And then suddenly, at the last minute, he was there; I saw him walking down the left aisle. A younger man directly behind him I judged to be Joyce's son, Giorgio, who had also trained for the opera and was said to be a fine baritone. The first glimpse was a bit of a shock; Joyce walked like a blindman. He looked straight ahead of him, with the rigidity of sightlessness, and leaned on his cane—doubtless the ashplant of *A Portrait of the Artist.* He was immaculately dressed—black tie, boiled shirt, and the famous "Latin Quarter" hat perched on his head. The two moved slowly down the thronged aisle, ignored by the audience, and sat down in about the twelfth or fifteenth row of the stalls. Joyce took the aisle seat. He shifted himself slowly into it. After a bit he removed his funereal hat, revealing abundant graying hair combed back and glistening. He peered through what looked like two pairs of spectacles, one superimposed on the other. The world had heard of his cataract operations. He was not totally sightless, but that evening he seemed like blind Homer; had he not written literature's queerest odyssey?

Once settled, he was immobile; he kept his hand on his stick. Then the lights dimmed. The orchestra began the fustian overture. I can't recall much of the opera. It was, I believe, the only Meyerbeer I ever heard, and the music seemed to me florid and old-fashioned. They drank; they roared; they stabbed; they chorused; they died. I had been nourishing myself on Bach and Stravinsky and Debussy, and somehow this opera seemed wrong. I deplored Joyce's musical taste; I felt that the Huguenots would hardly have sung so lyrically of their miseries; I did not care for historical violence and tragedy set to music.

John Sullivan finally appeared. He was in elaborate costume and had a tenorial embonpoint. Joyce didn't let him get out a single note. He began to applaud as soon as Sullivan was sighted, and we obediently joined and stopped the show. Sullivan had his recognition then and there, as if it were the final curtain. He could have sung badly. He could have hit false notes instead of all those fine ones Joyce had catalogued. Our part of the audience was assured beforehand of his greatness. As a matter of fact, he did have a fine voice, but it had sung better days. I expected a voice as reverberant as Caruso's. Sullivan's was smaller and distinctly lyrical (Lauri-Volpi's was smaller still)— and distinctly Irish. He could go up very high; he sustained his notes beautifully. He was, however, a stiff, heavy, overcostumed figure on the stage, and Meyerbeer's opera was pretty stiff too. It was when Sullivan had finished his first aria that I heard Joyce —clear, bell-like, high. The banned writer sang out, right up to the chandelier, "Bravo! Bravo!" I can hear him still. The banned writer applauded the "banned" singer. We brought down the house.

At the end of the first act, I wandered out for a closer glimpse of the literary virtuoso. I suspected Joyce would not stray far from his seat, so I descended the marble staircase to the horseshoe corridor on Joyce's side. There he stood, smoking a cigarette near the entrance to his aisle, surrounded by a group of friends. I watched (very worshipfully) at a distance, and I had a clear and undisturbed vision of my culture hero. He seemed tall; he was slim and carelessly elegant. His body curved in a slouch. He had put his "Latin Quarter" hat back on his head; it was slightly pushed up on his forehead. His clothes were well tailored, he wore pumps, and there was a certain daintiness and jauntiness in him despite the slouch. I had seen photographs of Joyce with a little goatee, but he no longer wore this. His mustache was closely trimmed, and the single great feature of his face was its owl-like, peering quality—those thick walls of glass seemed to shut everyone away from him. I could catch the tones of his melodious voice, but not the words. He talked; he never smiled. He appeared to me sad, weary, oppressed; he leaned on his ashplant with the jejune weariness of Stephen Dedalus, his body seeming hung loosely together. There was no suggestion in his manner that he was in any way enjoying this evening, in spite of its aggressive intentions and its clear triumph.

The rest of the evening was a repetition of all I have described: more Sullivanian high notes, more applause, more vocal variants on Joyce's "Bravo!" and "puur Jemmy in the stalls," as the virtuoso described himself with a hint of self-pity —Jemmy applauding "that long note he just delivered." We have Joyce's rendering of the evening in the "Banned Singer":

> Grand spectacular exposition of gorge cutting, mortarfiring and general martyrification, beleighted up with erst classed instrumental music. Pardie! There's more sang in that Sceine than mayer's beer at the Guildhall. . . .

And so on: the characteristic puns, the Irish jabberwocky. Joyce alludes to his claque a few lines after this in describing the *cliqueclaquehats* worn by three other tenors, Enrico, Giacomo, and Giovanni (that is, the dead Caruso, the fading Lauri-Volpi, and the elderly Martinelli). Sullivan must have had more applause than he had ever reaped in all his life; and always there came that splendid lyrical "Bravo!" which seemed to soar high, high up to the great frescoed ceiling. At the end, Joyce stood at his seat waving and cheering as if he were leading conquering troops to a great victory.

Had I been more prosperous then, I suppose I might have attended all of Sullivan's appearances that winter—or shall I say all of Joyce's? I know he was always there in his stall, giving his bravo signal to his cohorts. But I confined myself to the one evening of *Les Huguenots* and to the first performance of *Guillaume Tell*. Joyce was in his usual seat at the latter and I was in mine, and we mingled our applause as before. "Guillaume's shot telled, sure enough," with all the prescribed high C's, "for the odd and twentieth supererogatory time" (so we can read in the "Banned Singer"). "Aim well, Arnold," and Sullivan in the Arnold role hits his notes and "draws the breathblow: that arrownotes coming." Sullivan had his great evening, and between the acts Joyce smoked his cigarettes and talked gloomily (so it seemed) to his entourage. If the operas had bored me less, I suppose I might have been a more loyal claqueur, but I felt I had done my duty. I had lent my applause and spent my sous for Joyce's cause, and I suspect that when I applauded Sullivan at these gala occasions, I was, in the deepest part of me, applauding the other virtuoso, a hero not of the voice but of the pen. I would not be surprised that, in the deepest part of himself, Joyce's applause was as much for the banned writer as for the allegedly banned singer. For Joyce had linked himself wholly to his countryman's voice and read his own dilemma into the life of Sullivan—"this hardworking guy—long to lung over us." Having crowned him king of the tenors, Joyce, super performer of the writers, was satisfied.

Close-Up

My few memories, which are a series of vivid pictures but which may seem like a trip through a photo album when told in words, would be but half told if I did not say a little about the two ladies of the rue de l'Odéon. To this day I think of this short street somehow as feminized—not, as some Paris streets are, by *haute couture* but by its two noble tenants, both of whom have been recalled in various pages, not least in their own memoirs. The rue de l'Odéon: I look up from the Boulevard Saint-Germain and see at its far end the pseudo-Greek of the Odéon theater, today Malraux-cleaned and chaste like some ancient temple shining as if just built. I knew it in its down-at-heels days before and during the Second World War, and in the 1920s and early 1930s I browsed under its arcades in Flammarion's bookstalls. I remember the old Restaurant Voltaire at the left of the semicircle and, higher up, the Hotel Corneille, which in its time had harbored so many writers, including Joyce himself. If you walked up the left side of rue de l'Odéon in the direction of the theater, you would arrive very quickly at a French bookshop with the words LA MAISON DES AMIS DES LIVRES painted in large letters above the windows, and if you looked a short diagonal across the street you saw SHAKESPEARE & COMPANY in the same lettering. They were, if you examined one and then the other, twin bookshops, and if you entered them you recognized affinities and resemblances. Both were lending libraries; both were frequented by Latin Quarter students, French and non-French; both were presided over by interesting women who made friends with their customers. Much later in life I saw a picture of André Gide, wearing a beret, and realized I had often browsed beside him at Adrienne Monnier's. I seem to see Valéry there too, although I am not certain; one sometimes tends to falsify memory with photographs of the same places seen later. Adrienne Monnier's French lending library was a busy little shop, and I remember my first glimpse of her late in 1928; she has been much described, and we have Gisèle Freund's beautiful photographs of her. I see her now in her shop, or in Sylvia Beach's, or crossing the street in her long, nunlike flowing blue or gray garb—the round, soft, white-powdered face, the hair pulled back, her open-wide eyes. She reminded me of Flemish portraits, of rounded, large-eyed, reality-seeking ladies; all that she needed was the old-time ruff. Indeed, reading one of her little essays, I find she compared herself with such a portrait, from which I conclude that she probably dressed for the part. Her shop was always attractive, and yet it is hard to say why. There was no elaborate display: a few paintings and photos in such little spaces as were not taken by books, a stove, a straw chair; the books were covered with cheap tissue to protect them, since most of them circulated. I remember that when my first book was published I solemnly brought it to Adrienne and inscribed a copy for her. She insisted on reciprocating the gift and gave me the French translation of *Ulysses,* which she had published. I felt I had far and away the best of that bargain.

The story of Adrienne's shop was an interesting one. She had gone to England when young and learned to speak English (although I remember her speaking only French in her singsong voice). Her father had been injured in a train accident, for which he had received a large indemnity. He turned over some of this money to Adrienne, and she, booklover and constant reader, had the idea of opening a little bookshop at 7 rue de l'Odéon. She was twenty-two then (in 1915), which means that she was in her late thirties when I first met her. She was to remain in this one shop for thirty-six years. It survived the Second World War, closing its doors in 1951 because Adrienne's health was poor. (She committed suicide four years later in blank depression. Who today can say why?)*

I got to know Sylvia Beach over the years, and I remember her (as a whole generation of Americans must) in her well-cut suits and her bobbed black hair (Adrienne in the end bobbed hers too). She had a soft, musical voice and was one of the pleasantest women I have ever known. Much has been said about her difficulties with Joyce, and anyone who knows any-

* Her translator, Richard McDougall, in his lengthy biographical introduction to *The Very Rich Hours of Adrienne Monnier* (1976) gives us her suicide note. She took an overdose of sleeping pills to escape the effects of a disease of the inner ear (Ménière's Syndrome) which filled her head with noises "that have been martyrizing me for eight months."

thing about him and his money problems will recognize how much of a trial he must have been at times to his publisher. But I can testify that in all the years I knew her (I saw her often between 1928 and 1932 and again during 1936–37 as well as after the Occupation, when her shop was closed), I never heard her speak of him unkindly. She always spoke his name with respect; in fact, I never heard her say anything that did not enlarge the legend she had helped to create; she was, in fact, his public relations agent as much as his publisher. In the late 1920s he came much less frequently to Sylvia Beach's shop than in earlier days. Her customers always hoped to see him and asked questions about him, especially the summer visitors who arrived to buy their copies of *Ulysses,* and she was always patient, discreet, tactful. She could have set herself up as a flourishing avant-garde publisher. Many writers sent their manuscripts to her. But she remained the publisher of *Ulysses* and *Pomes Penyeach* and the little volume of comments on *Finnegans Wake* when it was still "Work in Progress." She remained in effect the publisher of a single author and in reality of a single work. She had never intended to be a publisher; she was one by circumstance. She had wanted to have her modest little bookshop, her literary foyer modeled on Adrienne's, but fame, in the figure of the tall, slouching Irishman with his cane and his arrogance, thrust itself through her doorway.

It was Sylvia who in the winter of 1931 sent me an invitation to attend a soirée at Adrienne Monnier's that would be devoted to a reading of the French translation of "Anna Livia Plurabelle." The passage had been rendered out of Joyce's liquid river-sounds into a strange, exotic Gallic equivalent. Joyce had presided over the translating sessions; it was translation by committee. One man wrote the text, but several translators were required—the combined efforts of Eugene Jolas, Samuel Beckett, Philippe Soupault, Ivan Goll, Paul Léon.

I arrive early. It is a damp Paris night. The shop is festive. The tables have been pushed aside; half a hundred chairs have been crowded into the front, where the window is the backdrop. I make for two low, curved seats in front and take one to the side, so I can see and hear everything and still be out of the way. I am distinctly conscious of myself as a student strayed into a literary party. I recognize a number of faces, the originals of photographs on Adrienne's and Sylvia's walls. But I know no one save my bustling hostesses. I sit quietly in my little corner. Adrienne takes her place in front of a music stand on which she has arranged the sheets of the French translation. Philippe Soupault is to speak. A tall figure glides swiftly in and places himself in the second low chair with the round arms just opposite, the twin of the one I am occupying. James Joyce is a few inches from me; I am looking into the sad face with the clipped mustache. Joyce's long legs almost touch mine. He looks larger than life, with his great owl-glass eyes, the most vivid thing I recall about him. Memorable evening. I sit as close to my culture hero as I ever got. Should I address him? What should I say? I am frozen. I am tongue-tied. I say nothing. I pull further into myself before the inscrutable and melancholy Irishman. When I recall the evening I remember above all the air of distance and aloofness of Joyce, the impassive countenance almost without expression. I am profoundly aware of the deep gloom in the man. He is shut in; he seems shut away. What could I say to him that wouldn't sound fatuous? The eyes are magnified and blurred. He is well dressed, informal; he slouches in his seat and leans his head on his hand much of the time. Philippe Soupault speaks with charm and liveliness of the translating sessions. He offers generalizations about "Work in Progress" and, if I remember rightly, speaks of the plastic qualities of English and the resistance of French to these very qualities. Then Adrienne reads the French text, in the accents of the Comédie Française, singsong, in her high musical voice, up and down, up and down, no low tones. She is wearing her long robes and has a white shawl thrown over her shoulders. She chants Joyce in French—strange, weird. The audience listens silently and respectfully. Her lips become a circle as she says the word *ondes.* Joyce sits without moving. I keep glancing at him, not knowing whether he is aware of me save as a juxtaposed physical presence.

Then Adrienne brings out a portable gramophone and winds it up. She plays the original passage as Joyce recorded it. It is one of the finest of all the recordings of what we now call "the spoken word." Joyce's genius for mimicry and his histrionic talent is in it. He is all the actor and also all the singer, and it is here that I can discover the sentient Joyce and his sentimental tenderness for words. *Are you not gone ahome? What Thom Malone? Can't hear with the bawk of bats.* Sylvia Beach had played the recording for me just after she received it, and she had obtained another copy for me. I remember how we had followed the text in the specially printed copy from which Joyce read it. It was set in large type so that he could see it with ease, and the effect was of large sheets of a medieval manuscript. The oversize letters hadn't prevented him from reversing some of the phrases, or skipping a word here and there. Now he sits, looking innocent and disinterested, as if listening to a stranger's voice, a poker face in the hush of Adrienne's shop. Oh, yes, I thought, the artist "refined out of existence, indifferent, and paring his fingernails." Was I reading something into the moment? This moment when I watched Joyce—I stared with impunity, he seemed so far away—and he sat there, head high, slightly cocked, jaunty, listening attentively but with no sign of being affected. I thought of it then, and think of it still, as a split second of literary history; and I am grateful that I had been vouchsafed a glimpse, a unique glimpse, of the author of *Finnegans Wake* listening to himself, to the strange and esoteric music of the words he had brought into being. I understood more than ever why this performing artist compulsively led his claque at the opera.

"Work in Progress" had seemed to me from the first the writing of a madman. It was, I thought, the futile creation of an energetic and endless *jeu d'esprit*. I had wondered again and again why Joyce was "wasting" his unique gifts in fashioning an entire book out of portmanteau words, the kind Lewis Carroll put together in "Jabberwocky." As successive sections appeared in the magazine *transition*, my bewilderment had grown; while some of the word nonsense was amusing and the puns in several languages were sufficiently outrageous, I had shrugged my shoulders, as the young will, and wanted to prescribe to the great man the books he should be writing. But from the moment I heard Joyce's recording of this section of *Anna Livia Plurabelle* I became a convert. I felt that there was method in the madness. It was during this time that Adrienne gave me an old 1925 issue of her avant-garde magazine *Le Navire d'argent*, which contained the earliest published version of *Anna Livia*. What startled me were sentences of "normal" English prose, and I suddenly had the idea of comparing this text with later ones to discover how Joyce was fashioning his work. I knew of at least four subsequent versions, and I collected these with all the zeal of a textual scholar.

The result was an article which I published in a Canadian monthly. I came on a copy of it recently; it is full of borrowed language, and I would never reprint it, but I suppose I can claim to have been among the first in the long line of academic *Finnegan* explicators, a kind of frontiersman of what has since come to be known as the "Joyce industry" in the universities. I am glad I wrote the article, for in it I recognized that "Work in Progress" needed to be defended against those who were pouring ridicule on it. Or, as I put it—as solemnly as Dedalus, with a certain pomposity, as if I were writing a leader for the *Times* —"what concerns us at the moment is method in 'Work in Progress': there is sufficient in it, I feel, to warrant a close scrutiny rather than a careless dismissal." The close scrutiny continues everywhere as I write these words. I find that I took a page out of Irving Babbitt to suggest that perhaps there was "a *mélange* of too many things, a confusion of the arts, akin to Father

Castel's *clavecin des couleurs.*" As I have said, my collation of
the text had been stimulated by the fact that in the *Navire
d'argent* version Joyce had written some sentences in straight
English, such as "Wait till the rising of the moon." But in subsequent versions (and in the pages of *Finnegans Wake*) this became "Wait till the honeying of the lune, love." The change
from "moon" to "lune" and the metaphor of "honeying"—thus
"honeymoon"—opened avenues of liquidity, and of pun and
suggestion. My article merely made a small point; it was left to
Harry Levin to write the first major expository essay, and when
Finnegans Wake was published, Edmund Wilson was to read it
with an ease that to this day few can cultivate. Thornton Wilder
was to be fascinated by it for years, finding all kinds of hidden
meanings until one day he felt he was being "had"—possessed
by the Joyce demon. Ultimately his verdict was *"Quelle fumis-
terie!"*

When my little article appeared, I showed it to Sylvia Beach
and she showed it to Joyce. She told me he read it with pleasure.
Later she gave me a photograph of him, which he had inscribed
to me—his and Sylvia's way of thanking me. Joyce at that time
was grateful for any commentary (however youthful) on his
work that did not ridicule it. We know how the book itself
finally came out at the moment of the Second World War, and
how the light and liquid sounds of the Liffey were drowned in
the roar of Hitler's guns. Today *Finnegans Wake* is in paperback, and a hardy new generation, trained in textual study,
takes it in vigorous stride. It is a work of the linguistic imagination and of fairy-tale quality. But as exegesis of it continues,
something else will be revealed. I have looked at the book often
enough to become aware that in it can be found both the most
and the least benign sides of Joyce. Joyce the monster, the
furtive and cunning, has used this poetic work to pay off all his
old grudges and debts as he did in certain pages of *Ulysses.* As
those to whom he was devoted figure affectionately in the book,
so he has also, like Dante, placed his enemies—or those he

believed to be his enemies—somewhere in the polyglot pur-
gatories of his word world. *Finnegans Wake* is both a work of
art and an act of revenge. It combines the brilliancy and the
madness of art. And I think in the end we will marvel that a man
should have so transformed the pettiness of the harbored
grudge into the humor and beauty of speech. *Finnegans Wake*
remains the greatest curiosity of modern literature. Generations unborn will learn lessons from it. But the book will also be
an object lesson in the perversities of genius, the compulsions
of art. There is simply too much of it.

City of Exile

In 1946, at Christmas, I did what now seems to me a curious
thing: I went to Zurich and visited the grave of James Joyce. It
was curious because I was then stationed with the U.S. Military
Government in Germany, a time when I was not inclined to
make sentimental literary pilgrimages. The war had just ended.
I was seeking ways to help Germans untainted by Nazism—
there were a certain number—reestablish a reasonably objective press, for better or for worse, in the U.S. zone. The Goebbels propaganda machine had perished in the holocaust of the
Chancellery in Berlin. Goebbels had committed suicide in that
great delusion of *Götterdämmerung* in which the Hitlerians
lived. They died in an ordinary fire, believing themselves in
Valhalla. The propaganda machine was wrecked; its communications were chewed up. It was very difficult to find reporters
in Germany who had not served the war makers. All that is
another story, and I find the years have tended to erase much
of it. It was a time of nightmare, after the speed and movement
and triumph of the Battle of France, and we tend to forget
nightmares. Perhaps one way to escape was to go to Zurich
when I got my first leave.

In Germany I lived in a hotel in the town of Bad Nauheim, where Americans used to take the baths for various ailments, notably heart disease. We had made it our headquarters and set up offices for the little news agency I had organized for Military Government's "Information Control Division." In the midst of this, as if I were reaching out to the sanity of another time, I found my thoughts turning to James Joyce. This was not altogether an accident. In the long evenings, in the bar at the Hotel Bristol, where we were billeted, time hung heavy on our hands; we drank watered German wine, and American officers talked of new wars to be fought. Here I found myself revisiting the past with an old acquaintance, Eugene Jolas, whom I had known in New York. He had been editor of *transition*, the avant-garde journal of the expatriates in Paris, and had been a friend of James Joyce. The dead writer's name came up often in our talk, although we spoke more often of war than of literature.

Eugene Jolas was a quiet and thoughtful man, born in New Jersey of French descent. His parents had taken him back to Lorraine as a boy and he had gone to the German schools, so he ended up a trilingual. This made him sensitive to word resemblances in different languages—to the question not only of how people communicate but how they express themselves. He knew the dada movement and was among the early exponents of surrealism in poetry. He wrote brooding poems of his own and opened *transition* to many kinds of contributors. I can still taste the German wines we drank in the lounge in which the military sat discussing how America should take on Russia. There was a good deal of army talk and barrack-room swagger around us, but Jolas and I talked of the life of letters. He had come to Germany as an American civilian to take part in the work of the Occupation and had agreed to be editor in chief of our news agency. Often in our talk we wandered back to the author of *Finnegans Wake*.

Late in the autumn of 1946, planning a furlough in which I

would escape for a while from the claustrophobic life of the German military compound, I talked to Jolas of my proposed itinerary in Switzerland. He urged me to include Zurich and to call on Joyce's widow. I could ascertain for him whether she was in need of financial help. Royalties had not always reached her during the war years. Zurich, for me, was associated with Jung, and even more with Joyce, for I remembered the "Trieste-Zurich-Paris" at the end of *Ulysses*. I thought of the way in which the Irish writer had suddenly been swallowed up in 1941, at the moment when all Europe was in flames. We knew then very little of his end. It had come during the deepest nighttime of the war, when all we cherished seemed laid on sacrificial altars.

Mention of Zurich had set Eugene Jolas roaming its streets in memory with Joyce, taking boat rides on the lake and walks on the Zurichberg near the zoo. Joyce was then writing the section of *Finnegans Wake* known as "The Mime of Mick, Nick and the Maggies," constantly elaborating and embroidering the text. One evening, as they walked near the zoo, he enchanted Jolas by quoting to him the nocturne of Phoenix Park from the "Mime"—its melting together of puns and poetry, seeking to create the animal sounds as they receded in the gathering night, a parallel passage to the nightfall passage in *Anna Livia Plurabelle:* "It darkles . . . all this our funnanimal world. . . . Ark!? Noh? Nought stirs in spinney. The swayful pathways of the dragonfly spider stay still in reedery. Quiet takes back her folded fields. Tranquille thanks. Adew."

"You must dine at the Kronenhalle and order a *vin du Valais,*" Jolas said, and he went on to praise the wine. The Kronenhalle restaurant had replaced in later years the Café Zum Pfauen of Joyce's earlier Zurich, chronicled by Frank Budgen. The Irish writer would dine, usually with Jolas, during this particular summer of 1932. Jolas remembered the desultory talk that continued for hours over the accumulating bottles of the Valais. "And be sure to take a walk by the Limmat," Jolas added. "Joyce always used to pun as he walked by it: 'See that! Isn't it the Limit?' "

So I found myself, during a frigid January in 1946, embarked on the classical literary pilgrimage—the visit to a hero's grave, a hero of letters, as one visits the graves of Keats and Shelley in Rome or the mountain grave of R. L. Stevenson in Samoa, or that of Rupert Brooke on Skyros, or (as I would later visit with Edmund Wilson) the grave of Henry James in Cambridge cemetery. I went by bus on a Sunday morning when a thick, buttery, bourgeois fog enfolded the stately city. I boarded the No. 5, which I was told would take me to the cemetery. It circled higher and higher in sepulchral mists, as in some modern eerie movie, some Poe-esque dream, until I was lifted out of swirling whiteness toward the clear air and blue sky. Below was the fogged-in city, and when I reached the Alte Kirche Fluntern, the sun, pale and moist yellow, peered out of the tenuous mists.

The cemetery was situated a few yards from the terminal on a gentle slope. It was not a collection of miscellaneous tombstones, stuck densely together, as in many cities, but an orderly park, with tall trees, wide paths, and disciplined hedges. It had large gates, and the snow had been carefully shoveled from the paths. To the right of the entrance was a long low building which looked more like a dignified residence than a cemetery chapel. It had a portico and white pillars. There was snow on the lawn and on the roof. In the chapel office a stout woman proffered a card index. I found the name Joyce, James Augustine (the Aloysius was omitted), Grave No. 1449. "Go up the center aisle," the woman directed, "and turn left in the fourteenth row." I went crunching in the frozen snow, past silent stones, past a row of graves dug a month before, while the earth could still be turned. They were boarded over now, awaiting the dead. Death seemed orderly and normal here, after Germany.

There were bits of ice and snow on the simple dark stone. I

had to rub them off to read the name and the dates, 1882–1941. There was no inscription. At this moment I found myself repeating the final words of Joyce's story "The Dead," with his picture of the snow falling gently, gently falling, on every part of the lonely churchyard on the hill where Michael Furey lay buried. And here in Switzerland, far from the Shannon and the Liffey, under mountain snows, lay the once elegant triste figure I had seen at the opera or at Adrienne's, buried with all his mysteries of creation and damnation, his aggressions, his madness. I had mixed thoughts, and they were only partly elegiac. I remember that what struck me most, as I thought of Joyce's world legend, was how little space it took to contain him, given the vast spaces of genius through which he had moved.

The church bells of Zurich began to ring their Sunday appeals to worshipers, in a symphony of metallic sound with varying rhythms, some distantly down in the city, some close, just beyond the tombstones. And then there crept a strange dissonance into this music. A loudspeaker began to blare a Strauss waltz ("Tales from the Vienna Woods"), and the noisily grating amplifier competed with the religious tonalities of the church bells, their deep clanging messages to the faithful that had sounded for decades and centuries. I remembered Jolas's words about the zoo; the zoo music and the church music blended as Joyce blended languages. The bells tolled, the loudspeaker music became shrill, and the sun acquired sufficient strength to start melting the bits of ice, so that tiny streams of water trickled down the dark headstone.

Later, when I heard the voice of Nora Joyce on the phone, I knew what Frank Budgen meant when he said Ireland herself was ever present at Joyce's side. She was deep-voiced but soft-spoken; the accent of Eire upon her lips delighted me. I felt her warmth even before I set eyes on her. She would not allow me to call on her; she insisted she would come to the Hotel Eden with her son to visit with me. I took this to mean that she lived in quarters poor or squalid and was ashamed to have me see them. She had her Irish pride. She was white-haired, her face lined and sad—a woman very Irish, of natural charm and dignity and of great simplicity. I was struck by her large, strong, bony hands, the hands of a woman of the people. Crippled by arthritis, she had clearly made a heroic attempt to pay this visit, instead of my going to see her. To me this was evidence of her strained finances. Wartime restrictions were still in effect, royalties and other monies were tied up, and I did learn that she lived on very little. Her son, Giorgio Joyce, in bearing and appearance—down to the long coat, the mustache, the glasses, and the way his thick hair was combed back—looked like photographs of his father in his Trieste and early Zurich days. We sat in the deserted and chilly sun-room of the hotel, and I heard the simple and sad chronicle of the last days of James Joyce. The name of Jolas had brought the son and the widow to see me; the message from him had been a spark of life in a dead past.

I have just reread what I wrote of this visit after I returned to New York. It was published as a small chapbook by Frances Steloff at the Gotham Book Mart. Between the lines of the past I recover much that I did not say—as if my emergence from the Army had created a frozen memory that only now has been thawed out. I can recover the Swiss light, the mountain vistas, the burgherliness of Zurich, and I wonder why I failed to describe Nora's shabby black dress and her arthritic rigidity. I mentioned none of this, nor the effect of frailty and forlornness, the anguish of memory that she communicated. I had simply remembered her gnarled hands. What I can see today, if I close my eyes, is the hotel lobby, the room, the big chairs. Mrs. Joyce asked for a hard-backed chair. We looked at one another, as in a council.

I still have the feeling of the snow-reflected light coming in through large windows; and I recover with ease, this above all, the constant surprise with which Nora Joyce greeted my appreciation of her dead husband: surprise that a stranger, in uniform, should want to hear about "Jim" and talk about him as if he were some great hero of legend—he who had been so mortal, so simply a husband (admittedly a difficult one). When I spoke of Joyce's growing fame, his posthumous life, then really just beginning, I talked of matters beyond her imagination— perhaps because she had not yet received the tangible proof of the royalities accumulated during the war years. She had known the improvident, demanding, mocking, depressed, moody, playful figure who, as she used to say, had such "a durrty mind." Our conversation followed the ground of the safe and the familiar; this was hardly the place for literature and literary criticism. We talked of rationings, of bombs sometimes falling inside neutral Switzerland, of other difficulties created by war, of Switzerland's isolation from the world. Mingled with these there would be a sudden memory of a picnic with the Jolases, or some glimpse of the old happy times in Paris. Infirm, stiff, dressed in her mourning black, with a seamed face lined by suffering and pain, Nora Joyce spoke of earthly human things in soft Irish accents. She refused the tea and biscuits I offered her, the meager resources of the hotel. Our interview was not prolonged. We exhausted our subject matter rather quickly. I could not ask the many questions that were on my lips; it would have taken hours of talk of a more intimate kind. Nor could I ask whether she was in want; something in her pride of carriage made it impossible to ask this even in the most covert way. She had told of the fall of Paris, the flight to Vichy, the long wait for permission to cross into neutral ground. Nor did it seem right to me to ask in particular what had become of Joyce's books and papers, though at a given moment she spoke of everything left behind and mentioned Paul Léon, dead in a Nazi concentration camp, through whose resources many of Joyce's ephemeral belongings were rescued. There was still much nightmare around us. And yet so much had been obliterated. I made no mention of the grave, not many miles from where we sat. We talked of living things—and of the difficulty of living.

It was different, I remember, that evening when I went to call on Carola Giedion-Welcker, wife of the celebrated architect; she and her husband had been friends of Joyce from the time of the First World War. There, in a finely designed and spacious house, was this woman of perception and intelligence who had written about the modern movement and had known the men of dada and surrealism, as her collection of paintings and objets d'art told me. She talked of the arrival of the Joyces in Zurich, at the beginning of the war, and the brief months of the writer's residence there before his death. M. Giedion was away, I think lecturing at Harvard, but she had invited one or two of Joyce's friends to join us. I recall in particular her description of how the Joyces looked as they descended from the train in Zurich —on December 13, 1940—after their journey from the French frontier. They had been pale and thin, in a state of weariness and melancholy and starvation. Their clothes had become too large for them and hung loosely from their frames "like an angular group in a Picasso drawing."

Madame Giedion was hospitable. She offered tea and cookies and grappa. Europe lived that winter in unheated houses, as if the war were still on. We sat in an icy room, with its modernistic furniture and its prevalent surrealism, talking of things of the spirit and trying to keep warm with the liquids that warmed our throats but not our fingers and toes. I talked with a doctor, a rotund gentleman who had been Joyce's physician during his last illness, and he described the perforated ulcer, the transfusions, the peritonitis (which drugs, soon to be available, might have healed). Doctors have a way of reeling off clinical history that is both fascinating and chilling. Then at one point, our hostess played Joyce's recording of the section from "Anna Livia Plurabelle" in *Finnegans Wake.* Suddenly his voice was in our midst—strangers who had met, as it were, at his ghostly beckoning. "Tell me, tell me, tell me elm." Was his alienated ghost listening somewhere in that cold room filled with warm voices, not least his own? I remembered how I had sat beside him when the record was played in Paris: Joyce listening to Joyce.

These were the fragments I gathered up later for "the last journey," having the help of a small book Madame Giedion had assembled of the last documents, the funeral accounts, a picture of the death mask in which Joyce's closed lips seemed fixed in a mocking grin. I had written with the aid of this book what was then a sketchy last chapter of the as-yet-unwritten life of the author of *Ulysses*. The author of *Ulysses*. . . . Yes, in our time Joyce had, in a curious way, succeeded in preempting Homer. I suppose if I were to ask a roomful of the young today who had written the *Odyssey,* their answer would be James Joyce.

The Injustice Collector

Writing now of Joyce, I find myself remembering Eugene Jolas's long silences in the bar at the Hotel Bristol. The period of the Occupation had no sense of triumph for me. There were too many graves, and the smell of the crematoria seemed to pervade every street, if not our imaginations. There was rubble on all sides; we stood always in the shadow of ruin—when there was enough of a building left to cast a shadow. We drank, we talked, we played cards, we rode, we walked, we whiled away long evenings. Jolas, as the editor of *transition,* had been in the very heart of the literary movements of the nineteen twenties in Paris at a time when I had hung on the periphery. Sometimes when I used to mention Joyce, Jolas would listen in silence. He half closed his eyes; he nodded his fine, large gray head—he looked always like some grizzled Roman senator of the time of Augustus who had anachronistically donned U.S. Army uniform. He listened to my immoderate and worshipful praises, and I came to recognize that Jolas said nothing because his memories were less enchanted than mine, that for a long time he did not want to flash any light of truth over my images and myths. One evening, however, he said a few words I have never forgotten. He was sipping his Rhine wine and smoking a cigarette in silence, his heavy body relaxed. In the outer room the tank corps major—for whom the war was over and who enjoyed playing at being hotelkeeper—was conducting the little orchestra he had assembled, pretending to be a bandleader. Jolas told me once more Joyce's alcoholic routine: his abstention during the daylight hours, his drinking of wine through the evening, bottle after bottle ("Ireland sober is Ireland stiff!") until he was anesthetized. His cigarettes would burn low in his fingers and blister them, but he would feel nothing. Jolas would take him home in a taxi, help him to bed, and find between his fingers the charred bits of paper and ash. "Great God, Edel," said Jolas, "great God! A man can't be a hero when you've seen him cold stiff, night after night." He said this suddenly with impatience, irritation, passion. And I think he wanted to convey to me, out of his own deep respect for his friend's work and his old-time attachment to him, that I should try to see Joyce as large as life and as large as his gifts made him—but not make him larger. If we pierce any artist's legend, we discover an all-too-troubled human. A reader always has the artist pure, undiminished by reality, but I suppose this is not necessarily having the artist true. Biography tells the truth, but it also dispels the mystery; it rubs off the magic. Life ceaselessly refuses to remain virginal; it offers us instead the joy of discovery and above all immunity from self-deception. Yet it is hard to forget a fairy tale. Legend lingers.

And so with time I have learned to see that the Joyce of my early admiration was a hero of a fairy tale written by myself and by himself. In middle age I found myself looking upon a different man, the man Jolas wanted me to see. The Irish writer was a strange, lost, troubled individual, weighed down by double guilt, split by conflicts. He had turned upon his two mothers, the mother who had given him birth and the church in which he was baptized. He turned as well upon his motherland. He had in him all the guilt of his aggression, all the aggression of his guilt. He could do almost anything with words; he could do nothing with his damaged self. The artist was divorced from the world, but not from the word. And so he built his own world of words. He was a poet who had the recording eye of a photographer, and he had an electronic ear. The rarer music of string quartets and of instrumental works seems to have said less to him than the music of the voice, the lilt of Irish melodies, the sentiment of ballads. He was the first and ultimate artist who both used and mocked the media. The music of word and song was contained in a being singularly distrustful of the world and of people. Joyce was cut off from human warmth, even of those close to him; they too knew what strange barriers of the spirit he erected. He had to organize his existence—instinctively, intuitively—with primitive superstition and magic so as to defend himself from the strange fears and omens he believed were constantly threatening him.

Much of this is implicit, but not explicit, in Richard Ellmann's life of Joyce. It was as if in childhood some strange experiences had occurred that left him both artist and monster. Joyce had taken form as a person in Clongowes, where he was a small, slight, nearsighted boy, handicapped among his schoolfellows. He was never with his peers; he was always the younger boy. The sense of his inferiority which made him assert himself with arrogance is described in *A Portrait of the Artist as a Young Man,* and also the growth of his defenses against physical weakness and nearsightedness. His sins bred guilt; inner violence became verbal violence. The two halves—the dissociated, alienated Joyce and the active Joyce—were kept from disintegration by the rituals Joyce organized for himself and by a kind of indomitable love of verbal beauty, in which he found the strength to save himself because it could express the ugliness within and be purgative. He was driven by nightmares. He felt that all his friends would betray him; he demanded complete loyalty yet never trusted those he could trust. I know of no other artist in the whole history of art who was so certain of his greatness before achieving it. Usually, artists win acceptance— and greatness—by what they offer to the world. The Joyce who left Ireland feeling he had been rejected had offered an intense rage, a gift of withering utterance, a precocious article on Ibsen, a few derivative poems with music in them, the "pure poetry" that George Moore defined. Suffering from an unflagging grandiosity and with the genius of his language, Joyce made the world yield to his demands. The world had owed a handout to his barfly father, who earned it by anecdotal charm and barroom blarney. Joyce surpassed his father a thousand times in the same maneuver. He is the supreme example of the artist in our century—before the bounty of the foundations—who was supported ultimately by a rich (at first anonymous) patron in England, Harriet Shaw Weaver.

Joyce the cadger, determined like Thoreau to live in his own way and make the world support him, convinced of his gift and his message and his vocation—Joyce-against-the-world wove a myth of the world-against-Joyce. He is portrayed for us faithfully by himself in the three volumes of letters we now have. We possess him in all his misery and heartbreak. I looked forward to these stout volumes, as one who cherishes the least scribble of a writer of genius, and Joyce's corpus consisted of so few books. His letters represent a large addition to the quantity of his prose. The impression I received from the first volume of the letters (followed ten years later by two more volumes) was of a man singularly unaware of the art of friendship or of the use of letters in human intercourse. He had loyal, devoted friends, but he was in reality a vampire; friends existed to be used. His correspondence has none of the easy give-and-take of the great epistolary artists: no generalizations about literature, no discussion of the work of his contemporaries to any significant extent, no hint of a literary idea or theory, only occasional flashes of the word audacities of *Ulysses* and *Finnegan.* He is very concrete, very demanding, utterly egocentric. By comparison with the letters of Flaubert, whose career and work in some ways resembled Joyce's on the side of craft, these are the hasty scribbles of a petty clerk, a rude egotist, rather than of a committed artist. They are the marginal fragments of Joyce's life, and not of his creative life. They say the things he had to scribble down for the minimal communication forced upon him by the daily demands of the world. But he would much rather not have communicated at all. What one hears in the two later volumes (published long after the first volume appeared) is a perpetual cry for money, for help, for love. The world is repeatedly proclaimed cheat and liar, and Joyce is its crucified martyr. The letters are a mixture of self-advertisement, charlatanism, pedantry, and arrogance. In this way Joyce fought his private demons.

The weight and abundance of these terrible writings of a desperate man risk a weariness to the spirit and to the reader's sympathy. Too much is told—more, perhaps, than is needed even for the purpose of truth and history. The anguish is made redundant. Stephen Spender remarked that if one does not keep in mind Joyce's sense of comedy, "he may find Joyce's letters oppressive and, in the long run, almost unbearable." When one comes to the essence of the matter, laughter is impossible. For the letters demonstrate more clearly than ever the pathological elements in the art of James Joyce. The writer was so alienated from the world, so cut off from empathy, that he could be ruthless with family, cruel to friends, surprisingly childish in his recurrent demands that the world give him ad hoc recognition. His talent, when he finally showed it, was accepted. Yet Joyce continued to cry betrayal, for in his alienation everything was pulled inward, into himself and his "madness of art." It is always Joyce on Joyce; and it is Joyce consuming himself in an eternal rage of art. For the Irish rebel, writing was a form of revenge against a host of imaginary foes—and he paid them off with "dagger definitions."

The essential story of Joyce's life has been given to us as that of an oppressed artist. He quit Ireland in poverty and anger, although many (including Yeats and Lady Gregory) held out hands of friendship to him. He wandered, pathetic and unheroic, until he settled in backwater polyglot Trieste and taught at Berlitz. He exploited his talented brother Stanislaus, one of the martyred siblings of literary history. And finally, with the aid of Ezra Pound, he pulled himself together and did his most characteristic work. Here his creativity found release. However, he refused to recognize that the world was quite prepared to accept him, even if it did not always admire *Ulysses* and scoffed at "Work in Progress," later *Finnegans Wake.* Harriet Weaver endowed him; the sympathetic ladies of the rue de l'Odéon, Sylvia Beach and Adrienne Monnier, published, protected, and cushioned him. He quarreled with everyone. He sued at the drop of a hat. He invited strife. He was one of the greatest "injustice collectors" of all literature. I think it could be demonstrated that Joyce needed the censorship and contumely of the world; he could thereby vent his rage and consider himself insulted and injured. Some of his letters read as if written by Dostoevsky's soliloquizing functionary in *Notes from the Underground.*

In particular there is much pathology in Joyce's erotic, childish letters to his wife, his common-law wife. His biographer speaks of "fetishism, anality, paranoia and masochism" but turns from Krafft-Ebing to praise Joyce's "Circean beguilements" and "vaudeville routines." No amount of self-mockery or literary heroics can conceal the sad, ugly truths. Strange laughter can still be the laughter of madness, and Joyce's wry comedy is a comedy of helpless megalomania. The artist filled with grandiosities walks "a way a lone a last a loved a long the" —as he tells us in the uncompleted final sentence of *Finnegans Wake* which leads us back to the book's beginning. It was one of his many insights into his personal self-containment. Another of his statements of his mental solitude is in *Ulysses:* "We walk through ourselves, meeting robbers, ghosts, giants, old men, young men, wives, widows, brothers-in-love. But always meeting ourselves."

He remains a curious memory. His eccentricities, which were those of madness, are often retold as if they were the inventions of genius; in part, I suppose, they were. His inwardness, his insolence, his world mockery, and his self-mockery make him one of the great curiosities of modern literature, which is what he will more and more become. It takes a certain kind of mind to give over endless pages simply to parody of cheap novels; it demands a curious kind of continuing obsessive hostility to mock the media as Joyce mocked them, although in mocking he acquired some of their cheapness. His is one of the saddest histories of modern creation: genius burning itself out always on a downward curve from transcendence to pettiness. Even the magical *Finnegan* ultimately palls. He is hugely overshadowed by other great creative figures of our time—Yeats, to name his countryman; or even, at another extreme, Eliot; and even, in her watercolory way, Virginia Woolf, who could mock quite as brilliantly but had more of the stuff of literary art in her because she knew where to call a halt, where to round out and shape a form. Joyce's poems are slight. His tales are neat but not inspired; there have been finer masters of the short story. His drama is impossible; only *Ulysses* and *Finnegan* dramatize for us the new time-and-space dimensions of fiction and the new subjectivity of our century—and they resolve themselves into parody, wit, and word games. I am reduced to saying that Joyce's one true work of art is *A Portrait of the Artist as a Young Man.* He is becoming largely a child of the exegetes, although he also serves the needs of literary politics and academic dissertations. That, however, shouldn't be held against him.

To the miseries of Joyce's inwardness were added the physical torments of a dozen eye operations for cataracts, poor health, partial poverty at first, and then self-impoverishment by a grandeur of spending. He had compulsive bouts of drunkenness. He had periods of depression during which he moved from "great irritation and impotent fury" to sudden fits of weeping. This is the haunted and driven existence of which we are made spectators, and with this there was Joyce's way—I suppose by the combination of helplessness and mockery—of commanding always a circle of friends hypnotized by his virtuosity and prepared to immolate themselves on his altar. They received scant thanks for their pains and are immortalized in the puns of *Finnegan*. Joyce wrote not for literature but for personal revenge. His motivations are confused, but there is something heroic in his ideal and in his sense of myth. He belongs to the witchcraft of words. He was Faust, but he thought himself Jesus—and Judas was everywhere.

I once heard an anecdote about Joyce told by an Englishman who remembered meeting, on a plane somewhere in Europe, a gentle and dignified woman who lived in Israel. In his conversation with her the name of Joyce came up, and she said that she had been one of Joyce's students when he taught at the Berlitz school in Trieste. She remembered him as well dressed and polite but that he also had, at times, a nasty and insolent tone. She spoke of him with some affection and described one evening when Joyce, coming out of the school with a few of his students, went with them to drink in a series of cafés. They drank much wine and were very happy together. In one place Joyce danced with her, lightly and gallantly. She had pinned a rose to her dress, and while they danced it fell to the floor. Joyce stooped to pick it up and, bowing, returned it to her with the words "I seem to have deflowered you." As the night advanced, Joyce became increasingly wine-happy. Long past midnight the group found itself in the central square of Trieste under a full, rich moon. The students were exchanging good-nights when the young woman looked about for Joyce. He had detached himself from the group and, lost to the world, was dancing those nimble steps which later were the delight of his friends on festive occasions. He danced in the moonlight with his enormous shadow that moved and darted with him eerily in choreographic arabesques, in rhythm to some music hidden within the man. She had never forgotten this moonlight memory.

The anecdote is unforgettable. This is the Joyce of literary history: a shadow larger than the man, a lone performer dancing with himself and his shadow, weaving in and out of his own rhythms, detached and lost in his own world, which is both a hodgepodge of history and a potpourri of language. The last words of *Finnegans Wake* come to mind as we hear the anecdote: *a way a lone a last.* It is the virtuoso sufficient unto himself, cut off from his fellows by his virtuosity, and by this selfsame virtuosity establishing strange and awesome communication with them. Joyce, wine-lost, dancing with himself by the light of the moon: the history of Joyce's art may be read in this act.

Psychopathology of Shem

So much I wrote of James Joyce during many years, until it seemed to me that I had summed up for myself the complexity of his flawed genius. Mixing my memories with such facts as I had, I illustrated some of his capers, each an acting out of certain psychopathological elements in him. But it now occurs to me that perhaps I need, at the risk of some repetition, to explain more fully what I mean by the "pathological elements" in the art of James Joyce. Perhaps it is appropriate to do so, for we are now at his centenary, a time for stock-taking, for retrospect and review.

I

The centenary of James Joyce's birth (1882–1982) comes at a time when his work, with all its audacities, virtuosities, and aggressions, has long ceased to be a novelty. *Ulysses* startled and mystified the literary world in 1922 and was promptly banned in many countries. Four-letter words were not then customary in print, printers often would not set them up in type, and the British did not like Irish insults to their royalty. The book was as fat as a telephone directory and often as unreadable: that is, it had to be worked at as one works at a crossword puzzle. There was no danger of its corrupting the young. It was full of literary inventions which are now commonplace. Joyce's verbal adroitness and music dazzled mature readers; yet even this shows signs of tarnish. Phrases such as "ineluctable modality of the visible" have been repeated too often. To be sure, we thought it very daring of Joyce to try to mirror within the pages of his book an entire day in Dublin—to catch the variousness, the hum, the interconnectedness of a metropolis. But we ignored the simple fact that in a rougher way, and with less artifice, the daily newspaper in cities around the world attempts to do the same. In brief, Joyce's central idea was more journalistic than literary; his desire to shock was quite as strong, and perhaps stronger, than his desire to deal with human situations, as Tolstoy did, or to inquire into the meaning of life, as Chekhov constantly does, or to decipher the subtleties of personal relations, as in Henry James. He had the temperament of a poet, the ambition of an artist, and the genius of a mime. Other writers derived useful literary stunts from Joyce; he had as marked an influence on literary complexities as Hemingway had on literary simplicities. His way of creating word panoramas, his use of Homer as analogue, his experiments with the "stream of consciousness," his tape-recorder-computerlike mentality, made his book a pastiche of the world's daily clutter, and his interest in excrement, dirt, smells, whether we liked it or not, made us aware that genteel literature had ignored for too long the physical bodies of men and women. His talent was brilliant but irregular. Once he started a parody or a mockery, he didn't know when to stop. He was like a juggler enchanted with himself, who throws more and more objects into the air to see how long a *perpetuum mobile* he can maintain. Joyce never learned the deepest secret of art—which many of his contemporaries knew: the limits of performance.

One tends to see him more and more as a performing artist doing tricks with language, rather than a writer seeking to express the mysteries of existence. Joyce would have argued that he did not want to express them; he wanted to "render" life, to speak it out. That was his privilege: but in doing so he announced himself a camera. And then he loved to build interminable mazes, both in *Ulysses* and in *Finnegans Wake.* These were so personal, so secretive, and so masturbatory, that his readers remained bewildered until he explained what he had done—or leaked the secret to others. Joyce's place in the Irish renaissance was not with a supreme artist like Yeats but rather with wits and public entertainers like Wilde and Shaw, who exploited their personalities. Wilde, to be sure, developed his Pateresque doctrine of aestheticism and even dressed the part; and Shaw lived on paradox, public utterance, and a kind of Voltairean wit. He at least was a consistent socialist who wished to remake the world. Joyce had no doctrine; the closest he came to it was in his announcement at the end of *Portrait of the Artist as a Young Man* that he wished "to forge in the smithy of my soul the uncreated conscience of my race." But we find no fulfillment of this vague promise—nor is it clear what Joyce considered the "conscience" of his race to be. And later in *Finnegans Wake* he reused the word "forge" in the sense of forgery. His personage Shem the Penman (Shem being Irish for the James of his own name) is both Joyce the writer and Joyce the forger. In a certain sense, writers, having only words as their medium, must forge their pictures of reality. Certainly Joyce's total writings show little concern for the "conscience" of the Irish but considerable concern with word matchings and word combinations, the higher pedantry cultivated by certain types of Irish nationals, usually in pubs. His double maneuver of ambition and pride was to achieve greatness and then demonstrate that he didn't give a damn for it, as when, having finally obtained a huge subsidy from Harriet Weaver, he took her to dinner and spent her money lavishly to show his independence —a little as if he had lighted his cigar with one of her bills. And a further maneuver—when perhaps he reached moments of great despair—was to vaudevillize himself, another way of attracting attention.

Joyce, in his constant efforts to give his readers the equivalent of photographs in words, confessed to having no imagination and apparently agreed with his alcoholic father's verdict on him: "if that fellow was dropped in the middle of the Sahara, he'd sit, be God, make a map of it." There was implicit confirmation of this when Joyce, in one of his moments of self-abasement, said he had "a grocer assistant's mind." This he demonstrated many times in *Ulysses*: Bloom is a measurer of reservoirs, compiler of statistics, dispenser of "useful information"; and it is illustrated in the biography by Joyce's need to know exactly how many steps led down into Leopold Bloom's kitchen in Eccles Street. He wrote from Trieste or Zurich to one of his sisters to count the steps for him. This is flatfooted policework—the imagination ousted in favor of reportage or record. We know that Joyce used not only place-names (many authors do) but the exact names of living people as well. No wonder his publishers balked. It may suggest the difference between this kind of literalness and imagination if we remind ourselves that Henry James, wishing to create a Massachusetts town, invented one in order to be relieved of "vain specifications." Joyce always needed the specifications, in the way a grocer's assistant has to be sure all the comestibles are in the delivery bundle.

Looking back over Joyce's hundred years, and attempting to see his "psychologic signs," what becomes visible is that the Irish writer suffered from more than the usual neurotic traits one finds in various kinds of gifted individuals. What his admirers have told and retold in anecdote about his eccentricities are symptoms of an intricate psychopathology. Joyce, alias Stephen, alias Shem the Penman, was a fragile man who spent his life building psychic defenses or maintaining those he built intact to keep himself from fragmentation. The madness of Virginia Woolf had its years of remission, during which she worked like an artist and achieved the body of work by which we know and admire her. Joyce's fight against disintegration was a chronic struggle on the edge of his personal abyss. J.I.M. Stewart, in his lively critical essay on the novelist, has pointed to this by observing that there is much in Joyce that appeals to "imperfectly critical minds," and he goes on to say that Joyce's flotsam and jetsam "offers ready entrance . . . to recondite researches and arcane solemnities—picking around, in fact, in the vast rag-bag of learning which Joyce's work may be viewed as constituting." He concludes that there is something "vulnerable in much discussion of Joyce . . . an approach fatally telescoping the pedantic and the portentous." What is portentous in reality is the evidence of Joyce's psychopathology, which criticism has blandly ignored in its failure to recognize that Joyce's creations are the more benign consequence of the systems and superstitions and the whole body of fetishes and tabus by which he lived. Primitive tribes create their particular law and order through systems of superstition and unearthly belief, and Joyce was often that kind of primitive within the civilization of his twentieth-century "dear dirty Dublin." In this sense we are concerned with an unfinished genius, a singular creative spirit formed out of contradictory psychological materials, some of which provided the power that drove him and others which acted as destructive elements within the achievement.

The vast literature on Joyce has tended to consider the intellectual side of his work: philosophy, theology, aesthetics, and his preoccupation with everyday life, city, church, family. But it has studied neither the intense emotions that drove these ratio-

nal disguises and the body of tabus nor the self-prescribed terrors that intruded into Joyce's daily life. I should elaborate in a
very general way what I mean when I speak of the psychopathology in Joyce.

When we use the word *neurosis* we mean the general anxieties and emotional difficulties which are our common lot; we are
all familiar with them. When these become sufficiently troublesome and interfere with adequate functioning and our daily
realities, we have a neurotic situation which in many cases lends
itself readily to corrective treatment by modern psychology.
We all have our neurotic quirks and private intuitions and
superstitions, and there are many writers who subsume them in
their writings: their outlet is the typewriter or the pen even as,
for less verbal individuals, there are the outlets of jogging or the
tennis racquet or other kinds of sport.

However, when we speak of psychopathology in an individual we are speaking of forms of what seem to be madness—
failures to see reality, the creation of entire systems to cope with
the sort of things tribal witch doctors treat: uncommon fears
and terrors and retreats from the given forms of society, with
resulting erratic behavior and psychic fragmentation. In Joyce
we discern on page after page of Ellmann's biography, a suffering helpless individual who behaves strangely and is invariably
building fears, anxieties, and hallucinations into verbal forms,
forms of clowning, and acquires the ability to laugh at the self
in moments of depression and terror.

One of Edmund Wilson's amusing anecdotes about Joyce
used to be how they first met. Wilson had written with admiration of *Finnegans Wake* and had unraveled many of its mysteries; Joyce was sufficiently grateful to want to meet him. During
a trip to Paris, Wilson was escorted by mutual friends of the
writers to Joyce's home. It was characteristic of Wilson, when
he met someone, to look at him with a sharp direct glance—
shrewd, inquiring, lively, and even diagnostic. He remembered
being greeted by Joyce in the entrance to his apartment, but

the Irish writer fell at once into a total silence. Nothing Wilson did could break it. They had drinks; everyone talked. Joyce seemed lost in gloom and blankness. Wilson fired questions; no answers. With the increasing embarrassment of all present, the party took refuge in conviviality and then set off for the restaurant, probably Joyce's favorite near the Gare du Montparnasse, Les Trianons. It wasn't until late in the meal, when Joyce had been loosened up by wine, that he finally spoke. With that particular Irish tone of his, he said to Wilson, "And why did you look so fixedly at my necktie when you came into my house?" Edmund promptly assured Joyce that his look had been directed not at the necktie but at the face above it; and he might have added that being a very short man, and Joyce being quite a bit taller, his eye level would seem to be necktie level. Joyce now became pleasantly conversational.

The anecdote, baldly told, illustrates Joyce's paranoid problems. He had promptly given unreal meaning to a simple reality: his mind read all kinds of hostility or evil, or at the least some kind of criticism, in Wilson's direct stare. To cope with such daily happenings, Joyce devised elaborate rituals, as we can see in his correspondence and in the accounts we have of him. Often these aberrations went to great extremes. Nearly always they were sufficiently harmless, although they could inflict discomfort upon other persons.

II

The pathology in James Joyce may have had its origins in part in his relations with a madcap aunt who lived with the Joyce family during its more affluent days. Readers of the *Portrait of the Artist* meet her on the first page of the novel, when Stephen is told he must apologize (he is then a mere child) and the aunt, Dante, as she is called, says, "O, if not, the eagles will come and pull out his eyes." The aggression is muted for the little boy— and it is a fear-inspiring way of talking to a child—by his early defense of language: what he hears, shutting out the terror of huge predatory birds, is the rhyme of "eyes" and "apologize," and he makes up the verse

> Pull out his eyes
> Apologise,
> Apologise,
> Pull out his eyes.

We encounter Dante (doubtless some childish form of *auntie*) in the pages of Ellmann's biography and learn that Joyce was exposed regularly during his early childhood to this quarrelsome church-ridden woman. We discover her "sitting on a throne-like arrangement of chair and cushions to soothe her chronically ailing back, wearing a black lace cap, heavy velvet skirts and jewelled slippers." She rings a little bell. School begins. Young Jimmy Joyce, the oldest son, sits at her feet to receive the elements of writing, reading, geography, arithmetic. She recites poetry. She talks of the end of the world as if it will come at any moment. For every flash of lightning during storms she makes Jimmy Joyce repeat, "Jesus of Nazareth, King of the Jews, from a sudden and unprovided-for death, deliver us, O Lord." Ellmann observes that "the thunderstorm as a vehicle of divine power and wrath moved Joyce's imagination so profoundly that to the end of his life he trembled at the sound." This is less a moving of the imagination than a profound ritual of fear and punishment, the inculcation into an impressionable and probably by then hysterical child of a fright so great that he needed elaborate modes of defense—the protective behavior of Stephen Dedalus—shown us in the *Portrait* and *Ulysses* as well as in Joyce's own phobias and fetishes. First there was prayer and confession, later defiance and rage. Ellmann chronicles Joyce's childhood games as if they were devised by a little genius rather than by a very sick little boy. The content of these games suggests the ways in which superstitions had infiltrated the Joycean psyche. The little boy directed the other children in biblical plays. As the oldest, he was in full

charge. In acting out the story of Adam and Eve, he gave himself the role of the serpent. He punished brothers and sisters by
forcing them to lie on the ground and placing a wheelbarrow
over them. Then he "donned a red stockingcap and made grisly
sounds to indicate that he was burning the malefactor in
hellfire." How real this hellfire was to him we may judge from
the sermons on hell in the *Portrait* and their devastating effect
on young Dedalus. He felt doomed to an eternity of punishment. To be sure, some children slough off such violence, only
half understanding the contents—but what we see is that the
play was a mix of eternal fear, aggression, punishment, and
terror. The child had a talent for "imagining horrors" in the
tales he made up—not a surprising consequence of this kind of
play. He frightened a playmate into great terror by telling him
that when children were naughty his "mother would hold him
head downward in the toilet and pull the chain." Such juvenile
sado-cloacal fantasies suggest a fostered malign imagination.
And this is why we must speak of the pathological content it
reveals. Numerous other instances could be given of these kinds
of fantasies in Irish Catholic schooling and play, but we are
concerned with their effect on a particular individual, James
Joyce. And yet a whole generation has read Ellmann as if Joyce
were simply a precocity indulging in good clean Irish fun.

Joyce did not outgrow his experiences of childhood. They
simply took other forms in later life. Within his public utter-
ances, Joyce was a mass of omens, signs, wonders. His paranoid
fancies came to direct his daily life. His guilt and fright at what
he himself imagined are documented, for example in Robert
McAlmon's memoirs. McAlmon recalls their going to lunch together. Joyce was superstitious over the way the knife and fork
were placed on the restaurant table, he was troubled by the way
McAlmon poured the wine, and when McAlmon spied a rat
running down the stairs of the café, Joyce exclaimed, "Where?
Where? That's bad luck!" which he promptly confirmed by
falling into a dead faint. Coincidences, for Joyce, were major

events and could be sources of extreme joy or extreme anxiety. *Ulysses* had to appear on Joyce's birthday: the story has been told many times of the extravagant lengths to which Sylvia Beach went to have a single copy brought to Joyce on that fateful day. Dogs were a source of terror to the novelist; and chronic panic, as we have seen, came with the least rumble of thunder. Dante Conway had left her mark. These signs and symptoms, these particular demons of a man who seemed a tower in letters, suggest a different person from the fearless and defiant young would-be artist (who is also afraid of rats and often alludes to them): the would-be maker of mazes; the individual who dreamed himself capable of finding wings like Daedalus and Icarus to fly him over the world—and away in particular from Ireland; the self-appointed hero who announces *Non serviam* to the "whole bludyn world."

III

Joyce also showed fear of Freud and Freudianism. He had read the Viennese master and absorbed many of his ideas about dream and fantasy. In *Finnegan* he turns his name into the word "freudened" in a sentence which also amusingly puns on Jung—"when we were young and easily freudened." Joyce, as we have seen, could easily be "freudened," but not only when he was young. He was ambivalent about Sigmund Freud. On the one hand he proudly pointed out that the name was his own, for Freud means joy in German. But when someone suggested in Zurich that he be analyzed by Jung, Joyce replied this was "unthinkable" and later said that psychoanalysis was "nothing more than blackmail."

One can understand that Joyce the loner would shy away from any suggestion that his psyche be explored: he would have to reveal too much, explore too much, and he carried too many burdens. Alienated though he was from the church, he said he would rather face the confessional than an analysis; and that, too, we can understand, for in the confession the unconscious is not explored. As early as 1916 Joyce had recognized the relationship between his dreams and his imagination—although, given his superstitions, he doubtless gave them distinctly paranoid interpretations. He kept a notebook in which he recorded dreams and often asked his friends for theirs and questioned them minutely on their ways of dreaming. Joyce's own verbal condensations, his discontinuities, his interest in free association, his use of the stream of consciousness, his mutilation and pastiches of language, his addiction to puns in more than one language, his large grasp of myth and symbol, and his ability to remember and recapture phantasmagoria—the dream phantasms of the *Ulysses* "night-town"—show a familiarity with psychoanalytical literature. Ellmann tells us Joyce was "close to the new psychoanalysis at so many points that he always disavowed any interest in it." His closeness to it was intellectual, and he could have understood it only on the surface, given his resistances. Moreover, he seems intuitively to have recognized that he needed his accumulated defenses—every superstition and good-luck charm he conjured up to protect himself from inner terror.

We may imagine that if Joyce had accepted Jung's analysis, he would soon have been told that he could not be analyzed; any analyst would have diagnosed the mental disorders that constituted his pathology. Since these disorders were highly compensated by Joyce's "systems," the armor of his defenses was well-nigh impenetrable. If they had been pierced, Joyce would have been toppled from the edge of his abyss. Without the barricades of his ego, he would have been reduced to the madness of his daughter, for he saw in her, as in a mirror, the projections of his own capacity for disintegration. To have accepted the idea of the unconscious would have involved releasing the minotaur in Joyce's private maze, breaching the walls that protected his passive-aggressive flights as well as the shabby cobwebbed guilt-and-punishment of his patchwork self.

We may judge from certain allusions in *Finnegans Wake* that

Joyce believed he was capable of analyzing himself. He would be his own protector. The spook voice in the *Wake* says, "Get yourself psychoanalised!" The characteristic anal allusion is made, and the response to the voice is "O begor, I want no expert nursis symaphy from your broons and quadroons and I can psoakoonaloose myself any time I want (the fog follow you all!) without your interferences or any other pigeonstealer." At another moment he assures someone, "You never made a more freudful mistake, excuse yourself!"

In speaking of *Finnegans Wake,* we must always remember that it was conceived and written as a dream book and that Joyce confronted in his cosmic way—the way of jumble and clutter held within a controlling frame—the "stuff of sleep and dreams," which he ridiculed as "the intrepidation of dreams," a reminder of Freud's classic work. In the *Wake,* the personages sleep through their long night floating in all history, all time, all eternity: the pubkeeper by the Liffey, a kind of Everyman, his wife, and his sons, Shem and Shaun. Languages, dreams, legends, myths merge and mingle and reflect a surreal world embodied and expressed in Joyce's constant effort to give every word multiple meanings, entertaining his readers and also taxing their patience. *Finnegans Wake* belongs thus to the century that has explored dream life not as magic, or as prophecy, but as the unconscious storytelling of men and women to themselves. Joyce envisaged *Finnegan* as a nightbook after the daybook *Ulysses,* and in this nightbook we meet Shem the Penman, the writer, word-giver, word-maker whose brother is Shaun the postman, a philistine who carries the words written by Shem. The two are also eternal siblings, Cain and Abel or Castor and Pollux; they embody the myths of brotherhood and brother rivalry; they are the dual natures of Joyce himself, Joyce the *renfermé,* as one French critic accurately characterizes him, and his word salads are not unlike the word salads of schizophrenics—with one remarkable difference: there is "Reason at the Rudder." One way of mocking the world was to create labyrinths, to make up puzzles, to keep the pedants writing footnotes, as Joyce mockingly said. Adaline Glasheen, in her *Census of Finnegans Wake,* observes that Shem and Shaun represent "men at war with one another and man at war with himself." Joyce was distinctly at war with himself.

If we look closely at Shem the Penman, we discern a strong resemblance to Stephen Dedalus—and therefore to James Joyce. As always, Joyce is writing the book of himself; he is the all-too-protean artist, and Miss Glasheen has described his display of self-depreciation and self-loathing. She remarks that both Shem and Shaun are loathsome but adds, "Joyce readers being bookish people are likely to feel that an Artist must be heroic when he is opposed to a Philistine." Self-depreciation can be a manner of self-inflation. Stephen Dedalus is most often portrayed as heroic, at least verbally, yet he commits no heroic actions. He simply rebels. He decides that he must "forge" his art in "silence, exile, cunning." This artist-in-the-making, whom we never see as a complete artist, is a morbid precocity, a sensibility, a *sensitif;* he is impelled to make factitious choices: country versus exile, religion versus art, freedom versus humanity. He is in reality modern alienated man. To be sure, many artists feel themselves alienated from their surroundings: they possess a heightened sensibility, they have few peers to communicate with, they are in a state of malaise which prosaic individuals can never understand, since they readily accept the world as it is. Joyce has recorded the stages of his sensory development as an infant, the passions of his adolescence, the passion of religion versus the flesh and of art versus religion, and finally the attempt to find some rudder of reason to control his passions.

There are explosive emotions in Joyce's autobiographical novel—his picture of a frail small boy set into a Jesuit school in an old castle with boys older than himself. Many pages are devoted to sensory perception. He smells everything, like a little dog: the water in the bathrooms, the cold night smell in the chapel, the peasants at the back. And then there is the tactile, of which we are given abundant example: cold and heat, damp and wet—"It would be lovely in bed after the sheets got a bit hot. First they were so cold to get into. He shivered to think how cold they were at first." It is only in the later part of the book, after his terror of the hell-fire sermons, that we reach the realm of the intellect, when Stephen attends the university. In the end he is ready to leave Ireland—but it is to be a self-exile. No one has banished him. His own edgy nerves, his hostilities, his rage deport him. He feels the world owes him a living; he often mistakes rage for art and for his genius.

IV

Shem the Penman expresses for us in many ways and in many puns Joyce's awareness of some parts of this pathology. At one point we find the phrase "the growing megalomane of a loose past," and also words such as "the shuddersome spectacle of this semi-demented zany." He tells us this as a joke; he jokes away the glimpses of truth. He speaks of "dislocated reason," and clearly alludes to his own compulsions when he speaks of "meticulosity bordering on the insane." The self-portrait in Shem—"a low sham"—touches hard and painful recognitions, disguised as puns. Shem "unconsciously explaining for ink-stands . . . the various meanings of all the different foreign parts of speech he misused." Shem, the sibling of Shaun (Joyce's brother Stanislaus), becomes all the opposites and contraries of Shem—yes and no, left and right, Jeff and Mutt, comedian and stooge. There is also right and wrong—but for Joyce there is "only the right and the wronged." He has to collect all the injustices he believes the world has heaped on him, and this in the face of his being one of the most endowed writers in Europe.

There is in *Finnegan* an entire litany of self-aggression and self-depreciation, in which Joyce suggests his schizoid nature—"you have become of twosome twiminds"—and pronounces himself "condemned fool, anarch, egoarch, hiresiarch, you have reared your disunited kingdom on the vacuum of your own most intensely doubtful soul." And he replies to Stephen Dedalus's declaration in the *Portrait*. Stephen had said, "I will not serve that in which I no longer believe, whether it call itself my home, my fatherland, or my church." In *Finnegan* the answer is, "Do you hold yourself then for some god in the manger, Shehohem, that you will neither serve nor let serve, pray nor let pray?" In Joyce's language to himself, Shem the Penman is without mercy: "Sniffer of carrion, premature gravedigger, seeker of the nest of evil in the bosom of a good word" and then "you with your dislocated reason . . . the dynamitisation of colleagues." The last is an acknowledgment of his payment of old grudges to old friends by introducing them in some scurrilous way in his text.

Joyce's portrait of Shem, the mythic penman, is filled with repudiations of himself, sometimes in a tone of reprimand and sometimes in a tone of indulgent vaudeville. But there remains one other place, outside the works, in which we can see Joyce's low self-esteem at work and the mixture of guilt and self-punishment, together with a parade of all his Krafft-Ebing perversions. I refer to the series of letters he wrote his wife at a crisis in their relations during 1909. They are published in Ellmann's *Selected Letters of James Joyce,* and they make curious reading for some and nauseating reading for others; it depends on one's reactions to such a wallowing in excrement, such a mix of sex and bodily function, together with a very considerable amount of masochism. Joyce had falsely accused Nora of infidelity, having listened too eagerly to Dublin gossip. Once he recognizes this, he is a character out of Sacher-Masoch's *Venus in Furs* or one of his other books, inviting Nora to take the role of the fatal woman, the fascination Joyce had, as an erotic sickness, with female domination. He pleads with Nora to be flogged; he reverts frequently to his "pantie fetish." He announces his masturbatory actions and fantasies. The world, to be sure, has long learned that one need not endlessly and boringly explore the physical varieties of sexual experience and the quest of man and woman for erotic excitements and intensities. But with Joyce, in these strange letters, the varieties seem to combine many confusions of sensuality, as if there existed a series of crossed wires, so that he writes in a feverish excited prose of the delights of simultaneous defecation and orgasm, a kind of "letting go" of all systems. One can spare readers much quotation—if they are interested they can seek the text of this series of communications; two passages alone should suffice to illuminate the psychopathology of which I have been writing, as it can be discerned not only in the work but in the life of the disturbed Irishman.

> I would love to have done something to displease you, something trivial even, perhaps one of my rather dirty habits that make you laugh: and then to hear you call me into your room and then to find you sitting in an armchair with your fat thighs far apart and your face deep red with anger and a cane in your hand. To see you point to what I had done and then with a movement of rage pull me towards you and throw me face downward across your lap. Then to feel your hands tearing down my trousers and inside clothes and turning up my shirt, to be struggling in your strong arms and in your lap, to feel you bending down (like an angry nurse whipping a child's bottom) until your big full bubbies almost touched me and to feel you flog, flog, flog me viciously on my naked quivering flesh!! Pardon me, dear, if this is silly. I began this letter so quietly and yet I *must* end it in my own mad fashion.

But there is more than masochism; there is fetishism as well:

> Are you offended because I said I loved to look at the brown stain that comes behind on your girlish white drawers? I suppose you think me a filthy wretch.

In the next letter the compulsive Joyce pursues the subject:

> I am sure my girlie is offended at my filthy words. Are you offended, dear, at what I said about your drawers? That is all nonsense, darling.

I know they are as spotless as your heart. I know I could lick them all over, frills, legs and bottom. Only I love in my dirty way to think that in a certain part they are soiled. It is all nonsense, too, dear, about buggering you. It is only the dirty sound of the word, I like, the idea of a shy beautiful young girl like Nora pulling up her clothes behind and revealing her sweet white girlish drawers in order to excite the dirty fellow she is so fond of; and then letting him stick his dirty red lumpy pole in through the split of her drawers and up up up in the darling little hole between her plump fresh buttocks.

A sensitive civilized reader will cry "Enough!" and wonder whether these letters might not have been allowed to remain in their archive, available in the age of Xerox to those who wish to study Joyce's scatology. Ellmann feels that this correspondence commands respect "for its intensity and candour, and for its fulfilment of Joyce's avowed determination to express his whole mind." He seems here to be treating them as if they belonged to literary art rather than to private communication. He is being rather disingenuous in his passage which attempts to chaperon and defend Joyce's epistolary scatology. It in reality defines itself. Ellmann writes in his preface to the selected letters:

> Frank as these letters are, their psychology can easily be misunderstood. They were intended to accomplish sexual gratification in him and inspire the same in her, and at moments they fasten intently on peculiarities of sexual behaviour, some of which might be technically called perverse. They display traces of fetishism, anality, paranoia and masochism, but before quartering Joyce into these categories and consigning him to their tyranny we must remember that he was capable, in his work, of ridiculing them all as Circean beguilements, of turning them into vaudeville routines.

Traces? Technical? It is silly to speak of Joyce as a technical fetishist or a technical masochist, and there certainly wasn't anything the least bit technical about his paranoia. These may be Krafft-Ebing's diagnostic labels, but to attempt to make us think that Joyce was copulating for artistic purposes is to misun-

derstand his entire nature. We can appreciate Ellmann's desire
to explain away his hero's bedroom capers. But the issue lies
elsewhere. Joyce, in his varieties of sexual behavior, was acting
out his lifelong pathology—acting it out in his private letters
and later in the *persona* of his Leopold Bloom. Indeed, John
Glassco, who was something of a specialist on the aphrodisiacal
pleasures of whippings and sex, has pointed out that Joyce's
choice of the name Leopold for Bloom was less accidental than
might seem. The man who gave the language the word *masochism* was named Leopold von Sacher-Masochi, and we know
from Ellmann that his books were in Joyce's library at the time
of his death. Leopold Bloom displays the same mix of fetishism,
paranoia, and excrementary delight amid his dreams of glory,
punishment, and self-abasement in the night-town episode of
Ulysses.

V

Portraits, sketches, caricatures of Joyce come to us in the
high-verbal of *Finnegans Wake,* a long circular self-confession,
a picture always in words. But there exists one cartoon which
translates his words and self-mockery—his wobbly self-esteem
—into visual tracings.

One day, the Spanish painter César Abin came to do a sketch
of Joyce for *transition,* Eugene Jolas's journal which was publishing portions of "Work in Progress." Abin drew a conventional man of letters, sitting in front of his books, with his pen
in his hand, his eyes visionary. It was a tolerable if awkward
likeness. The books, the pen, the entire drawing seemed to
Joyce too solemn, too simple. He began telling Abin what to
draw, and presently he was involved in a collaboration. At
Joyce's instruction a different picture was drawn: Joyce was
shown in a large semicircle as if he were doubled up by cramps,
with his feet dangling among wisps of cloud. His body ended up
shaped like a question mark—the eternal enigma he regarded
himself to be and was to himself as well as his audience. His

*The Joyce-Abin caricature of James Joyce
drawn to the author's specifications*

blinker-like spectacles were on his nose and the tip of his nose collided with a star. Under Joyce's dangling feet Abin drew a terrestrial globe labeled "Ireland." The globe was made to become the large dot completing the question mark. On the head of this free-floating Irishman among the clouds, suspended over Ireland and a large Dublin drawn as Ireland's heartland, was placed a battered cobwebbed Irish derby. There were cobwebs in the hollow of Joyce's chest—that is, near the region of his heart. Shoved into the left pocket was some sheet music. The title printed on it was "Let Me Like a Soldier Fall." There were patches at the knees and a patch on the sleeve. Joyce's mouth is turned down. Stuck into the front of the bowler is the portentous figure 13.

For two weeks Joyce kept on making suggestions to César Abin until he was satisfied. Eugene Jolas tells us that the star in front of the nose was inspired by a critic who had called Joyce "a blue-nosed comedian." And so in this Icarus-like cartoon we may discern, behind its conscious humor and self-denigration, the Joycean comedian and the Joycean self-image. A patchwork cobwebbed Irishman, suspended over Dublin, and an enigma. The cobwebs are strategically placed, almost as if Joyce felt that his head was a cluttered attic and the region of his heart a cluttered storeroom. Thirteen was his number, his fate, the crown of his superstitions. And he is a comedian who thought himself capable of Daedalus-like flight with wings of his own making. He is also Ulysses, the hero who must fall like a soldier, a hero who sings of his glories, as Homer sang of Odysseus. He made himself a question mark, Jolas told us, "because friends had told him once that his figure resembled a question mark, when seen standing meditatively on a street corner." This fell in with his own sense of his being a maze-maker, an enigma-creator, enigmas he unfortunately had to explain to others, since no one understood them. Joyce leaked the method of *Ulysses* to Valéry Larbaud, and some of the secrets of *Finnegan* were divulged to Jolas, McAlmon, and other friends. They spread the good word of how clever Joyce had been. In this way we see behind the fun of caricature the conflicted, suffering, self-disparaging genius. The flaws in his personality are the flaws in his art—and anyone who has carefully read *Ulysses* knows the quantities of cobwebs in that work.

III

TRISTIMANIA:

THE MADNESS OF ART

In honoring the name of Benjamin Rush, we honor a doctor who happens to be one of the signers of the Declaration of Independence. He is among the Founding Fathers of the United States; he is also the father of American psychiatry. George Washington was dedicated to unifying Americans and freeing them of their transatlantic bonds. Rush wanted to free Americans from the bondage of their mental ills. In the midst of a struggle to achieve universal freedoms of mind and spirit, he sought a particular freedom for the possessed and brought to bear on this goal the scientific spirit of the Enlightenment, with which he had become imbued during his studies in Europe. The price of revolution and glory in times of national outrage and public elation is a mixture of genius and madness. Wars, triumphs, and national dedication are compounded of the sublime and the paranoid, of megalomania, and of despair. Rush addressed himself to the manifestations of what were then generally described as "diseases of the mind."

I am led to these observations by a dream that Dr. Rush recorded. Like all good psychiatrists—even then—he listened to his own inner voices as closely as he listened to those of his patients. The dream dates from the period of national triumph; it seems to be of 1785. Rush dreamed that a great crowd was surging about Christ Church in Philadelphia. He approached. A man had climbed the steeple and was sitting on the ball just below the weather vane. Rush asked what was happening and was told that the man on the steeple had discovered he could

control the weather. He could call up sun and rain and cause
the winds to blow from any direction. In effect, he claimed
mastery of the weather vane. It was no longer an indicator; it
was a directed instrument. The man held a trident in his hand
like Neptune and flourished it as he shouted his commands.
Alas, the elements refused to comply. He called for rain; the sun
shone, and the streets were dry. He called for wind; Philadelphia was becalmed. The trident wielder after a while showed
signs of agitation, then he sank into a deep depression. "The
man is certainly mad," the doctor told a friend in the dream. At
this moment a messenger dressed like Mercury descended from
the steeple carrying a banner; on this Dr. Rush read the Latin
device *De te fabula narratur*—"about you a story is being told."

It takes a distinct kind of genius to supply an interpretation
within a dream. Rush wrote in his account of the dream, "The
impression of these words was so forcible upon my mind that
I instantly awoke, and from that time I determined never again
to attempt to influence the opinions and passions of my fellow
citizens upon political subjects." In his prompt reading of the
dream, Rush recognized, both within sleep and on his awakening, who the trident wielder on the steeple was. It was himself.

Admirable dream, in its power, its drama, its myth! In broad
terms we could say it was a doctor's dream—a doctor who tells
himself that the curing of his patients is often dictated by forces
beyond his control, or one who is troubled about his ability to
control his own feelings. It was also a dream of a politically
minded man, as Dr. Rush showed in his remarks. Beyond personal statement, it was a dream for revolutionary America—or
of a Britannia that claimed to rule the waves. The dream was
prophetic in its warning against national megalomania. It said
that neither people nor nations alter historical forces. Even the
symbol of the weather vane has its relevance in our time; we
remember the Weathermen who blew themselves up with
their own explosives in Greenwich Village. In its direct mes-

sage, the dream said that man proposes and God disposes and the laws of probability—if there be such laws—usually prevail.

A few years later Dr. Rush wrote down another dream. This time he was elected President of the United States, a good dream for a Founding Father. At first, probably out of some undetermined feeling of guilt, he declined; it was too high an office, he said. Then he reminded himself that he would have a glorious opportunity to prohibit drunkenness in the United States. This rationale persuaded him to accept. Congress yielded; prohibition was passed. And the country revolted. Petitions showered upon "President" Rush demanding repeal. As Dr. Rush sat in the council room, an impudent stranger came up to him. Americans, he said, would not submit to Rush's "Empire of Reason." Echoing the former dream, the stranger said, "You might as well arrest the orbs of Heaven in their course as *suddenly* change the habits of a whole people." He told "President" Rush to "retire from your present station and go back to your professor's chair and amuse your boys with your idle and impracticable speculations." Rush called for the ouster of this impudent man and awakened in anger—and in relief.

Once again the doctor had rehearsed a dream of personal and national megalomania, the fear of emotions running wild, of legislators and dictators who seek to defy the national conditioning. This dream, too, was prophetic, as we well know. Prohibition and its evils are still remembered. In both dreams, Dr. Rush told himself that the power of God can never become the power of man. We might in more direct form say that it can be very frustrating for man to try to play God.

I

I report these dreams of the remarkable Dr. Rush because they are related to the subject I have chosen for the annual lecture that honors him. My subject is the madness of art. Art has a certain relation to the more benign forms of megalomania;

many are the artists who sit on the weather vane and bid the weather to change, who, like Milton, put words—magnificent words—into the mouths of both God and Satan; who, like Dante, tell of the voyage of the poet to the regions of the Inferno, there to visit figures Dante assigned to hell.

James Joyce believed that he could seize one day, June 16, 1904, out of all eternity and confine it in a single book of 800 pages, possessing only language and intellect for his task. God made this world, Joyce seemed to say in *Ulysses,* but I, the poet, with the power of my craft, can grasp a moment out of all history and preserve it in words. He did this brilliantly enough, in his obsessive-compulsive madness. The work's audacities captured the literary imagination of Joyce's time. New critical perspectives may revise its literary value now that it has reached its seventh decade.

That is an illustration of one form of the madness of art, actually a moderate and creative sort of madness. The artist, the word-wielder (words become the trident), tries to summon up life, feeling, and experience in poems and plays; to speak for all men and women while speaking as an individual, to become the voice of humanity or of the Devil. We could say this of painters who cover great ceilings with mythic representations, of sculptors who rear mighty statues and monuments, or of the anonymous builders of ancient times who set pyramids in the desert and posed the riddle of life in the massive bulk of the Sphinx.

Beethoven called up the thunder of Zeus in symphonic roar; Turner painted season and storm, using only pigments and light; and Shakespeare was as close to realizing word omnipotence as any writer in the literatures of the world. He wrote in the language of the mortal, but he made it sound like the language of eternity. He dealt with concretions of history and power, and as Dr. Rush observed, he wrote an "inimitable history of all the forms of derangement, in the tragedy of *King Lear,*" that extraordinary poetic rendering of the senility of kingship. Rush quoted the following to illustrate his statement:

Better I were distract;
So should my thoughts be severed from my griefs,
And woes, by wrong imaginations, lose
The knowledge of themselves.

These words contain the drama of mental illness—the attempt to escape into "wrong imaginations" so as to escape miseries of the mind. By implication, the words also contain the drama of artistic madness. Artists, too, seek to sever themselves from griefs and woes; artists, too, can lose the knowledge of themselves. But they do so, shall we say, with the right imaginations instead of the wrong. The difference lies between disintegration and integration. Their fantasies become poems and stories; their rage is channeled into rhetoric; their griefs and woes become imagined tragedies. Dr. Rush, in his pioneer work *Medical Inquiries and Observations Upon the Diseases of the Mind*, hoped that his readers would "excuse my frequent reference to the poets for facts to illustrate the history of madness." Poets, he said, "view the human mind in all its operations, whether natural or morbid, with a microscopic eye; and hence many things arrest their attention, which escape the notice of physicians."

The doctor called agitated forms of depression "tristimania" —a mania of sadness—because he felt that this word was more accurate than "hypochondriasis," then used to describe many mental ills. He remarked how people in deep despair often decide they are the victims of all sorts of illnesses; this they carry into realms of illusion. That is why the term "hypochondriasis" was used. The doctors of Rush's time tried to prove to their patients that they were inventing all their extravagant ailments —that they did not have snakes in their innards, had not been secretly disemboweled or robbed of their cranial matter—but it was useless. However much these patients imagined their illnesses, what they were *not* imagining was their depression. "Tristimania" is a good word. It may be inaccurate in a diagnostic sense; yet I find it has descriptive value. It helps describe the component of depression in art, for nothing is more chronic among writers than their sadness. Turn where we will, we find them writing elegies upon the passing of time, of glory, of life. *Sic transit gloria mundi.* All artists seem to want to inscribe this motto on the door of their imagination.

I I

In 1893, Henry James, an American whose historical imagination reached back to the Enlightenment, wrote a short story called "The Middle Years." He was a brother of William James, who set up the first psychological laboratory in the United States.

In the tale a novelist named Dencombe is at a seaside hotel getting over an illness; he sits on a bench looking at the ocean. He thinks that "the infinite of life had gone" and compares that which is left to a small glass engraved like a thermometer. His years are now measured; they have acquired boundaries after seeming boundless. The sea is all surface and twinkle, but Dencombe finds it "far shallower than the spirit of man." Weakly he opens a package he has received. It contains the novel he finished before his illness, titled *The Middle Years.* He does not recognize it. He has another thought: Why did he write fiction? Why didn't he seek the romance of life in the acts of life instead of in the acts of words? It has taken him so long to perfect his art, and now he thinks, "Ah for another go!—ah for a better chance!" Another go—a better chance! We do not have to be too diagnostic to remark on how sad is this character and how depressed the author who thought up this character and this story—a story about art and aging and the depression of illness. James was fifty when he wrote it.

There is a doctor in the story, a young man who has recently taken a medical degree and is attending a wealthy hypochondriacal lady at the hotel. Dr. Hugh, as it turns out, is a devoted reader of the great novelist, whom he rescues from a fainting spell on the beach. Chance "had brought the weary man of letters face to face with the greatest admirer in the new generation." The admirer is described as "a bristling young doctor—he looked like a German physiologist," and "a representative of the new psychology." I may say, speaking from the pages of biography, that William James had studied in Germany, had taught physiology after taking a medical degree, and had published his *Principles of Psychology* three years before James wrote this story. "The Middle Years" embodies the novelist's wish for his brother's attention and love, which he never had, because William James the scientist was critical of his artistic junior, who played with the facts of life in words instead of putting them under a microscope.

In the tale, the novelist wants to revise his novel. He is a "fingerer of style"; he alters the text. "Another go" would give him the opportunity to rewrite, to rewrite his life, as it were. An attachment develops between Dencombe and Dr. Hugh; when the doctor is dismissed by the rich lady for his inattention, he decides to devote himself entirely to the novelist, who is obviously dying. The conversation at the deathbed between patient and doctor has mythic qualities. The novelist muses, "The thing is to have made somebody care. You happen to care. You happen to be crazy, of course, but that doesn't affect the law." Summoning his last strength as his life ebbs away, the novelist says to the doctor, "A second chance—*that's* the delusion. There never was to be but one. We work in the dark—we do what we can—we give what we have. Our doubt is our passion and our passion is our task. The rest is the madness of art."

III

The madness of art: these words spoken by the dying author in the story contain the essence of tristimania. They are weighted with a sense of mutability, and they recognize a supreme reality. There *is* no second chance. What we lose—we lose. What we do cannot usually be undone. As in Dr. Rush's dream, the artist cannot change seasons, years, or lives, however great the dream's force; the mysteries and secrets of the creative life remain hidden within the artist's power of metamorphosis, the imaginings of new—individual—forms of reality that are his own. To those who are not artists, this kind of imagining may seem madness. "The Middle Years," one of Henry James's many fables for writers, was addressed to all men and women who invest their tasks with passion. The particular madness in literary creation resides in the need of the writer not only to have experiences, which is enough for most people, but to sit down and write them and even change them, as Canaletto painted scenes of Venice but reorganized the buildings and scenes into Venetian scenes of his own or as Dante took the Christian concepts of heaven and hell and made them creations of his mind. This is the art of transposition as well as metamorphosis. Weaving between illusion and reality, dreaming dreams that are reality, seeing realities that are dreams, the writer writes of personal secrets and mysteries, often in language obscure to many readers. In this, too, the writer seems to suffer from a form of madness, as Samuel Daniel's "Are They Shadows That We See?" illustrates:

> Are they shadows that we see?
> And can shadows pleasure give?
> Pleasures only shadows be
> Cast by bodies we conceive,
> And are made the things we deem.
> In those figures which they seem.

The person who is neither writer nor dreamer, the individual who lives each day without the verbal obsession, needs neither paper nor pen to express strong emotion. A great deal, no doubt, is suppressed; but often if a person feels melancholy he or she knows the value of a shot of whiskey or a glass of beer and the companionship at the corner bar; men and women know how to release anger on a tennis court or some other form of violent exertion. They have discovered a multitude of ways to lighten their emotional burdens. Not so the artist, who uses particular and highly individual pigments, clay, sound, words, to disguise and muffle or transform whatever deep-seated feelings imperiously demand issue. We might consider this a form of self-healing; often what is created in this way can, as Aristotle knew long ago, heal others.

It must be understood, to underline and frame my picture of artistic melancholy, that I am not arguing the outworn thesis of Cesare Lombroso, who saw a close relation between art and insanity. Nor do I seek to sustain the long debate of our time, initiated by Freud, on the nature of art and neurosis. I leave genesis and diagnosis to others. I recognize that art has other components than depression. I do not for a moment ignore the libido force that probably subsumes all others. However, within the harmony and beauty of most transcendent works, I see a particular sadness. We might say it is simply the sadness of life, but it is a sadness that somehow becomes a generating motor, a link in the chain of power that makes the artist persist, even when having lived an experience, to transform it within his or her medium.

Franz Kafka used to say that writing was a form of prayer. Of course this is not so for most writers, but it was for him, and his saying this tells us a good deal about his troubles. He needed to write in order to supplicate, to appeal, to defer to cosmic powers beyond his reach, even as for others writing is a form of conquest, a form of winning love and admiration and universal approval, or simply a way in which the artist writes a letter to the world. Many are the uses of art, and most important are its uses to the individual artist. There come moments, for certain writers, when the tristimania gets out of control; at that moment we have our suicides of art, Virginia Woolf or Hart Crane or Sylvia Plath. Other artists, made of sterner stuff, resist the anesthesias or the ocean's oblivion; they defy the death impulse by finding words for the inner struggle. I long ago suggested in a paper on Willa Cather's novel *The Professor's House* how she transformed the depression of her middle age into a parable of the self. In writing out the suicidal fantasies of her fictional professor at the end of this novel, she seemed to have resolved the moment when, as she said, "the world broke in two." She no longer had to commit suicide.

The best known literary "case" of our time is, I suppose, that of Virginia Woolf, who is most often called a manic-depressive and who tried to do away with herself repeatedly, yet whose drive to health mounted with each creation—only to descend again when the creation was completed. She had a vision of "a fin rising on a wide blank sea," as a poem or a novel rises seemingly out of nowhere. This suggests both the strength and blankness—the word is hers—of her creative struggle. Her death by drowning was a kind of return of the fin to its native element.

I come back to Kafka for a moment, to his sense that he was praying when he wrote. A capital memory of Kafka's childhood was of his having one night kept his father awake by demanding repeatedly, as little children can, a drink of water. The father, never a temperate man, abruptly locked his son out on a balcony and went to sleep. I believe that this trauma, doubtless reinforced by others, became the central myth of Kafka's life. We can read it in the first sentence of *The Trial:* "Someone must have been telling lies about Joseph K. for without having done anything wrong he was arrested one fine morning." In the childhood episode, Kafka did not associate his unreasonable cries for a drink of water with the punitive action taken by his father, the form of "arrest" and jailing imposed on him. He saw all of life thereafter as a kind of arbitrary arrest—filled with arbitrary punishment, arbitrary fathers, arbitrary governments, arbitrary Gods.

I V

To write of Kafka in this way is to suggest perhaps that the depression we find in art has its genesis in some fundamental early hurt or "wound." Certainly the trauma theory is valid in a limited way, but it is not my intention to rehearse etiology. Any trauma, as we know, is surrounded by a history; accidents of childhood do not always occur full-blown, save when unforeseen in such catastrophes as war. I take it as a postulate, even an axiom, that by the time the creating personality has acquired adult being, a great fund of melancholy has been accumulated. It clamors for release. We can hear it in all the tumult in Schubert and Schumann; it is sounded for us in the cosmic cadences of Beethoven; it comes at us from almost every page of poetry.

"After thirty," wrote Emerson, "a man wakes up sad every morning . . . until the day of his death." The sadness is often there long before the age of thirty. We see it in Dickens, who was put to work in a factory at a tender age. Kafka's terrifying episode on the balcony can be found in his "letter" to his father, which is replete with remembrances of arbitrary parental rule. If we search carefully I think we would find that central to the melancholy of Virginia Woolf was not the sexual play to which she was exposed at a tender age (she might have even enjoyed that) but the inconsolable loss of her mother when she was fourteen or fifteen. This was reinforced by a series of other deaths in the family; the sense of loss and desolation was cumulative, and the will to death grew stronger as she grew older.

We need not cling to the trauma theory this late in the century; all trauma is related by the web of attachment and detachment and by interaction with figures surrounding any child. I will add only that I consider it one of the misfortunes of the stumblings of psychology toward illumination that the adult language of sex has been applied to children. The tragedy of Oedipus is now a child's so-called oedipal fantasies; "depression" and "incest" are linked in the pages of textbooks as terms for conditions that would much better be described in the language of displacement of affection—and mourning for separation—appropriate to childhood.

I am dealing with the phenomenon of mourning I find in art.

How to cure it, let me add again, belongs in the domain of psychiatry. Most artists would rather not be cured. What happens in art is something quite unique. A pattern of repeated experience is wedded to a very early and unfathomable gift of sensory harmony; a sharpness of the ear and of verbal memory; a capacity to link like with like, which is the artist's symbolic imagination; and a thousand other experiences of color and shape, the imprint of the physical world upon the senses, which no computer of the most cunning construction can unravel or duplicate. Beyond this endowment, there is continuing life experience. That experience (I do not want to make it sound simple) contains within it joy, calm, anger, violence, deprivation, and depression—depression sometimes so profound that it gives the artist so endowed the few options of, for example, Levin or Anna in Tolstoy's *Anna Karenin.*

The death wish is strong, but art, in most cases, provides an exquisite way of reshaping the pain of experience into wholeness, health, and harmony. I suppose a supreme example of such a struggle in our time is to be seen in T. S. Eliot, who by writing *The Waste Land* found an archetypal way to express his tristimania. Dante expressed it in the noble simplicity of the descent into hell and then the return. Eliot's descent can be charted in his early poems. They are monologues of frustration, impotence, and intellectual frigidity. Weaving into this early melancholy, we now know, were personal feelings of inadequacy, deepened by the failure of his marriage. The resulting frustrations—who knows how many and how powerful—engendered the symbolic poem of a wasteland, expressing the impuissance of the poet, who lives in a world in which there is so much to be said that has already been said for him. The montage of quotation in Eliot is but another statement of frustration, and the waste-world is inhabited by hollow men who go through rituals. This is the poet making poetry out of his deepest sense of powerlessness and performing an affirmative act of creation.

Within each depression, as we know, there is a wish for death.

The work of art often, so to speak, stands between the artist and extinction. Eliot, writing out of his personal myth of the world's dehydration, was actually writing of the dehydration of the soul. After *The Waste Land* gave him a fame that seemed for the moment empty, Eliot moved even closer to expressing death in "The Hollow Men." Here is the very apathy of depression, a mania of sadness carried to its farthest shore, beyond which there can be only extinction. The verses end in a toppling of towers and the babble of nursery rhymes.

Most often, however, the poet has resilience; there is always another poem to be written. After the descent there can be either annihilation, a lingering in hell, or ascent. Virginia Woolf, in her repeated need to reassert her life as each of death's boundaries was reached, found herself invariably thinking of a new novel. In Dostoevsky we see a similar cycle. It takes its form in his devotion to the story of Christ, to death and resurrection. I do not doubt that Dostoevsky's having had grand mal epilepsy gave corporeal shape to this powerful myth: each epileptic fit was annihilation, each awakening a rebirth. At the moment of the onset of the seizure there were the split seconds of aura, which made the world seem a magnificent work of art.

We can multiply examples. We can see the deep melancholy in Flaubert; the driving misanthropism of Maupassant finding its outlet in a kind of sexual suicide; the self-destructive personae of Oscar Wilde; the compulsive escape into storytelling, made routine, by Trollope; the euphoria of the comic writers, all clowns grimly smiling at man's vanity and choking back their tears. I would focus, however, on Tolstoy, whose profoundest novel I feel is not *War and Peace*, in which we have a distinctly depressed hero, but *Anna Karenin.* It has been read and is read as a novel of a grand passion, of a love that transcends social boundaries, of the wages of sin, which are death. I do not read it only in this way. *Anna Karenin* is a supreme novel of tristimania. That is its real subject, behind the stories of love and marriage and unhappy families and unhappy lovers.

Most readers remember Anna as a creature of beauty and radiance, an embodiment of the *ewige Weibliche,* the eternal feminine, as we see her at the great ball, at the center of the scene. She falls in love with Count Vronsky, and their passion consumes them, especially Anna, for Vronsky is an empty man. As always, passion collides with reality. We read of Anna's mounting despair and her terrible fantasies; we see the disintegration of her composed societal self. The beautiful, seemingly poised, and self-sufficient noblewoman has no inner resources. Once the society on which she leans and where she found her identity is removed, she too is an empty vessel. She throws herself in front of a train with the suicide's characteristic aggression against the world: There, thinks Anna, as she falls, I will punish him and escape from everyone and from myself. The classic fantasy: annihilation of self is annihilation of the world and one's supposed enemies.

Readers have been so caught up in the passion of Anna and Vronsky and the qualities of the love story that they pay less attention to Levin, whose history runs parallel to that of Anna. Levin is interested in managing his estate, in farming, in his peasants. He likes hard work, yet it leaves him dissatisfied. Even his marriage, a good one, does not suffice. After the death of his brother, his depression comes to the surface. He tries to distract himself, but he cannot escape his despair. He sees the light only after a long and sustained inner debate. Then, grasping that for every man there is nothing in store but suffering, death, and forgetfulness, he makes up his mind that life is impossible and that he must either interpret existence so that it does not present itself to him as the "evil jest of some devil" or shoot himself. Levin does not shoot himself. He does not throw himself in front of a train. He accepts the jest. Anna represents the depression that ends in self-annihilation. Levin represents the depression of the existentialist who knows what he faces and that the options are his. He will muddle through.

We can go beyond this in literary psychology to ask ourselves:

Why did Tolstoy write such a novel? The biographical facts are available. Tolstoy was going through a profound crisis when he was working on *Anna*. He was an acclaimed artist, a master of his craft, but his soul sickness ran deep. He seems in this work to have split his tristimania into the feminine and the masculine, the artist side of himself and the practical land-owning nobleman. A depression split into two is still depression. The artistic feminine side is killed off in the novel. To take a great leap, to defy the social order in which Tolstoy was bred, was too much for him; the emotions and the internal clamor are therefore stilled, and the rational side prevails. Anna dies; Levin lives on in existential despair; and Tolstoy lived on, abandoning his writing for some years and adopting a simplified Christianity, mingling his religious feeling with his agrarianism. Ultimately he returned to art, to write "The Death of Ivan Ilyich" and *Resurrection*. Death and resurrection: the titles tell us that the debate continued until he was over eighty years old, to the day he died. Symbolically, he lived out the death of Anna in a railroad station, but without her violent act. Trains and horses—the leap and the journey—speak in Tolstoy as symbols of the eternal struggle of art and ideas in this man.

A part, then, of what Henry James called the madness of art resides in the artist's search for some exit from the labyrinth of the imprisoned and despairing self—the verbal structure, the philter, the anodyne that will somehow provide escape and surcease. There are times when a work of art can provide total healing; it has happened in certain instances. Often, then, the artist ceases to produce. The single book, the single play, the series of poems, have given full expression to what needed to be said. Ralph Ellison's *Invisible Man* seems to be such a work, although we must not prejudge Ellison's potential productivity. It is a case of the artist moving from personal struggle and imagination into reality and then having no further need or impulse or material to go on shaping fantasies. The classic example, I suppose, is the French symbolist poet Arthur Rimbaud, who revolutionized French poetry between his fifteenth and twentieth years and then became a merchant in Ethiopia. He died unaware that he was a poetic legend in France.

In the literature of the United States, I have always felt that an ambiguous element enters: advertising and success sometimes kill off our young geniuses; they are not allowed their catharsis. Exalted prematurely, they develop a success-neurosis. On the other hand, I have always found the case of Edith Wharton illuminating. She felt imprisoned by wealth, society, and her conventional and sterile marriage. Having written a novel about this imprisonment, *The House of Mirth,* in which her heroine commits suicide, she was able to go on to self-realization as a woman of letters. She discovered the life of passion and the passion of life. I think she continued to write more out of habit than out of fundamental drive. Writing was an exercise, a form of emotional calisthenics for her fine intelligence and her admirable lucidity. She had become accustomed to verbalizing her experience; nothing else sufficed. Only *Ethan Frome* and *The Age of Innocence* among her later works come close to the intensities of *The House of Mirth.* These later books contain all of her skills and distinctions without the early crystallization of feeling.

V

Let me reiterate: it has not been my intention in describing the madness of art to suggest to psychiatrists that art is an illness. I speak simply in the sense in which Max Beerbohm, asking someone to meet him in a certain pub frequented by writers, warned his friend he would see a good many depressed people sitting around the bar. "These," he said, "will be the writers."

Many great artists are aware that they live with their devils and struggle constantly to make their peace with them. Rilke refused psychoanalysis, saying, "Leave me my demons." Joyce recoiled when Jung offered to analyze him and scoffed in his special way about "Doctor Jung the Swiss Tweedledum who is not to be confused with the Viennese Tweedledee, Dr. Freud." I think both artists intuitively realized that to dispossess themselves of their demons would strip them of the defenses they had built up from their earliest years and leave them vulnerable. The opposite of these are the men of talent who, unaware of the demonic within, have through psychoanalysis discovered their demons in a process of self-examination. Edwin Muir was such a man. A writer and translator, he emerged from a period of analysis as a distinguished poet; he had discovered the lyrical side of himself that he had suppressed for many years.

My concern has been with the phenomenon of depression in art. It might be said that I have perhaps emphasized the obvious. One might argue that the pursuit of happiness, as Benjamin Rush's contemporaries formulated it, was indeed a "pursuit" and that one did not find the womb a place of eternal bliss, although this is generally assumed. I rather think that in the womb the babe, nourished by the mother, is imprisoned in the mother's physical and mental feelings, that we find here a preparedness for both the bliss and bale of the human condition. In literary art, however, we find the human condition articulated for us as nowhere else. Take any anthology and read poems at random and you cannot but be struck by the underlying sadness even in poems of joy, the constant reiteration of the pain of love, the euphoria that can be a mask of despair, the common recognition that we smile but we also sigh, that we laugh but also shed tears, and that the shedding of tears is itself an act of need and of release. Shakespeare assured us in one of his moods that "present mirth hath present laughter," but a few lines farther he hits us with a truth we all know too well, "Youth's a stuff will not endure." In "Lines," Tennyson, filled with delight by memories of childhood, after a few words of rediscovery finds

> Gray sea banks and pale sunsets—dreary wind,
> Dim shores, dense rains, and heavy-clouded sea!

What majestic desolation of feeling! Turning at random in a search for relief, I plunge into the "lamb white days" of Dylan Thomas's "Fern Hill" and see how he was "happy as the grass was green." Moving with him through his sun-long days and moon-long nights, I nevertheless reach the last two lines:

> Time held me green and dying
> Though I sang in my chains like the sea.

Death sits beside every one, but death seems to have many incarnations in the lives of poets, who summon him as an ever-present stranger at the feast. In "How Do I Love Thee," Elizabeth Barrett Browning counts the ways of her love freely, purely, "with the passion put to use/In my old griefs, and with my childhood's faith." But her last line is a prophecy of parting: "I shall but love thee better after death." Then we have Edna Millay, the waif of the 1920s, summoning in "What Lips My Lips Have Kissed" the elegiac—for all poesy seems to be elegy:

> I cannot say what loves have come and gone;
> I only know that summer sang in me
> A little while, that in me sings no more.

I will not continue this game of random questing for poetic melancholies. Why need I when I can turn to Keats and find his supreme "Ode on Melancholy," an epitome of the death-in-life and life-in-death of the artist. I need not quote to you his enumeration of the anodynes for his mourning—nightshade, yew, beetle, death-moth, and Lethe for disremembrance, out of which he sails into the world's life, but I would quote the following:

> Then glut thy sorrow on a morning rose,
> Or on the rainbow of the salt sand-wave,
> Or on the wealth of globed peonies;

Or if thy mistress some rich anger shows,
Emprison her soft hand, and let her rave,
And feed deep, deep upon her peerless eyes. . . .
She dwells with Beauty—Beauty that must die . . .
Aye, in the very temple of Delight
Veiled Melancholy has her sovereign shrine.

When the lament for passing youth is sung, the poet may survive to rage with Yeats upon his aging. The list of those in art who never reach old age is long; some drown themselves en route in the grape or in drugs; others flee this world; still others simply sink into impotence. When the artist survives, however, full of power, and turns to self-contemplation, the depression of aging permits a towering rage like Lear's against the prisoning of great powers in senility of body and mind. In "Sailing to Byzantium," Yeats wrote, "An aged man is but a paltry thing/ A tattered coat upon a stick." Sometimes this rage of art produces the greatest works of all.

Few are the artists who reach this moment, who work through their aging and end with the serenity of Oedipus at Colonnus. But when they do they give us supreme and enduring art. I think of Michelangelo, his powerful old hands still forcing marble to yield to his dreams; of Henry James fashioning his three greatest novels; of Yeats's sinewy poems that replace the romantic hesitations and despair of his younger self; of Johann Sebastian Bach working on the art of the fugue. It is as if there is a final summoning of powers and divinities, a final cosmic laughter against the ultimate. Perhaps this is after all "the better chance"—not reliving the old life but rewriting it into a *vita nuova* of the years of mastery. Such artists preempt "a place in Time infinitely more important than the restricted one reserved for them in space," as Proust said. Out of world sadness, out of tristimania, immortal and durable things are brought into being.

PORTRAIT OF THE ARTIST
AS AN OLD MAN

> SOCRATES: I consider that the old have gone before us along a road which we must all travel in our turn and it is good we should ask them of the nature of that road, whether it be rough and difficult, or easy and smooth.
> —PLATO, *The Republic*

In his conversations with Goethe, Johann Eckermann records a ride to Erfurt on an April day in 1827. Goethe, then seventy-eight, looked attentively at the landscape and remarked, in passing, that nature is always filled with good intentions, but—one had to admit it—nature is not always beautiful. By way of illustration, he then began a disquisition on the oak. Sometimes an oak, crowded by other trees, grows high and thin, spends its freshest powers "making it" to air and sunshine, and ends up with an overblown crown on a thin body. Then there is the oak that springs up in moist and marshy soil. Overindulged and squat, it is nourished too quickly into an indented, stubborn obesity. Its unfortunate brother may lodge in poor, stony soil on a mountain slope; lacking free development, it becomes knotty and gnarled. Such trees, Goethe said, can hardly be called beautiful—at least they are not beautiful as oak trees.

Then Goethe described to the recording Eckermann the perfect oak. It grows in sandy soil, where it spreads its roots comfortably in every direction; it needs space in which to feel on all sides the effects of sun, wind, rain, light. "If it grows up snugly sheltered from wind and weather," said Goethe, "it becomes nothing. But a century's struggle with the elements makes it strong and powerful, so that, at its full growth, its presence inspires us with astonishment and admiration."

I

The author of *Faust* was speaking a piece of autobiography as his eightieth birthday drew near: he had been one of the

fortunate oaks of literature. Few can claim such favored circumstances; still fewer survive to full growth; if they do, they
consume many years struggling toward light and sun, or are
undernourished like the mountain oak, or grow obese from the
effects of a soil too moist, a climate too lush. Nature has its own
ways of inhibiting and stunting art, of forestalling the ripeness
of age. Many artists, mere saplings of promise, are cut off in
their precocious youth. And those who survive often remain
aging versions of what they have been during their earlier years
—that is, individuals who repeat their performances and grow
rigid and stale. They have consumed their originality. We can
count on our fingers the few artists who surpassed themselves
when old, as Goethe did. Among painters, Rembrandt comes to
mind. His autobiography, begun early, is spread over many
canvases—those marvelous paintings of himself. They show him
in jaunty youth, all plumes and velvet jacket; in middle years,
with increasing disorder in costume, but the face powerful and
arresting; and finally we look upon him watery-eyed and be-
draggled; but what a magnificent old man! How sure and fine
is his self-realization as he confronts his visage in old age! The
early swagger gives way to a mixture of resignation and resentment; as an old man he paints himself with an ever greater
honesty; the feather and cape have long ago been set aside.
There remains only the truth. The artist addresses himself to
these truths: the truth of appearance and the truth of feeling,
the reality of wrinkles, the delicacy of the bulges under his eyes
as they catch the light, the face now set in irreversible lines, yet
suggesting wisdom and experience, the acceptance of all life,
the recognition that it is usually the journey and not the arrival
that matters. The artist as an old man knows that life will not
offer him any better chance. There is only one, and his art has
been that chance.

In looking at the splendid finished oaks—in visual art, Leonardo or Michelangelo, Titian or Tintoretto; in music, Bach or
even the gnarled Beethoven—we must remind ourselves that
some of these men did not live as long as men live today. But

art has its own life span. A finished Mozart died in his unfinished thirties. One thinks of Rimbaud, whose growth as poet came to a stop before he was twenty, although he lived on in the world of commerce; or of the Romantics, such lively saplings, who withered or were suddenly cut off close to the ground. The portrait of the artist as a young man is usually the picture of an unfinished artist, one who may not end up as an artist at all. I am convinced that the fictional Stephen Dedalus, arrogant and poised for flight, in his coldness, secrecy, cleverness, had in him nothing but a potential virtuosity. He was all anger; he was mindless with rage. He wrote a single poem, not a very good one, but he called himself an artist and wanted the world to give him its bounty before he had given the world any proof of his worth.

Portraits of artists as young men speak to us with what Henry James called a hungry futurity. The portrait of the artist as an old man, on the other hand, is that of the finished oak, standing strong and sometimes beautiful in nature, with a developed and nourished past. Most questions have been answered. The storms and stresses are over. The pain of growth, the anguish of aging, have been surmounted; the radiance and suffering have ended in triumph and fulfillment, even if sometimes in penury and want. Biographers of the young are in a forest of saplings; biographers of the old stand in clearer land, amid a finished forest—a beauty of maturity. All is not perfection; but then nature, as Goethe has taught us, is unsymmetrical, prodigal, often a game of chance.

With aging, spontaneity disappears; it belongs to the earlier flowering, to one's thirties and forties, sometimes earlier, as with Mozart. The aging artist is left at sixty-five or seventy with the resources of the past but with a diminished future. The need to advance and to achieve has been superseded, leaving old memories, old strengths, perhaps hidden powers previously held in check but still available for release in a new kind of freedom; and at the same time a freedom curtailed by physical change—a waning resilience in the mind, a tendency for fantasy to become circular and repetitive, and last, but far from least, curtailments of memory. The system seems overloaded; it resists taking too many new things aboard. Memory is often momentary—we forget as we walk from room to room. The old life, the lived life and also the unlived, are remembered with greater clarity; somehow the earlier years still claim vivid possession. Perhaps, with death nearer, we cherish beginnings rather than endings.

In gifted individuals there can emerge with aging certain kinds of compensation: a cumulative synthesis of earlier riches, combined with freedom brought by acceptance, faith, resignation, a willingness to recognize the inevitable. The atmosphere may be more rarefied, but it is more panoramic. Parents and friends are gone, and if there are children they have departed their separate ways. The future offers one thing: the reality of death, the unknown. Artists are human. They cling to life (if they don't surrender to apathy and indifference) and this means they cling to their art. "No one believes in his own death," Freud has told us. In our deepest unconscious we have lived and continue to live as if we were immortal. That is a law of life—without it everything would seem worthless.

But in our conscious selves we are having glimpses at last of the finite. Arbitrary and accidental things fall by the way. Within the creative being there remains a timeless world; and the artist lives on, as all creative men and women do, for the continuing creative act. In Hawaii a few weeks ago I watched a ninety-three-year-old woman, a distinguished artist, wearing blue jeans covered with paint and turpentine, climb a ladder to a scaffolding to retouch a mural on the wall where it has found its final home. The *doing* has primary importance, within whatever limitations the artist encounters. There are always expediencies. When Gauguin, at whatever age, ran out of canvas, he painted on sackcloth. When Henry James developed writer's cramp, he learned to dictate directly to the typewriter. This in aging is much more exciting than the question of survival—a question which has become academic. One has survived. The question now is of the new career, and as my tired fingers use a typewriter I dream of the new word processors which promise to lengthen my writing life. There is also a summoning of new powers, the final powers of synthesis—as if one has lived one's whole long life to be strengthened by the insights and fortitudes of experience. Old men and old women learn to accept the incomplete. They now know that total order can never be achieved in any life. Each day brings new disorder. Youth may be able to say more than it knows; age tends to leave a great deal unsaid. What is said has an achieved simplicity, a beautiful starkness. The commitment now seems to be to one's past. The sense of the past has become enlarged; one has a longer backward reach, and it is seen in its largest outlines, for again the trivial and the accidental fall away and one discovers essences. The intelligence no longer wants to cope with mass and detail; it holds instead to illuminations. These yielded us Bach's art of the fugue, Beethoven's late quartets, Yeats's final poems.

In literature we find many kinds of aging. One thinks of Coleridge's genius spread in incompleteness and steeped in opium; of Landor's dramatic senility; of Browning in London, prosaic and drowsy after the great poetry of his early years; or of Carlyle's rage and dyspepsia and brilliance. Let me sketch the portraits of three writers—two novelists and one poet—who bridged the nineteenth and twentieth centuries. Let us look (as far as biography ever can) at what each represented. Each is a special case, as artists are bound to be. In our empirical way, we might find in these transcendent cases some common illustrations of artistic experience, some crises of the imagination and of being, often observed in men of high resource and development. These may permit us to understand, perhaps in a heightened way, some part of the human drama and human values in aging, or what we now call gerontology.

II

I choose as my first case a Russian master, Count Leo Nikolayevich Tolstoy. He was born in 1828 and died at eighty-two in 1910. He seems at first glance one of Goethe's splendid oaks. He grew up on a large estate, a nobleman, with full opportunity to sink his roots deep into native soil. The young Tolstoy, as well as the old, revealed certain traits and conflicts that embodied the most characteristic struggle of man: the struggle between instincts, which demand freedom, and civilization, which insists upon controls.

Tolstoy never knew his parents. His mother was dim and ghostly, probably a screened remembrance, for she died before Tolstoy was two. His father seemed large and authoritative, but he disappeared when Tolstoy was eight. French and German tutors, a series of maiden aunts and cousins, and the life on his estate provided the future writer with an enormous sense of freedom, yet a freedom hedged with emotional restrictions. Tolstoy had the privileges of a young aristocrat at large in an accepting world. He had a life of ease that is reflected in all his works—in the lives of Pierre and Andrei and Levin. Yet how deeply troubled a spirit he was, a spirit brooding and confused. It is a cliché that the nineteenth-century Russians were "melancholy Slavs"; certainly the articulate among them gave the world a sense of yearning and weariness, a chronic soul-sickness. "What is life?" they all seem to ask. "What does it mean?" And they give troubled and deeply human answers. Tolstoy had an aloofness that enabled him to see more clearly than most. He also had the egotism of his privileges, and a curiously low self-esteem, so that his art gave him no solace. It seemed to him a plaything. He was a novelist who wanted to be a philosopher. He wanted systems—for by systems alone could emotion and impulse be strongly harnessed. When young, every time he encountered any subject, he experienced an urge to write a treatise on it. Whatever came to hand—religion, music, philosophy, history, conduct—required rules: rules of life, rules for himself and his busy, compulsive, driving mind, and of course rules for everyone else. Some vast inner reservoir of personal grief and insecurity, some strange fear of allowing himself to feel, although he was extraordinarily aware of the feelings of others, made him a prodigy of self-prohibitions, which were, in the aristocratic way, promptly undermined by self-indulgence.

The child Tolstoy was brought up by a clan rather than by emotionally identifiable parent figures. While that practice is highly successful among some primitive peoples (making children feel that every home is their home), it gave this aristocrat a sense of drift in his youth, even of rootlessness. And how difficult to be a realist who prefers lofty, abstract thoughts about God and society! How exact, how accurate, were his observations when he walked into a room! He could note the button on a cloak, and it could tell him things about the wearer; he could capture fleeting expressions on faces, see the fumbling finger, the jerk of the shoulder—he could see *into* people, and their lives, and how they handled their affairs, and could remember all they said. He loved nature, the sensible visual world, although he lacked a style in putting down what he saw on paper. Yet how could he reconcile all these realities with a kind of inner despair, a God who made life seem arbitrary—and offer only death as a solution?

By sixty Tolstoy was world famous, the author of *War and Peace* and *Anna Karenin* as well as of many tales and tracts on how to lead a good life—according to Tolstoy. He was a Thoreau grown old, a foreshadowing of the future Gandhi, all for nonviolence and passive resistance and self-immolation; the Kingdom of God, he said, was in man. He preached simplicity and chastity, yet could not escape the call of passion in the large bed at Yasnaya Polyana, where he fathered thirteen children. After his passionate middle years, sex was still imperious; but when passion was spent, he tended to see his wife as a temptress and blamed himself for his weakness. He entered old age with the step of a patriarch—the long beard, those world-weary wrinkles, a flat nose like that of a prizefighter, a gnarled oak of a man with lively eyes that looked searchingly, always seeking. This man, who seemed to have all the fulfillments of life, somehow felt a lack—of what? Something was missing, as seen in the frown, the rages, the enthusiasms, the prophecies of this rustic primitive genius at large on his lands amid his peasants and disciplines. *"Tak chto zhe nam dyelat?"* That was also the title of one of his major essays: "What then must we do?" What *was* there to do? Endowed with abundance, could he give away his property? Put his copyrights in the public domain? Recognize that money is not important? Be a vegetarian? Have no part in the exploitation of man by man? Forswear smoking and self-indulgence? Lead a life of chastity?

He was a bundle of strivings, as Thoreau might have said, but somehow he always checkmated them. "I tell others what to do," said Tolstoy, "but I don't know what to do myself." Some sense of worthlessness, some need to hold himself in low esteem, gave him also a brooding fear of his mortality. He was afraid of death—this man who could understand and feel so much of life. He was the aristocrat in spite of himself, jealous of his prerogatives, yet also insisting he was the friend of the people, at heart closest to his *muzhiks,* his peasants, who never understood what he talked about and suspected his generous impulses. The young Chekhov, visiting Yasnaya Polyana, remarked that Tolstoy's idea was to put himself on the level of the plebeians; what was necessary, said Chekhov, was to educate the plebeians to a higher plane. Tolstoy was indeed a bundle of strivings and contradictions. He was an ardent Slavophile, but he also loved the West; he was hostile to private ownership, but he kept up his estates and added to them, living as a man of wealth. In his youth he was a compulsive gambler, like Dostoevsky; but he repaired his losses ultimately with vast royalties from his writings. He never questioned the fact that so many peasants worked for him and his large family. He abhorred the eating of meat, but he could spend long days hunting. He ate vegetables and grains but had sudden spurts of gluttony. He lectured his peasants on the evils of tobacco and dug a ditch and made them throw their pipes into it. Then, returning to his study, he reached for a *papirossa,* a cigarette. He was orthodox and devout, but he defied the church and was ultimately excommunicated. In *The Kreutzer Sonata* he told the world it must be chaste; he quoted Christ and said that a man who lusts after a woman commits adultery deep in his heart. But at that very moment he made his wife pregnant with her thirteenth child.

We must not dismiss Tolstoy as a hypocrite, any more than we would Thoreau for building his hut in a symbolic loneliness, less than a mile from his mother's home. Something more profound is at work in such a genius. His sense of chaos and his sense of order are mixed. His feelings are too strong, at times overwhelming, driven by a constant depression from which there seems to be no escape. That depression is written into Tolstoy's fiction. In *War and Peace,* for example, Andrei, a nobleman filled with despair, goes off to the Napoleonic Wars and is wounded. Lying on the battlefield, he looks up into the great immensity of blue sky (who, reading that page, can ever forget it?) and feels the futility of existence. He has an extraordinary yearning to die, and when he returns to his father's estate, he abandons life; it is a kind of abandonment of the life-struggle, the life-will. The other side of Tolstoy is in the ever-questioning Pierre. A gambler—anarchic, dissipated, made serious by war and suffering—Pierre wants to reform everything, to transform a cluttered world into a rational order. One side of Tolstoy has to die; the other lives and suffers. Anna Karenin—the feminine side of Tolstoy—throws herself under a train when her great passion has run its course. Passion must be punished. But Levin, like Pierre, goes on living. So Tolstoy sought to kill the art within himself and to live on in a kind of existential brooding, an eternal muddle. Levin, too, considers killing himself but decides he must make the best of God's world. His meditations on suicide are taken almost verbatim from Tolstoy's personal journal, in which he wrote:

> I was unwilling to act hastily, only because I had determined first to clear away the confusion of my thoughts, and, that once done, I could kill myself. I was happy, yet I hid away a cord, to avoid being tempted to hang myself by it to one of the pegs between the cupboards of my study, where I undressed alone every evening, and ceased carrying a gun because it offered too easy a way of getting rid of life, and yet there was something I hoped for from it.

What strikes us in particular is Tolstoy's psychological sagacity; he understands how people feel, and he has a gift for novelistic detail. But in his life he does not apply this sagacity to himself. Even when he says he wants to die, we see that he doesn't really want to—he must put his thoughts in order first. A gun is too easy; apparently he must find something more difficult. This is a man who wants martyrdom, wants someone else to kill him; a soul caught between the empyrean of speculation and a drive to exactitude, yet in reality a soul struggling with passivity, self-indulgence, egotism, unable to reform itself —asking for external forces to deal out justice. From this we may understand how unhappy was Tolstoy's old age. In the midst of his great fame, a world hero, he was a fount of despair. His quarrels with his wife and children are legendary. The Countess Tolstoy was a long-suffering woman of much ability, and Tolstoy's deep dislike of women often emerged in their struggle. In his later years he dwelt, as always, on death but never believed he would die; and although he wrote, on the one hand, his later masterpiece "The Death of Ivan Ilyich," he also wrote the novel entitled *Resurrection.* Life was a purge. Purged, one had to be resigned—until the caldron within boiled over again.

Tolstoy's power as a writer did not diminish with age, but it did not grow. He discovered himself always in his work, yet got no comfort from it. He had no faith in art, no belief in his uniqueness. While in his search for a faith he chose a primitive form of Christianity, he recognized he could not practice his preachings. He tried. And when he broke his own rules there were remorse, self-laceration, and ultimately blame to be placed on the world around him. Again and again he told himself that a man of his beliefs had to live them—that he had to leave his cushioned ease, his servants, his home, and go forth and lead a saintly life. Still, the aristocrat in Tolstoy could not bring himself to become one of God's athletes, a missionary, a martyr. When he finally left home, it was too late. He was eighty-two, and his departure was a symbolic act of death. He became ill as he journeyed by train with his youngest daughter. He died in a railroad station, like his heroine Anna.

Tolstoy's patterns of life reverse the usual patterns of the aging artist. For example, he wrote his autobiographies at the beginning instead of the end of his career. *Childhood, Boyhood, Youth,* his fictional trilogy, made him famous in his twenties, as if he had, in the full force of his manhood, to relive his beginnings. Middle age embodied the years of his richest life—indeed, they had a plenitude that would have sufficed for most men, most artists. The Russian writer raised a large family, experimented with education and farming, and wrote his world masterpieces with consummate power, if not always with an economy of art. But his inner melancholy, his indulged self, brought him to crisis and, as we have seen, to fantasies of suicide. His old age was in reality a chronic crisis that he never resolved. Edmund Wilson argued that his proclaimed love of mankind and his particular religion seem "an arid self-directed exercise that simply raises the worshipper in his own self-esteem." Tolstoy was an angry, forbidding man of high gifts, a Jeremiah—perhaps a supreme example of an artistic power that did not suffice. In tune with the realities of most humans in the crowded scenes of his existence, Tolstoy could not be in tune with the realities of his self.

III

To leap from continental Russia to continental America for our second writer is to take a great leap indeed. Yet while environment and circumstances may differ, artists are made of similar stuff. Henry James, who was born when Tolstoy was fifteen, lived to be seventy-three, dying six years after Tolstoy's death. Looking at their parallel lives, we see that whereas Tolstoy came out of feudal Russia, Henry James was a grandchild of the Enlightenment that placed America on the road to a kind of unenlightened egalitarianism. His grandfather had made a fortune in Albany, New York, and James, like Tolstoy, had a spacious childhood. Tolstoy grew up in a family clan; James had loving parents, but he had awareness of clan as well, both in the big grandmotherly house in Albany and in teeming New York City, where as a small boy playing in muddy streets he saw pigs rooting in the gutters and chickens walking in Washington Square. The novelist's father was like a Tolstoy in reverse. Tolstoy wanted rules and regulations to curb his freedom; Henry James's father defied the rigidities of Calvinism and preached the joys of a sensual life as against religious restraint. But in the way of puritanical Americans, the elder James's sensory adventures were tame and intellectual. Simple joys sufficed. Tolstoy had chastening experiences in the Crimean War; Henry James, the future novelist, shrank from the violence of the Civil War, suffering more from a case of nerves than from physical disability. He was exposed early to European culture, acquiring a cosmopolitan spirit without ever having had to be a provincial. Although allowed to enjoy his senses, he also inherited an idea of duty and possessed a desire for fame, fortune, and glory, which he would win by the pen, like Balzac. James did not have Tolstoy's exposure to all kinds and conditions of men in war and peace. James came to life through literature; Tolstoy came to literature through life. Such an epigram, however, would over-look the fact that an artist with a "grasping imagination" and an observant eye can often feel all life, and see it, more powerfully than the one who plunges directly into it.

What I find significant is that while Tolstoy in his twenties wrote his first novels out of early memories of childhood and youth, James wrote his first novel (at thirty, after ten years of apprenticeship) out of maturity. It deals with a young artist who feels he has to choose between art and passion and is defeated by passion. Tolstoy had gratified his sexual needs from the first, with mistresses or in brothels, but he was a clumsy lover. Sex for the puritan-conditioned James was suppressed, controlled, turned into a problem of conduct—made a part of the art of life. James feared mistresses and read about brothels in French nov-els. From the first, his concern was not what to do with the world, which Tolstoy wanted to change into a pastoral, sim-plified Christian one, but how to make it into a work of beauty and art. James's philosophy was that of a man in search of aes-thetic freedom; Tolstoy's was that of a man who feared freedom and legislated for himself out of his own intelligence. James, like Balzac, accepted life—he wasn't the least bit philosophical. In an early essay, he is specific about this. Life, he writes, is a battle.

> Evil is insolent and strong; beauty enchanting but rare; goodness very apt to be weak; folly very apt to be defiant; wickedness to carry the day; imbeciles to be in great places, peoples of sense in small, and mankind generally happy.

But there was also for James one singular reality, that

> the world as it stands is no illusion, no phantom, no evil dream of a night; we wake up to it again for ever and ever; we can neither forget it nor deny it nor dispense with it. We can welcome experi-ence as it comes, and give it what it demands, in exchange for something which it is idle to pause to call much or little so long as it contributes to swell the volume of consciousness. In this there is

mingled pain and delight, but over the mysterious mixture there hovers a visible rule, that bids us to learn to will and seem to understand.

The world was a spectacle, supplying abundant raw material for art. All the writer had to do was to be artist enough—self-critical, exigent, sentient. The rest was a matter of craft.

With his sexual drive channeled into his art, James felt no need to marry. He was secretive, private, intimate; even his notebooks are impersonal and professional. The young artist kept strict watch on his passions. He preferred to make love to his obedient and yielding muse. His early novels are novels of society, of the world, of art; they do not deal with love. His first masterpiece, *The Portrait of a Lady,* is about a young American woman, richly endowed when compared with her European sisters, trying to "affront"—that is James's word—her destiny. But it is her American destiny to be affronted; she is too innocent, too ignorant, too unfinished. James made himself the historian of the unfinished American woman, and the American girl, and won early fame. He worked hard; he fled loneliness by social mingling; he lived an intense, busy London life, a perpetual student of "society." Middle age came upon him unobtrusively. And with it he experienced the first crisis of his aging.

As with Tolstoy, something remained unfulfilled in spite of success. We can see this in James's turning to naturalism and trying to write deterministic novels in the manner of Zola. He wrote *The Bostonians, The Princess Casamassima, The Tragic Muse:* novels in which the inner statement is that the world is unkind to sensitive young persons; it is a brutal, philistine world that expends its gifted children and discards them. When these novels failed, he told himself that perhaps he would do better as a playwright. Certainly he would make more money. He tried for five long busy years to write for the theater. This brought him into backstage reality, a corner of life concerned, in a practical way, with illusion; and James, the man of the writer's study, felt out of his element. One play was produced and was a modest success. The second, on which he placed all his hopes, was ill received by a rowdy gallery. James himself was booed when he came out to take a bow. January 5, 1895, was the night that marked a fundamental break, a crucial turning point, in James's life. He was fifty-two, and at that moment his world broke in two.

In the ensuing five years we can read what seems to be characteristic of the history of every great artist—that moment when latent depression smothers the creative individual. In this crucible the artist faces the ultimate test: survive or go under. It came to T. S. Eliot early, and he wrote *The Waste Land;* it was a chronic state with Tolstoy, never resolved. It came to Henry James in the moment of high drama when the gallery howled at him (as he said) like a bunch of savages. We need not rehearse the stages of his depression. He did not write about it; perhaps he was aware of it only peripherally and intermittently. He went about London performing his "forms of expression" as if nothing had changed. But the changes are revealed in what he wrote. He wrote a series of short stories about authors who are private successes and public failures—one called "The Death of the Lion," another "The Next Time." His authors in these tales are always "too good" for their public. The public does not understand them. Then, during these years, James wrote a dozen ghost stories. He lived in a ghost world. He talked of the "black abyss" of the theater, spoke in images of drowning, of trying to keep his head above water. He wrote a novel about a child murdered by drowning. Now, in middle life, he did what Tolstoy did at the beginning: he went back to childhood and set down a series of stories about children victimized by an adult world that appreciates neither their delicacy of feeling nor their fresh perceptions. James's middle-age crisis fascinates us by what his imagination brought forth; the great thing about his despair was that he did not stop writing.

To understand Henry James's old age, we must learn one thing more. In this period, in which his emotions regressed to his childhood, a past of ghosts and extrahuman happenings, he cured himself by his work. Each story released some of his anxiety, discharged his anger, made him feel strong again. In this healing process of art, he opened himself at last to love. He had been a bachelor, a man for whom physical drives were submerged in a drive to power; now, meeting a young American sculptor in Rome, he was able to love him. It was a new experience, a tense and deeply felt moment, and a bitter one. His egotism of art was breached.

He was then fifty-seven. Isn't it "too late, too late?" he asked himself. In his notebook he wrote, "Youth, the most beautiful word in the language." But his youth was gone. He had believed that he had passed the time for passion—and yet at last he could feel it. He felt the pain, the pity, the absence of the beloved. The great thing about Henry James is that, face to face with a truth, he was able to accept it. He did not rebel like Tolstoy and try to drive passion out as if it were the devil. He wrote a novel on the theme of "Live all you can" and called it *The Ambassadors*—the story of an elderly American like himself who comes to Paris to take a young man back to America, to his mother, but decides the young man is better off living his own life abroad. In his novel he comes to the question of determinism. He doesn't ask, "What is life?" He accepts life. The question he asks is how much of life one can live within the restraints of civilization. One may not be technically a free man; one may be a slave of instincts, drives, conditionings. One is formed by heredity and environment, but one has *the imagination of freedom,* or, as James calls it, "the illusion of freedom." In his old age James was prepared to live by that illusion.

After *The Ambassadors* came *The Wings of the Dove,* a novel in which a young heiress, knowing she must die, feels that she will have "lived" if she can allow herself to love. It is the heiress's fate to be deceived, but she does, in a manner, live. And finally James wrote *The Golden Bowl,* his last novel, summing up his experience and his wisdom. In this work he sees civilization as a series of grandiose myths created by human beings to mask their rapacity, their deceit, their cruelty, their ability to deceive themselves. The myths are often beautiful falsehoods, designed to hide primitive, cruel things. In living by myth— that is, by imagination—we open the way to knowledge, to codes and forms of life that impose decency, honor, generosity, love.

While writing his last novels, James recognized and faced his solitude. Without a wife, without children, spending long months in a rural retreat, he could say to a young man who asked him about the art he practiced, "It is a solitude, an absolute solitude." He did not mind growing old, he said. "I quite love my present age [he was fifty-six], and the compensations, simplifications, freedom, independences, memories, advantages of it. But I don't keep it long enough—it passes too quickly." He also added that it takes a whole life to learn how to live, "which is absurd if there's not to be another in which to apply the lessons."

When a younger friend pressed him about his life and asked him what had been its "point of departure"—from what point had he indeed set sail?—he answered:

I am face to face with it, as one is face to face, at my age, with every successive lost opportunity and with the steady swift movement of the ebb of the great tide—the great tide of which one will never see the turn. The gray years gather; the arid spaces lengthen, damn them!—or at any rate don't shorten; what doesn't come doesn't, and what does does. . . . The port from which I set out was, I think, that of *the essential loneliness of my life*—and it seems to be the port also, in sooth, to which my course again finally directs itself! This loneliness (since I mention it!)—what is it still but the deepest thing about one? Deeper, about *me,* at any rate, than anything else;

deeper than my "genius," deeper than my "discipline," deeper than my pride, deeper, above all, than the deep counterminings of art.

The answer for James was not a return to the melancholy from which he had suffered. He returned instead to America, after an absence of twenty years; he revisited his childhood and youth. He wrote then his moving record, *The American Scene,* mingling memory and nostalgia with prophecy, predicting city blight, waste, ecological ruin, showing in this work an acceptance of himself as old and as having the clairvoyance of his years. He wrote short stories until he was almost seventy; and only then did he embark on his autobiographies, after the death of his brother and emotional rival, William James. He revised minutely his major works for the New York edition, as if he were attempting to live his creative years all over again. He brought together his travel essays. His last ten years were a kind of shoring up of all his writings. This is not to say that his aging did not have unavoidable difficulties. It was not easy for an addicted artist, who had worked every day—from his youth—at his writing, to allow himself the luxuries of indolence demanded by his body; to find his physical strength refusing to match the strength and liveliness of his mind. Henry James had his measure of tristimania as he had to face and accept physical decline.

His supreme statement as an old artist is to be found in a letter that he wrote at seventy to Henry Adams. He had sent the second volume of his autobiography to Adams, who for years had been sour with age and disillusion, a disappointed member of a great clan. James's words to Adams ring out as a summons not to bend before the infirmities and physical insults of aging:

> You see I still, in the presence of life (or what you deny to be such), have reactions, as many as possible—and the book I sent you is proof of them. It's, I suppose, because I am that queer monster, the artist,

an obstinate finality, an inexhaustible sensibility. Hence the reactions—appearances, memories, many things, go on playing upon it with the consequences that I note and "enjoy" (grim word!) noting. It takes doing—and I *do.* I believe I shall do yet again—it is still an act of life.

For Henry James, aging was "still an act of life" and there was no surrender. "Art makes *life,* makes interest, makes importance," James wrote, exalting the transfiguring imagination. When he lay dying, he insisted on dictating certain reverberating phrases, and when unconscious, in his last hours, his hand still moved spasmodically over the sheet, as if he were writing. He died in full belief of the power of art, its beauty, its immortality.

I V

That idea of art, of great art, as being a supreme form of life brings me to my third portrait of an artist as an old man. William Butler Yeats is the very archetype of a late flowering and late power, and a towering, controlled rage,

> What shall I do with this absurdity—
> O heart, O troubled heart—this caricature,
> Decrepit age that has been tied to me
> As to a dog's tail.

He is writing at sixty-one:

> Never had I more
> Excited, passionate, fantastical
> Imagination, nor an ear and eye
> That more expected the impossible. . . .

We are beyond the miseries of Tolstoy, the active acceptances of Henry James. This is a rage of art and a use of this rage to make poetry. In a letter to Olivia Shakespear, written when he was fifty-seven, Yeats described his feelings: "I am tired and in a rage at being old. I am all I ever was and much more, but an enemy has bound me and twisted me so as I can plan and think as I never could, but no longer achieve all I plan and think." Where is such mental energy to go when the body refuses to follow? Yeats grudgingly accepted aging—he had to—but he also defied it and *used* it. He insisted on finding new crystallizations of thought; his anger pushed him to overcome physical lag by a great luminescence of thought and feeling:

> That is no country for old men. The young
> In one another's arms, birds in the trees
> —Those dying generations—at their song.
> The salmon-falls, the mackerel-crowded seas,
> Fish, flesh, or fowl, commend all summer long
> Whatever is begotten, born, and dies.
> Caught in that sensual music all neglect
> Monuments of unageing intellect.

We can paint a large portrait indeed of a man who could insist upon "unageing intellect" even while seeing himself as a comic pathetic figure.

> An aged man is but a paltry thing,
> A tattered coat upon a stick, unless
> Soul clap its hands and sing, and louder sing
> For every tatter in its mortal dress.

Yeats sang. He sang the tatters in a kind of revenge upon the indignities heaped upon the body. Wherever we turn in those last immortal poems in *The Tower* and *The Winding Stair* we find the old man surpassing anything he had written in his younger years. We encounter the symbols of his old age and the images of his old age; they are not repetitions of images called up by his younger self. They speak out of awareness of the past, his deep national feeling, his sense of himself within his race and as seer and singer. He writes of spirals, gyres, staircases to be climbed, a freedom and loftiness that defy horizontal decay. In his youth he had sung high romance and the Celtic twilight.

Hands were pearl-pale, water was foamy-oozy, the dawns were passioned and shod in gold. Beauty there was in abundance, and his lyric sense had a tapestried splendor. His later style is free of book language and romantic convention. The poet uses the spoken word: belly, bum, sop, pun, bowels, randy, codger, leching, warty. He is free in describing passion and sex. He no longer finds euphemisms for the flesh; it is no longer made ethereal. He undergoes one of the fashionable gland operations of that time, the Voronoff monkey-gland graft that promised rejuvenescence, but one wonders whether Yeats needed so literal a step-up of his hormones.

To arrive at such power of utterance, and such heights of vision, Yeats had passed through struggles as profound as those of Tolstoy and James; one might almost say such struggles belong to the laws of art. In his reveries on his childhood and youth (he wrote his autobiographies at fifty), we can read of his years of uncertainty, the wavering between action and dream that we find in so many poets. Like James and Proust, he worked through his childhood in middle age. He had the sexual inhibitions of his Protestantism and a natural fear—it has been called shyness—of women; he had his saturation in the myth and folklore of Ireland, derived in part from his mother; he had the extraordinary clarities of his father, who was a painter—that is, an artist aware of his son's vocation. There had been years of melancholy and depression, and an obsessive love for the beautiful Maud Gonne, who was hard and conspiratorial and revolutionary, as only the Irish can be. Yeats saw her beauty; it blinded him, in a poet's dream of ideal love. In middle life when he was writing his autobiographies—seeking, as it were, the inner sources of his life—he married (in 1917 at fifty-two). With this settling influence and with parenthood (and the end of the First World War), he entered upon the fulfillment that we can read in his verse. It was not a question for Yeats, as it was for James, of "too late, too late?" but rather one of facing and using the growing truth that his body could not keep pace with his lively surging mind. He made his verse and prose and his plays instruments of intellectual assertion as powerful as any we have had in our time. He had by degrees (and long before his marriage) overcome his sexual fears. And he had by degrees (one can read it in the books about him and in his own autobiographies) found a course between action and dream. The truths of poetry confronted the truths of life. Yeats's marriage led to his writing a book called *A Vision*—a strange search for the meaning of the occult, the invisible spirits of his unconscious guiding him to his newfound destinies; a search in which his wife, who had the talents of a medium, participated. For all his belief in some of the old wives' tales of spiritism, Yeats's essential strength lay in his constant ability—and need—to cut through to reality. "We make out of the quarrel with others rhetoric," Yeats wrote, "but of the quarrels with ourselves poetry." His was, we can now see, the most powerful voice in English in our time speaking in behalf of life's mysteries as against scientific realism—the old battle of the naturalists and the symbolists raised to the plane of high poetry. *A Vision* must be taken seriously in spite of its mystifications, for with each insight Yeats seems to be touching, in his poetic way, truths given us in other forms later by Freud and Jung—above all, his recognition of the power latent in the unconscious. Yeats in his terminology describes this as "an energy as yet uninfluenced by thought, action, or emotion." We might say he is here defining the id. So, too, Yeats understood the nature of the personal myth each man and woman creates, the *persona,* "the image of what we wish to become, or of that to which we give our reverence." He was touching the borders of self-belief and self-concept. He defined the creative mind as "all the mind that is consciously constructive" and called the environment, the general state of physical being of humans, their "body of fate"—a packed, deterministic statement, even if not so intended, in which another might discern the built-in societal and moral values we forge as ego and superego.

I have a memory of Yeats one evening in Montreal, at his

hotel: the shock of white hair, the clear, questioning eyes, the restless animal pacing in his room, the vigor—the boundless vigor—the pounce of an animal all instinct and superb control, control of everything he said. We talked of Joyce and D. H. Lawrence; he wished to see the best in both. It takes a long time, he said, for a poet to be understood: "we wear our metaphors and rhythms . . . poetry grows slowly; the novel reaches the public with immediacy." Yeats the public figure was but a surface; he spoke in his verse by a sounding of primitive depths —like Conrad, he could tap his unconscious. It is the old Yeats, filled with the pride of his animal power, who could conjure up the beating wings, the shudder in the loins, the earthly visitor from Olympus:

> God guard me from those thoughts men think
> In the mind alone . . .

and he prayed

> That I may seem, though I die old,
> A foolish, passionate man.

He wanted "an old man's frenzy." He was ready to remake himself, till he would be Timon or Lear or Blake beating upon the wall—"an old man's eagle mind." The image of the old man reduced to a coat, a tattered garment, the clothes of a scarecrow, comes to us always as a bit of outraged defiance, yet Yeats feels it to be "a comfortable kind of scarecrow."

> You think it horrible that lust and rage
> Should dance attention upon my old age;
> They were not such a plague when I was young;
> What else have I to spur me into song?

When he went to Stockholm to receive the Nobel Prize, Yeats looked at the medal that came to him with Sweden's bounty; it showed a young man listening to the Muse. Yeats thought: "I was good-looking once like that young man, but my unpracticed verse was full of infirmity, my Muse old as it were; and now I am old and rheumatic, and nothing to look at, but my Muse is young. I am even persuaded that she is like those Angels in Swedenborg's vision, and moves perpetually 'towards the day-spring of her youth.' " Let us remind ourselves that when the Angels of Swedenborg kissed, the kiss was a burst of flame.

Yeats flamed, and the flames were brighter for his being old. He had never flamed as much in his youth.

V

A Russian, an American, an Irishman: three towering writers —one coming to us from an old feudalism, the second from a new ill-at-ease egalitarianism, the third from a land in chronic revolt. Their lands made them; but their personal beings offer us certain general truths that belong above nationality to the universality of the emotions, out of which poems and novels are made. They had in common, all three, the melancholy and despair so often heightened in the lives of artists; each of them had large funds of the egotism of art; they shared man's libidinal drives—sated yet never controlled in Tolstoy, repressed and channeled into art in James, liberated by middle-aged domes- ticity in Yeats. Tolstoy wanted to be always virginal; James late in life accepted passion as feeling and learned the meaning of love; Yeats recognized the sexual drive and its power by refer- ence to man's primitive state, saying that Christianity had sub- stituted a virgin womb and an empty tomb for the more inclu- sive phallicism of earlier religions. In their fundamental attitudes toward freedom, we can see in James and Yeats a struggle against the shackles society imposes. They speak of art as the greatest freedom—or, as James put it, the "illusion of freedom"—to be cultivated by man. Tolstoy, coming from a land that was only beginning to learn the meaning of freedom, was a man of rules, laws, precepts. What John Butler Yeats, the father of the poet, once said seems applicable to our three artists: that poetry embodies an *absolute* freedom in which the inner and outer self can expand in full satisfaction, but that in religion "there is absent the consciousness of liberty."

If we look at these states of being in all three men, we recognize that aging and creativity are closely linked, that there exists a creative aging. In certain instances, aging is a way of crystallizing and summarizing the life of art and the achievement of art. And when—amid the new despair and infirmities that aging brings—the artist has experienced fulfillment of certain old unfulfilled needs, then there is an expanding power of mind and utterance that can lead to the supremacies of art. When staleness, drink, drugs, or mere cessation does not occur —for these are often common among younger and middle-aged artists—the artist who has endured and suffered and transcended those sufferings becomes one of the transcendent beings of art. Without fulfillment there is misdirected rage: this was Tolstoy. With fulfillment there can be a rage of doing: this was Henry James. And a rage of power, renewed and enlarged by the very process of aging, which becomes in itself the creative force of the old artist: this was Yeats.

Of our three artists it was Tolstoy, so superb in his art, who was incomplete in spite of his outer aspect of venerability and his enormous vitality. Melchior de Vogüé said of Tolstoy that he was "a queer combination of the brain of an English chemist with the soul of an Indian Buddhist." A rum mixture, no doubt —a confusion of specifics with universals. I am haunted by the image of that railway station, of Tolstoy setting out on a literal journey at an age when most artists have already completed their travels. Tolstoy's end was death at a wayside station; Yeats's was a sailing forth to Byzantium, into the glories of the imagination; and in James's final works we find the imagery of voyage and exploration, Columbus and Amerigo—and the narrative of Arthur Gordon Pym. Out of the sadness and decrepitude of aging, Yeats and James, and those who believe in art, make a hymn to life; they sing life where Tolstoy sang despair; they sing acceptance where Tolstoy sang repudiation. They acknowledge despair, they acknowledge their instincts and their feelings, and grow old without the rigidities of aging. Within the tattered coat upon the stick there is a radiance—the same radiance as in the self-portraits of Rembrandt grown old.

Endure what life God gives and ask no longer span;
Cease to remember the delights of youth, travel-wearied aged man;

and, as you travel, say again with Montaigne, "It is not the arrival, it is the journey which matters."

ABULIA AND THE JOURNEY
TO LAUSANNE

Critics have remarked, in their sequential analyses of T. S. Eliot's poetry, on its Dantean pattern: they have seen a symbolic descent into Hell and a gradual emergence through insight and faith into a kind of Purgatory. In an essay written in 1959, I went further than this and sought to demonstrate Eliot's underlying depression as a source of his spiritual journey; however in the absence of biographical evidence at the time, when the poet was still living, I did not wish to make deeper soundings. My 1959 experiment touched the surface of Eliot's chronic melancholy. The relevant psychological question, now that we can discuss him with greater freedom, was: Why did the poet experience so profoundly the waste and corruption of human existence—the sinister, dark, and empty streets of modern life, and the mechanical modes of modern sexual feeling, hostile to the beauties and wonders of God's creation? In other words, where lay the origins of the depression out of which Eliot's poetry came into being? It is too banal to assume that his life's despair sprang simply from his poetic sensitivity before the uglinesses created by man, or that it derived from his sudden plunge into the world's realities from the earlier Paradise of his youth. Poets do feel more than most persons; that is why they are poets; and their feeling leads them to say much more and at their best to say it memorably. They are barometers of society's emotions; but to say this is to offer too general an answer to my precise question. In his poetry Eliot reveals, with perhaps the greatest poignancy of our century, humanity's enormous failure to find a new spiritual life in our technological world. This has prompted Stephen Spender to point to a paradox: Eliot's "choice of eternity is so obviously preferable to that of life on this earth that it is difficult for him not to make actual living less than second-rate." And the cities tumble:

Falling towers
Jerusalem, Athens Alexandria
Vienna London
Unreal

I

The biographical material that has accumulated since T. S. Eliot's death justifies our now inquiring, What was Eliot's original Paradise from which he fell with such eternal anguish? Who and what did he mourn? We now can discern through the period immediately preceding *The Waste Land* the effect on him of his impulsive marriage, the ensuing breakdown and failure of his will, his *aboulie,* as he called it (he used the French form), which he described as "a lifelong affliction." What was this prolonged abulia? How had it been a lifelong affliction? No one has asked this question. And there has been only one inquiry (by a psychoanalyst) in a diagnostic sense into the psychotherapy T. S. Eliot underwent in Lausanne in 1921. On the literary side, we have recently had uninterpreted recitals of the events of Eliot's life as we now know them. When these events are explored and analyzed—and this is our task in literary psychology—we may be enabled to understand some of the sources of Eliot's profound and unending depression and his life's struggle to overcome his inertia of the will. I propose to retrace Eliot's spiritual journey in the light of our new evidence. Since Eliot asked his second wife, Valerie, to discourage the writing of a full-length biography, we must content ourselves with an adumbration of his early *rite de passage,* relying still on the supreme evidence available to us, the emotions expressed in his poems and plays.

Modern psychology, as well as modern literature, tends to assume that a child's period in the womb is a paradisial period. "Before babe born bliss had," James Joyce alliterates in the maternity hospital scene of *Ulysses.* But we still know very little of the prenatal dramas enacted in the womb. The assumption is that the embryo, living a sheltered life, a passive life, for the only time in its existence enjoys all the benefits of sustenance and growth without the pain of living. In the womb the fetus achieves growth protected from the world's bombarding stimuli and remains in a state of general beatitude, occasionally perhaps going through the motions of a symbolic yawn (has it yet learned boredom?) and, as its mother knows, stretching and kicking a bit. Is this the closest we come to utopia? How immune is the embryo from the mother's emotional shocks and the mother's physical discomforts? We know it is not immune to maternal addictions to drugs or nicotine, and perhaps also to the mother's moods, her moments of happiness or distress. Some kind of life is communicated through the mother to the physical, nervous, emotional entity in the making. We have tended to see the growth of the embryo as a reenactment of Genesis. Then comes the moment of birth. Is it an expulsion or a liberation, a deprivation of paradise or a freeing from a troubled uneasy environment? The passage through the gates into this world has implied for us the time of Adam and Eve, and the moment of entry into life on our earth is the moment, in the biblical sense, when we receive our heritage of man's punishment. We are placed squarely on the road (if we combine Dante, the poet Eliot accepted, with Milton, the poet he originally rejected) to Inferno and Purgatory. The innocence of childhood, the period of youth, may still contain a residuum of the seemingly lost paradise; some of the early protection and care may be prolonged among the more affluent during periods of adaptation and growth. I suppose the final loss of these vestiges of the Edenic time occurs at adolescence. At that moment, as presumed equals among equals, we are supposed to stand on our own feet and take our way among our fellows without the supports previously provided, unless (as in Adler's observations) we feel ourselves unequal to such responsibilities.

Some such psychological picture has in part been drawn with great subtlety by Ernest Schachtel in his book *Metamorphosis,* one of the more profound works of psychological exploration of our time. Schachtel went beyond Freud to study the fundamental dilemma of birth—jokingly described as the choice we must make between "a womb of our own" and a "room of our own." Schachtel wrote:

> Growing up in a concrete society and culture drastically narrows the patterns of relatedness to the world offered to the growing child. On the other hand, it makes [it] possible for him not to get lost in the infinite possibilities of his world-openness, but to find, within the framework of his culture and tradition, his particular structure of relatedness to the world.

This is the struggle all humans undergo in a society where civilization has established boundaries and resistances. It is the greatest and most important subject of art.

There are individuals, Dr. Schachtel tells us, who refuse to accept a relatively separate existence from their paradisial past. They feel frustrated and angry. They long impatiently for some magical substitute that will restore their "lost childhood." Such individuals are "embedded" in their history; they deprive themselves of time present by looking always for time past, or for a problematical future they dream will be a kind of utopia. They are poised indeed between past and future: the present is a horror, a continuing hiatus. And when this becomes chronic and pathological, we are likely to have exactly what T. S. Eliot described as *aboulie:* loss of the will, despair and apathy—that apathy we hear in "The Hollow Men." This fantasy of the future explains also Eliot's conservatism. Some seemingly stable past makes him an enemy of change. Change implies revolution; he prefers history and tradition; it is always in the past, it can lead to some "still point"—in a word, to beneficent stasis. The structure of time experience is wholly changed for such individuals. In seeking a conservative replay of an old experience, the wish is for a future that will contain a repetition of the past. Schachtel points out that Samuel Beckett's *Waiting for Godot* embodies such a wish; it offers a picture of embeddedness in which there is chronic hope that things will change for the better, and with this waiting there is also a wish and expectation of magical change by an external agency.

The fight against embeddedness can create terrible anxiety: the innate human need to be active and to face immediate life situations is, in such individuals, in conflict with their sense of helplessness and their frustration. Schachtel observes, "Man's anxiety in leaving embeddedness is the one most powerful antagonist of his world-openness. It wants to confine him in the embeddedness of the familiar so that he will not experience the awe and wonder of the infinitely new and unknown." The drama of being born, therefore, is a catastrophe for some, while for others it is the rising of a curtain on the wonders of the world. Small wonder that there are millions today whose quest is to be reborn. But the truth is that we are born only once. It is new experience, *after* this birth, which is mythic rebirth, so that every day we live opens opportunities for the continual renewal of experience.

II

Thomas Stearns Eliot was born in 1888 in the prosperous city of St. Louis. He was the seventh and last child of the middle age of his parents. His father, Henry Ware Eliot, a wealthy brick manufacturer, was forty-three and, while strong and active, was already deaf and so seemed remote and distant to his youngest child. Eliot's mother, Charlotte, an *exaltée* and religious poet, was the same age. One daughter was already in college, and Eliot's youngest sibling was eight. He was distinctly "baby," and we may extrapolate that there was little challenge for the child in the obsolete nursery where from the first he was lonely master. His parents could not allow the arrival of this unexpected child to change their way of life; having children was by now for them an old and past experience. The new child seems to have been valued and cared for and cherished, but in the circumstances of belated arrival found himself in a world of peculiar reality, and one that encouraged his fancy. Like Joyce and Auden, he was very much with elders.

The Eliot boy (with the eager bright eyes and pouting, almost prissy, lips we see in an early photograph) was handed over to a kind surrogate mother, an Irish nurse named Anne Dunne, whom the poet remembered with affection. It is clear that the baby and the growing little boy had much feminine affection and tended to be treated at times as a wonder child, a kind of special late gift of God. This was reinforced by certain physical ailments, in particular a hernia which kept him from sports. He received the fundamentals of Christianity. His ancestors had been Unitarian clergy, and his grandfather, William Greenleaf Eliot, founded Washington University in St. Louis and was its president. T. S. Eliot, who never knew him, thought of him as "the head of the family—a ruler for whom in absentia my grandmother stood as vice regent." A godly grandfather, a remote deaf father, an older mother and older siblings—Eliot was conditioned from the first to adult talk, elderly authority, gravity, and, it seems, also to passivity. He had his attendants as if he were a young Prince Hamlet. There were lively summers in New England that gave him a deep sense of America. Supreme in his life, it appears, was his exigent poetic mother:

> The rule of conduct was simply pleasing mother;
> Misconduct was simply being unkind to mother;

What was wrong was whatever made her suffer,
And whatever made her happy was what was virtuous.

These words from *The Family Reunion* may be an extreme picture, but they convey a considerable depth of ironic feeling. On her youngest son, Charlotte Eliot placed the mantle of her own poetic strivings. He was to perform the work she longed to perform, and he had to win the world's praise and acknowledgment she most desired. The sense of family, ambition, importance, success, the idea that one performed noble works and deeds—some such inner myth or quest for a Holy Grail was built out of Eliot's childhood experience and determined the spiritual drama he would live.

Eliot remained in this sheltered environment until he was seventeen. He then went to a prep school in Massachusetts and on to Harvard, where he published early verse in student magazines. A vivid bit of testimony exists in a letter from Bertrand Russell, who was visiting Harvard in 1914. He wrote to Lady Ottoline Morrell after a weekend party in Cambridge, "My pupil Eliot was there—the only one who is civilized, and he is ultra-civilized, knows his classics very well, is familiar with all French literature from Villon to Vildrach, and is altogether impeccable in his taste but has no vigour or life—or enthusiasm. He is going to Oxford where I expect he will be very happy." The quick observant philosopher had recognized—one wants to say diagnosed—the presence of what Eliot himself would later define: his abulia "no vigour or life—or enthusiasm." Mr. Prufrock had already taken shape.

The abulia at first lay below the surface, for Eliot lived in a paradise of endeavor; the young struggle among peers for an active life enabled him to take boxing lessons, go to parties and dances, make friends—but he remained fundamentally shy and withdrawn. Eliot's Harvard years are well documented. We know that he was highly regarded and went on to write a doctoral dissertation. He was at the university from 1906 to

1910, and after receiving his Master's degree he went to Paris. His French experience seems to have been liberating—that is, it opened him somewhat emotionally. He read much French poetry and had a close friendship with several young Frenchmen, one named Jean Verdenal, who was later killed in the war and to whom "Prufrock" was dedicated; but there were also Jacques Rivière, the critic and later editor of *La Nouvelle Revue Française,* and Henri Alban Fournier, better known by his pen name, Alain-Fournier, who was writing his modern classic novel *Le Grand Meaulnes,* published in 1913. Eliot studied French with him. There has been speculation that Eliot became involved in a homosexual affair with Verdenal, but given his temperament and reticences there seems little likelihood that he found this kind of sexual liberation. On the other hand, Paris offered him a rather negative kind of conservatism: the vigorous and indeed brilliant prose of the fanatic fascistic anti-Semite Charles Maurras, who believed in the restoration of the French monarchy. Maurras's remarkable polemical style reinforced Eliot's innate conservatism; certainly some of his banal ideas about Jews and foreigners and his political elitism stem from this source.

Eliot's travel and studies brought him for the first time into a wider cosmopolitanism and gave him a wider vision of civilization's distortions and cruelties than he had known in St. Louis or at Harvard, or during those New England summers where family and home sheltered him from the world's brutalities. At Milton Academy and at Harvard he retained the security of his position in the social scale. His family gave him an adequate allowance, and he was free to pursue his aesthetic and spiritual life—above all, the life of poetry. *Prufrock and Other Observations,* which emerged out of these years, suggests, in its first bold tradition-smashing image, the simile of the sky as an etherized patient, Eliot's own sense of becalmed inertia and powerlessness—and in all probability his sexual neutrality of the time. And we may speculate, with "Prufrock" before us, that Eliot lacked the spontaneous response which the less sheltered young possess in their relations with the opposite sex. We must remember that he had been brought up with all the Victorian constraints in a period of the enforced separation of the sexes. "Prufrock" suggests that the poet was as unprepared to receive the affections of the male as of the female. Like Prince Hamlet, "man delights not me—no, nor woman neither." His early vivid poem about Saint Narcissus seems to point rather to adolescent self-gratification.

> Then he knew he had been a fish
> With slippery white belly held tight in his own fingers,
> Writhing in his own clutch, his ancient beauty
> Caught fast in the pink tips of his new beauty.

Like Proust he could experience the aesthetic side of masturbation.

Such conjectures about Eliot's earlier psychosexual life offer us no sign of any attempt on his part to break out of the paradise in which he experienced loneliness and inertia of the self, within the circle of his family. Joyce, a very different sort of *sensitif* and product of a more primitive and impoverished narcissism, sought physical initiations directly in the brothel.

What we see in T. S. Eliot from the first is his extraordinary gift for discovering visual images to give body to his emotions —the center and source of his genius, and never held in the bondage or constraint of his rearing. If the poet was physically passive, there was no passivity of the mind or the imagination; he could be aware of his environment, and he allowed himself subjective sensual experience—and his senses and mind were in constant harmony with his gifts of expression. We must note the high significance of his use of the word "observations" in *Prufrock and Other Observations.* He observed very much as his puritan predecessor Henry James had done: the eye could supply experience. Moreover, Eliot's mother's dedication to verse offered sanction and support for his active use of his gift of expression. But like Hamlet—or like Henry James—he could not act physically. As he became increasingly aware of the sinister streets and dark retreats of life, and as the world began to intrude into his early paradise, he was able to voice his Prufrockian ambiguities, his pose of an older man afraid of experience, unable to cut loose. The mermaids would not speak to him —and he apparently was afraid to risk speaking to them. He was an active creator who could seize what he observed and felt and subject it—through powerful mental organization—to a bold and free imaginative process. But this imagination was in turn harnessed to a quasi-dormant body that had never been prepared to fend for itself or minister to everyday needs, so greatly had his life been facilitated. He could not stand alone. He needed support. This was the T. S. Eliot (observed by Bertrand Russell) who in 1914 summoned up all his energies and plunged into what seems an impulsive and wild attempt at destructive self-assertion—how could it have been otherwise for a New England Hamlet?

III

Up to his twenty-sixth year—until 1914—T. S. Eliot had led the quiet life of a young gentleman, the leisurely preparation for a career of erudition and writing, in the tradition of his university-founding grandfather. Little had been required of him by his family save that he pay attention to his ancestry, his position in society, and his muse. With the advent of the 1914 war, the prized child with the Mona Lisa smile and acquiescent spirit suddenly took a series of steps no Eliot was supposed to take. He changed all his well-laid plans—the family plans he had accepted for himself. He announced that he did not want to return to America. He had completed his doctoral dissertation but saw no reason for taking his degree. And quite suddenly, during the late spring of 1915, he married an English girl named Vivien (or Vivienne) Haigh-Wood, whom he had met at Oxford a few weeks earlier.

There was understandable astonishment among the Eliots in St. Louis. The exemplary and model, fastidious and obedient Tom Eliot was suddenly transformed in their eyes into a wayward, defiant, and irresponsible youth, obviously in a state of Circean crisis in his mid-twenties. He was not only throwing away an honorable career at Harvard but shattering all the family codes. There had been no formal engagement. The parents had not been consulted or their consent obtained. Eliot's decision to remain abroad was contrary to the family tradition. The son's actions, moreover, demonstrated a decisiveness and determination no one would have expected from his hitherto compliant passivity. The family blamed the young woman—and probably was right. If Eliot needed support in order to act, he had found it. However, he crossed the submarine-haunted Atlantic to explain his conduct and his decisions. His bride did not accompany him. She saw no reason to risk her life when the U-boats were waging their predatory warfare, nor had she any urgent need to meet in-laws who disapproved of her without having met her. The confrontation of the rebellious son and his elderly parents could not have been easy, and it provoked a great deal of anger and bitterness. Now the gates of T. S. Eliot's prolonged Edenic existence slammed shut behind him, and he was for the first time thrown wholly upon the world and his own resources. His father cut off his allowance, and the poet found himself at twenty-seven in a delayed rite of passage, an abrupt transition from the serenity of his childhood and youth and young manhood into a season in hell. He was living through the age-old conflict between parents and children—between conformity and revolt—which would become the subject of some of his major critical essays. But to understand what had happened an important question must be asked. If we allegorize his bride as Eve—it was she who proffered the apple—who, in Eliot's Eden, was the serpent?

In order to discover the major character, the *deus ex machina,* we must resolve still another problem of a psychological order. Eliot's sudden revolt appears inconsistent in an individual who suffered from inertia of the will, and had suffered for as long as a quarter of a century. He seemed the least likely of rebels, the most conservative of traditionalists. What did he derive from the Tree of Knowledge to provide the opportunity for his Fortunate Fall? Character change is never abrupt, and we know that T. S. Eliot, in spite of his seemingly impulsive rebellion, could not rid himself of his abulia overnight. He was in every way the same Tom Eliot as before, the reticent, shy, unadventurous and rather uptight American he had pictured as Mr. Prufrock. There had been, however, a singular alteration in the field of force in which Tom Eliot moved. That force was embodied in a fellow American with a little pointed mustache and beard and aesthetic clothes whom we might see as a kind of serpent in Eliot's domestic drama.

His name was Ezra Loomis Pound, a generous, impulsive, knowledge-giving, active—indeed, pushing—proselytizing poet and would-be poet-maker from Idaho. The speedily Londonized young Ezra, full of doctrine, energy, and bombast—a prodigy of initiative—provided the kind of *energization* T. S. Eliot's passivity needed, the kind that Vivien was attempting to provide for Eliot's apparently timid sexuality. The two poets met in 1914. In no time at all, Pound was converted by Eliot into chief surrogate for "family." Eliot was, in reality, no less dependent on others now than he had ever been. There was however a significant transfer of dependency. He was still incapable, in his shy inert way, of initiating or undertaking the promotion of his career or his poetry. Pound became, as if by magic, father, mother, mentor, guru, confessor, public relations counsel, and catalyst for Eliot, the very chief and leader of the rebel angels in the American literary counter-establishment— Pound's Establishment, to be sure.

From the moment he read "Prufrock," Pound recognized Eliot's genius—"the best poem I have yet had or seen from an American." In his doctrine-giving midwifing way, the serpent in Eliot's obsolete Eden bestowed on his younger protégé his own sense of self-reliance and power in his art while remaining a poetic crusader as well. More important was a certain stiffening of the Eliot selfhood, although in reality, as I have remarked, Eliot's need to lean on others for the mundane carrying out of the kitchenwork of life, as he had leaned on his family, was reinforced. Pound held out to Eliot the promise of fame, independence, fortune, success, and triumph with an assurance to which Eliot naturally responded from behind his own mask of strength and humility. Within the humility there was the drive to power imparted by his poet mother, an unflinching ambition. Virginia Woolf perceived this and recorded in her diaries "great driving power somewhere . . . a very intricate and highly-organized framework of poetic belief." Pound had cranked the motor of this driving power. "Beneath the surface," Virginia Woolf shrewdly notes, "it is fairly evident that he is very intellectual, intolerant, with strong views of his own and a poetic creed."

It was Pound who insisted that Eliot had to achieve some form of selfhood. He must not lose himself on the American continent. Eliot did not need urging. The serpent made friends with the Eve of the Adamic Eliot. Some even said Pound encouraged his younger friend in his decision to marry an Englishwoman; it assuredly committed Eliot to expatriation.

Pound's revolution was being staged in the very seat of eight centuries of English poetry, which America—save for Walt Whitman—had imitated as if no other kind of poetry could be made. In England and in Europe, the "new" could confront the old. There was no "old" to confront in America. This had been the experience and precedent of Henry James. What Pound could not know was that the beneficent side of his serpentine seductiveness created in the young man from St. Louis a traumatic ambivalence. Eliot had no desire to upset the old secure deep-puritan New England side of himself. He was attached to his St. Louis–Cape Ann–Harvard backgrounds. Ezra seems, however, to have brought home to him that this kind of domesticated paradise was no proper shelter for dynamic poetry. To "make it new" one had to break out—burst open—as buds burst open in "the cruellest month" of April. At this moment Eliot embodied his soul crisis in the impersonal intellectualism of his essays. His masterly "Tradition and the Individual Talent," in its very title, suggests to us how extensive can be the flowering of unconscious urging. He was the individual talent; tradition was his family and his past and all the centuries of recorded imagination he had assimilated into himself. He offered the dictum "novelty is better than repetition," but he also knew what one wasn't supposed to repeat changelessly from the past; and the essays of these difficult years embodied in his first prose book *The Sacred Wood* in 1920 speak for his creative self: the probing of the metaphysical poets, the place of Milton, the problem of Hamlet. The seemingly remote but pressing inner world of his creative self is articulated. Why the essay on Hamlet at this juncture, titled "Hamlet and His Problems"? It is as relevant as the essay on himself and tradition which he so majestically depersonalized. In *Hamlet* there is the absent father, the present mother, the gloomy meditative prince who finds it so difficult to act, given his dilemma. "We need a great many facts in his biography," wrote Eliot. "We should have to understand things which Shakespeare did not understand himself."

What Eliot did not understand himself is that he was enunciating the real function and the real purpose of the very kind of biography he tended later to dismiss. For the biographer, with his evidence before him, sees a body of data the subject has never been able to assemble. So too Eliot's evocation in these primary essays of "the dissociation of sensibility" (which became the catch phrase of a generation of imitative critics) suggests to us the dissociations that were going on in Eliot himself. Eliot felt a need he could not fathom to dissociate the sensibility that troubled him from the high problems of intellect. It could be demonstrated, I believe, that the "objective correlative"— that precise formulation he arrived at in his essay on *Hamlet*— spoke for his climactic need to break with, yet retain or compromise with, his past.

The essays in *The Sacred Wood*, in their totality, were the objective correlative of T. S. Eliot's crisis. They are admirable prose expositions of a personal dilemma buried within re-created literary history and literary criticism. And the long poem he now contemplated would be the objective reality, the metamorphosed images of his troubled and confused feelings, those anxieties that drove him deeper and deeper into his state of melancholy. Once again we can ask (paraphrasing Yeats), How can we know the thoughts from the thinker, the essayist from his essay? How build a bridge between talent and genius and the long past of the race (race being family)? This was the genetic soil in which Eliot planted the trees of his personal sacred wood. Eliot was seeking reconciliations, while he was embroiled in the life of wartime Britain, and the answers to the imperious demands of his physical drives, which seemed to end in the impotence of his marriage and his tattered relations with his difficult, uncompromising, and uncomprehending family. And now he needed also the hard cash of existence; he had at last to live by the sweat of his brow, as God had ordered Adam to do at the gates of the lost Paradise.

Eliot's past, his personal passivity, as distinguished from the activity of his creative imagination, made him expect his new young wife to be all that his sisters and his mother and his nanny had been in the earlier phases of his pilgrimage—the shelter and umbrella of his St. Louis days. On this ground we may see that a terrible mismating had occurred. We have evidence of his dependency on Vivien almost from the first. She, on her side, expected (especially at that time) to be dependent upon her husband. She was neurasthenic and hypochondriacal, hardly the sort of woman capable of sustaining the pressing

weight of Eliot's contradictory needs—those of the imagination
and of the body, when they were coupled with lingering infan-
tilisms within his psyche. She had probably expected a more
assertive husband. The result was inevitable: a series of continuing collisions. Eliot's demands were chronic and private.
Vivien's were often cruel and public. These induced a sense of
humiliation in the delicately strung poet. We note the lines in
The Waste Land:

> "My nerves are bad tonight. Yes, bad. Stay with me.
> "Speak to me. Why do you never speak. Speak.
> "What are you thinking of? What thinking? What?
> "I never know what you are thinking. Think."

They decidedly gave on one another's nerves.

I V

Virginia Woolf, in her diaries, describes the Eliot of this period as "all caught, pressed, inhibited and my word what concentration of the eye when he argues." Eliot was, she wrote,
pale and marmoreal, but she added that she laughed "in the
grim marble face and got a twinkle back." Vivien understandably found this marmoreal personality inhibited and inhibiting:
Virginia could laugh but Vivien had to live with it. And the
picture of Vivien in the Woolf diaries seems to provide the
counterpoint to Eliot's frozen state—she is described as
"washed out" and "worn," and also "so scented, so powdered,
so egotistic, so morbid, so weakly." Bertrand Russell, who had
an affair with Vivien early in Eliot's marriage (with Eliot's apparently passive complaisance), called her "light" and "a little
vulgar" and also an "adventuress." Russell believed she had
married Eliot "to stimulate him, but finds she can't do it." And
Russell adds that Eliot was "ashamed of his marriage." Lady
Ottoline saw Vivien as "second rate," saying also that she was
"playful" and "naïve." Aldous Huxley described her as "an in-
carnate provocation." When Virginia Woolf remarked to Eliot

that "missing trains is awful," his answer, for all its seeming irrelevance, was, "Yes, humiliation is the worst thing in life." He had somehow missed a train and felt humiliated, powerless, impotent. In truth one should sit in judgment on neither; their incompatibility is what the evidence loudly proclaims.

Such glimpses of the pair through others' eyes suggest chronic checkmate. "The ivory men make company between us," was a line in the original *Waste Land* that Vivien asked Eliot to remove. He did so, only to restore the allusion to their game of chess after she was dead. Soon after the marriage, Eliot had tried his hand at teaching; he disliked this and gladly shifted to a position in Lloyds Bank, where he worked for almost a decade in the colonial and foreign department. This kind of work provided stability and routine in Eliot's otherwise temperamentally volatile days. In the evenings he wrote book reviews and essays and gave an occasional lecture. In this way he eked out a living. He, as well as his wife, developed assorted symptoms—headaches, insomnia, fatigue—"the objective correlative," we might say, of their pent-up rages and guilt. Pound, perhaps with some feeling of guilt as well, but also in his usual maternal way, tried to create a consortium among Eliot's friends; they would pledge a certain sum as an annual subsidy and so free him from the irksome routine of the bank. But we may wonder whether Eliot really wanted to be free. It was the marriage, not the bank, that was his prison. He would say later that a regular position in an office with prescribed tasks was a useful way of controlling a writer's life. Aldous Huxley saw him at the time as "the most bank-clerky of all bank clerks."

Such was T. S. Eliot's life predicament by 1919. These years were by no means barren. In spite of his psychic burdens, he published, with Pound's aid, *Prufrock and Other Observations* in 1917; a collection of his poems in 1919 containing "Gerontion," and another collection in 1920, *Ara Vos Prec;* and the volume *The Sacred Wood.* He had spent the four years since his marriage working against the grain, but he preferred this to taking steps to resolve the impasse of the marriage itself. The marriage was in a rut; he was in a rut. His life had dried up. Ottoline found him at first "dull, dull, dull" and spoke of his "even, monotonous, voice." He seemed to have lost all spontaneity. She also found him "sharp and narrow and much of a stick." Aldous Huxley, meeting him in 1917, saw him as "haggard and ill-looking as usual." His psychosomatic symptoms increased. A process of erosion seemed under way, and in the midst of this despair and depression came the shattering news in January 1919 that Eliot's father had died in St. Louis.

The extinction of the parent finalized the break of 1915. Beyond normal grief at the loss of a key figure in his life—a formidable, distant, godlike figure—Eliot seems to have been jolted by deep feelings of guilt. Perhaps he had lived in some dream of ultimate reconciliation. Now it could never be. He blamed himself in many ways, and like Hamlet his grief exceeded the bounds of traditional sorrow for the departed. He suddenly felt a Hamletesque need to prove himself, to justify himself. And he had a feeling that he must rejoin his mother and share his grief with her. The war was over, but a trip to the United States, even with leave from the bank, would give him at best ten days or a fortnight's visit. He persuaded his mother that they would have much more time together if she came to England. She agreed and journeyed with one of his brothers and a sister. This was the moment, then, of "the family reunion." Her presence, far from aiding Eliot's spirit, only created new anxieties. As might be expected, Charlotte Eliot, now in her seventies, was not inclined to approve of Vivien or the marriage even in the atmosphere of reunion and the recapturing of older and happier feelings. Eliot accordingly found it practical to send Vivien off to the country. During this period, in which the poet (still continuing his daily duties at Lloyds) sought to integrate his fragmented world, there appears to have been instead considerable emotional regression. His days were filled with the ghosts of his family past; or, as he put it, "the new and old relationships involve immense tact and innumerable adjustments." What adjustments could there be in a reunion built around remorse, mourning, melancholy? All was discontinuous and somehow "unreal." When his mother finally returned to the United States, Eliot was on the verge of a breakdown. He said he was "shaky" and had "gone down rapidly since my family left."

V

With considerable difficulty, Vivien finally induced Eliot to consult a neurologist, since he seemed in general physically sound. Her theory was that he was suffering from a case of nerves. In the manner of the time (and much in the way Virginia Woolf was treated for her chronic depression), the doctor prescribed three months of complete rest, a vegetative life, above all no mental stress—as if a troubled mind could be put out to pasture. Eliot tried dutifully to obey. He obtained sick leave from the bank and went to the seaside, to Margate. As might be expected, he took his melancholy with him. Having been able, however, to shake off some part of his abulia for positive action (with the aid of Vivien), he decided to seek further help. He remembered that Julian Huxley and Lady Ottoline had been treated for depression by a Swiss psychiatrist named Roger Vittoz at Lausanne. He accordingly wrote to Huxley and told him of his dilemma. The British doctors, he wrote, appeared to specialize "either in nerves or insanity," and he added, "I am satisfied . . . that my 'nerves' are a very mild affair, due not to overwork but to an *aboulie* and emotional derangement which has been a lifelong affliction." He added that "there is nothing wrong with my mind."

A capital revelation, yet all who have written about this phase of Eliot's experience have not paid attention to it. His saying he had an "emotional derangement" and that it had been "lifelong" suggests that he had distinct awareness of the way in which his psychic life was formed. His use of the medical term *aboulie* meant that he had grasped how he suffered from frozen volition—"paralysing force, gesture without motion," he would say in his poetry. This kind of paralysis of the will—a sort of supreme passivity—reminds me of Kafka's Joseph K. in *The Trial,* who suffers a total "arrest" of being. The word *arrest* has been taken literally by many critics, but nothing in the novel resembles police arrest: Joseph K. is free to come and go, and like Eliot he worked for a bank. Within the bank he functions adequately since everything is prescribed. Outside the bank, he is unable to perform any action without appeal to others. R. D. Laing has described an analogous condition in language that reminds us of *The Waste Land:* finding in a patient "an overall sense of . . . emptiness, deadness, coldness, dryness, impotence, desolation, worthlessness." Eliot, in his pathology of despair, could not be in a spontaneous relation with the world. Still, in this moment of partial remission, he could muster sufficient will to seek some issue from his impasse. Julian Huxley in due course replied affirmatively about Vittoz, and Eliot told him that the Swiss psychiatrist "sounds just the man I want."

We know that Eliot had spoken of his need to do a large piece of work. He took with him to Lausanne a great part of the manuscript of his long poem or series of poems that would become *The Waste Land.* In it he included certain earlier poems. He apparently had in mind a poem sequence embodying early and late work—early and late emotion. It would be unified by a common theme and certain connecting passages, as if what had come out of his earlier life belonged also to the "wasteland" he had now reached. The poem was—and would be—filled with discontinuities, as in cinema; the manuscript seemed to be a gathering-in of much old feeling, irradiated by the tumult and intensities of his present "season in Hell."

In mid-November 1920 Eliot made the journey to Lausanne from Paris, where he left Vivien to wait for him. We find mention of the Vittoz methods of treatment in Lady Ottoline's journals, and in the letters and writings of both Aldous and Julian

Huxley; an account has been given also in the scientific paper written by Dr. Harry Trosman of Chicago in which he explores the "psychological antecedents and transformations" preceding *The Waste Land.* The Swiss doctor was an "original" in his healing, neither Freudian nor Adlerian nor Jungian, though he may have taken some cues from Vienna. He had been in practice since 1904 at Lausanne. His education had thus been pre-Freudian. One gains the impression that certain of his ideas came closer to Buddhism and Yoga than to modern psychology —a psychology that was then, during his own active years, still in the making. He was a religious man filled with strong Christian feeling, an ideal therapist for an American grandchild of the Unitarians. Eliot would have shied away from Freudian directness, which would have seemed to him an unwarranted invasion of his privacy. Indeed, a letter exists in which Eliot speaks of psychoanalysts as "coercive," an error which reflects his reticences and misunderstandings of the difference between "directive" therapy and the basic therapies of self-discovery.

The moral and confessional atmosphere of Vittoz and the doctor's practical approach to forms of problem-solving seem to have evoked a positive response in the passive poet. Vittoz believed that he could feel the patient's "brain waves" by laying his hand on the patient's head. The laying on of his hand was a paternal, almost a religious gesture, and to an Eliot in mourning for his father it could give comfort, relief, reassurance. This kind of old-fashioned treatment, akin to phrenology and "animal magnetism," was of less importance in the Vittoz rituals than the latter's attempt to reintegrate and reinforce some forms of mental control in patients like Eliot who had reached a high degree of physical immobility and psychic apathy.

The poet had come wanting to be helped, and the therapy seemed to meet his needs by the mixture of the personal touch and the impersonal puzzles Vittoz seems to have given Eliot to solve. Lady Ottoline describes in her journals such "integrative psychology" as "a system of mental control and concentration."

She had liked Vittoz's attentiveness, his poise, his way of asking her to sort out her "instincts." He gave her puzzles to do, such as eliminating letters in certain words or removing numbers from a set of numbers—forcing her to look attentively at the shape and density of letters and figures. Julian Huxley had been given similar problems and believed that performing them did assist him in obtaining greater control of his depression. These we may judge had the same kind of mystifications which the Koan of the Zen masters pose for their pupils. The problems helped draw Vittoz's patients out of self-absorption and narcissism and put them in touch with simple fragments of reality, even if these were garbled words or scrambled ciphers. He also made his patients perform physical actions "consciously and voluntarily"—that is, he made them seek "conscious mature control of body," something which sufferers from abulia lose. Aldous Huxley, who was not treated but who studied the psychologist's writings, tells us that "Vittoz obtained good results in simple neuroses by making patients fix attention by performance of some simple act like raising the hand." We may speculate that Vittoz pulled Eliot—at least for the time being—out of his inertia and his negation of the self into a modicum of awareness and recognition of his own body and its environment. Such acts properly carried out demand use of the will—one has to will the raising of the hand and the observing of it—and therefore they were effective in at least temporary remission of the abulia. Vittoz used an amalgam of patient-waking techniques, mingled with his own benign, sympathetic manner. By this means he provided a kind of supportive therapy. What he could not erase, and probably was not aware of, was the extent to which the patient became dependent on him—that subject over which Freud worked so long to find the proper distances and modes of handling "transference."

Vittoz dealt with manifest things. A modern analyst looking on Vittoz's practice would be inclined to regard it as temporary and palliative. One must add, however, that even temporary help of this kind, given the primitive state of psychiatry at the time, could have practical and beneficial results. Eliot, in the midst of Vittoz's therapy, was able to begin work again, and the work in itself was a kind of unconscious self-therapy. In Lausanne he wrote perhaps the most brilliant part of his poem, the final section of *The Waste Land*. And a letter to a brother tells us that "the great thing I am trying to learn is how to use all my energy without waste." The use of the word "waste" at this moment comes out of the poem he was writing and suggests a deeper meaning to the title—the idea of squandering as well as desiccation. Eliot added, in his letter to his brother, that he was also learning "to be calm when there is nothing to be gained by worry, and concentrate without effort. I hope that I shall place less strain upon Vivien, who has to do so much thinking for me." He reported that he felt "very much better and not miserable here." And he added he was well enough to be working on a poem. Vittoz had clearly helped remove some of Eliot's psychical stress, with the result that he had a grip on himself once more.

VI

Eliot rejoined Vivien in Paris in January 1922. He brought with him his long sprawling manuscript and delivered it to Ezra Pound. The unifying idea of *The Waste Land* seems to have come to the poet in Lausanne, when he wrote "What the Thunder Said." It was inevitable that the irresolution from which Eliot suffered should be reflected in his poem—the Ur-manuscript reveals his indecisions. He clung to fragments that gave the poem the effect of a mosaic or palimpsest of feelings old and new rather than a flowing, unified creation. "These fragments I have shored against my ruins." So reads one of the moving final lines, revealing Eliot's awareness of the way in which he had created his mosaic.

The poet left Lausanne still standing amid the fragments and discontinuities of his life and work, but with a sense that he had arrived at a certain wholeness. Once again he intuitively reached for the help he needed. As he had turned to a healer for his abulia, so now he turned to a fellow poet for the inspection of his fragments. Ezra Pound had been playing his midwifely role for some time in his relations with Yeats and Joyce, among others. He now assumed this role, with his customary zest, for Eliot. He could look at the long poem in a coldly objective way; the emotions were not his, the struggle had not been his. Where each line spoke to Eliot out of inner history, the lines spoke to Pound as they usually do to a skilled copy editor: their content was the felt verbal-visual of poetry, and Pound could cut, rearrange, see where concision was possible and how the continuities of Eliot's experience could be made to flow. He relieved the poem of its sprawl. He urged deletion of three insertions that included a lengthy Sea Narrative, "Death by Water," later contracted to ten lines, a section written in imitation of Pope, and the vigorous early poem "The Death of Saint Narcissus," half a dozen lines of which Pound retained. These sections seem indeed like excess cargo when we read the final version. The "Narcissus" poem, published later with Eliot's early poems, gives us his insights into the narcissistic side of his abulia and his understanding of his self-absorption and self-negation, for he discusses with considerable power the orgasmic masochism of certain kinds of religious visionaries.

Eliot accepted gratefully most of Pound's changes and deletions. His own poetic essences remained. They were enhanced by Pound's adroit trimming of much excess shrubbery and digression. The most moving portions of *The Waste Land* had been written during Eliot's deepest struggles with his inertia. The poem was speeded for publication and came out that year, and Eliot found himself famous. Fame, however, is not always a cure for a man weighed down by a heavy burden of guilt and despair. He had sought a supreme summing up, a rebirth of his spirit, a kind of resurrection of his earlier visionary life and his quest for peace implied in the last words, "Shantih, Shantih, Shantih."

T. S. Eliot had found the energy and will to complete the large work he had set himself: but in spirit he still lingered in the inferno of his life, or at best had just begun the slow climb through purgatory. The Vittoz therapy had broken his inertia but there were relapses, and my 1959 picture of his continued struggle still remains valid. Another four years were required. During this time Eliot touched the bottom of his abyss when he wrote "The Hollow Men." The poem is of 1925, when Eliot had a long illness, and it is in 1926 that he seems for the first time to plant his feet on the purgatorial steps. In that year he was baptized and accepted into the Church of England. He also became a naturalized British subject. Church and State are one in England, and the naturalization was corollary to his baptism. The slow progress of recovery now really began. He did not separate himself from his wife until 1933. There followed the long years of religious poetry and dedication that led him to the *Four Quartets;* he spent indeed all the years of *l'entre deux guerres* in his private journey through purgatory. By this process he rescued himself from a state that might have led another individual into a monastery and eternal silence. To what extent Vittoz found a chink in the armor of his abulia it would be difficult to say. But after many years there would be a reconciliation, in life as in his poetry, with more sensuous modes of being and the warmth of his second marriage; this we may read in the dedicatory poem of his works to Valerie Eliot, set down not long before his death.

VII

Did T. S. Eliot ever resolve his abulia and his Hamletesque failures in action? He had leaned on Vittoz, to be sure. But then we all inevitably lean on doctors, whether we are passive or not.

There are moments when the mysteries of physical being must be taken to medicine or to psychiatry. He had leaned on Pound —but then all writers turn to editors who read their copy with an uninvolved and unprejudiced eye. And was he not leaning on religion? Certainly we can say that his faith and his ever-growing fame were supportive during Eliot's more serene years. Nevertheless, I would suspect that Eliot only partly overcame his lifelong depression, however much he surmounted his abulia—surmounted it to make his all-important second marriage. He found ways of lightening his burden and his poetry, and his grasp of his own dreams and fantasies through his image-making enabled him to perform a constant kind of self-analysis. One may postulate that Eliot might have gained from modern psychoanalysis a great deal of reinforcement of his religious and spiritual life, providing he could find an analyst of the very highest skill capable of keeping pace with his verbal and imaginative power. There are few such analysts. However, his resistance was a serious obstacle; and his religion and his self-release helped him instead to regain the energies required for his poetical-critical works as well as his newfound career as a publisher and later his experiences as a playwright. Virginia Woolf, leaning on her husband, Leonard, during her two decades of creation between the wars, was enabled to write her novels during remissions of her melancholy. In the end that melancholy ended her life. Eliot seems to have entertained suicidal fantasies, but his tristimania was of another sort. One suspects that his fantasies were rather a wish for release than for extinction. The release came in his religious poetry, his sense of a future life rather than an impotent present. And his re-marriage, as I have observed, restored "time present" to him.

And so we can see in Eliot's work—from the early poems, even those discarded from *The Waste Land*— the particular life curve of the poet, the journey of the psyche which resembles those journeys Jung described: descent, ascent, rebirth—the great religious archetype given permanence by Dante and dramatic power by Milton. In Jung these journeys seem too general, too wide of application. Each journey is, in reality, different. Eliot's had in it a profound identification with Dante. The Italian poet was his Virgil during his season in Hell. The inward journey was consummated by one of the supreme poetic craftsmen of our time, possessed of a remarkable visionary imagination. A full biography of Eliot, if it is ever written, would have to go much further than I have ventured in this account. We would need a more intimate picture of the first marriage than we possess, although we obtain many glimpses of Vivien in the memories of her friends and acquaintances. We would also need a careful picture of Eliot's struggle to find a foothold in England—his years at the bank and the inner conflicts that brought on the breakdown and the crucial journey to Lausanne. It would be less difficult to document his years in Chelsea, where he lived in the sedate Victorian Carlyle Mansions, in an apartment under the one Henry James occupied at the end of his life. (It was Eliot's little joke that he sometimes heard the Master in the late hours pacing the floor.) He shared it with an invalid friend, John Hayward, a gifted amateur who wrote little, but kept an archive, now preserved at Cambridge, of considerable biographical and bibliographical importance. What we would need above all would be a full and searching inquiry into the foundations of Eliot's Christianity and his insistence that the power of the Kingdom of God has to prevail over the human failure to establish a kingdom of man. We would explore in this context the extent of Eliot's own anti-humanistic feelings. Narcissus cannot "live men's ways," and so he becomes "a dancer before God." Eliot's life is very rich and filled with human mysteries. Is it also a dance before God? If we can use that characterization, we must say it was an endlessly imaginative and intricate dance.

Finally, we would have to explore his visionary sense, his way of imaging his fantasies, the "reality" of his imaginings and his forms of symbolic statement—a quality he shared with Joseph

Conrad. All dream is symbolic statement, and Eliot understood that his visions were "a disciplined kind of dreaming." Like Coleridge he believed in the "Reason at the Rudder" behind his phantasms. Eliot's world view was painful, and his sense of the corrosion of civilization was intense. To reread his poems and plays is to be filled with an ineffable sadness. The drum beat of mankind's doom pulses through line after line, and in a world of war and holocaust and nuclear bombs—in a world of decay, degradation, destruction, and the withering of earth's fertility —we may yet discover that Eliot's anti-humanism—that is, his insistence upon the primacy of the Kingdom of God instead of the primacy of man—was a kind of prophecy of the future. For Eliot, it would seem, man was too much of a barbarian to be allowed self-rule or authority over the dominions of the earth. The supreme tabus of a Divine Order and a religious faith, Eliot seemed to say and believe, were needed in the republics of ignorance and the commonwealths of terror. In its essence, Eliot's message was that humanism can only be possible when man becomes human; that the creations of man's imagination —including his religions—alone can constitute for man, as we know him, the Divine Truths by which his spirit has managed to survive.

THE MADNESS
OF VIRGINIA WOOLF

In Virginia Woolf's "A Sketch of the Past," written two years before she died, a dream is remembered: "I dreamt I was looking in a glass when a horrible face—the face of an animal—suddenly showed over my shoulder." Virginia wasn't even sure that it was a dream. It had so much reality that she half believed it had happened. "I have always remembered the other face in the glass, whether it was a dream or a fact, and that it frightened me."

Who can now say out of what depths of memory and the unconscious, out of what sublimated feeling and perception, this fusion of evil and horror and shame emerged in the mirror's frame like a photograph in developing fluid. There was her own face—and then "the other face." Was it the me and the not-me? Was the animal face guilt, self-loathing, madness? The questions are not asked or answered; but a few lines farther Virginia tells us, "The looking glass shame has lasted all my life." As a grown woman she could not powder her nose in public. It meant taking a mirror out of her bag and looking into it. It also meant risking a glimpse at the face of horror. "Death was the glass! Death was between us!" So she had written in a fantasy of a haunted house.

I

Virginia Stephen's nature and temperament, and her lapses from sanity, have been laid to her father's temper and emotional aggressions, to her mother's sudden death when Virginia was still a young girl, and to boyish sexual treatment by one of her half brothers, to which she was exposed while a child. She herself spoke of "violent moments of being." And certainly aggression, death, confusion of infantile sexual feeling, in a child and woman of particularly intricate perceptions, can damage an entire life and sometimes lead to madness. But we must not simplify. Between the lines of "A Sketch of the Past" we obtain some glimpses into the tragic—and also heroic—story of Virginia Stephen's struggle long before she became Virginia Woolf. What were the violent moments? Three are juxtaposed for us in her sketch of Cornwall summers and the mirror in the Talland House hall into which she could look only on tiptoe as a child. On the shelf beside the mirror one day Gerald Duckworth, then sixteen, placed Virginia (she was probably five or six), "his hand going under my clothes; going firmly and steadily lower and lower." She stiffened and wriggled. She was helpless, with the inarticulate anger of a child; she felt frustration and "dumbness," and the mounting anger was apparently unexpressed. There had been an earlier and forgotten episode which someone told her, of her "being thrown naked by father into the sea." Leslie Stephen, we may judge, would have failed to make this into a moment of fun—it was not in his nature; there must have been surprise here, too, and the same kind of helplessness. And then there was the moment when she wrestled on the lawn with her older brother, Thoby, and he pommeled her. She wanted to hit him with her fist, but "why hurt another person?" So she told herself. She suffered the violation in silence. Within, we may judge, she was a childish vessel of wrath. "I have remembered it all my life."

Her "private parts" explored by the older boy; thrown into the sea naked by her strong, bearded father; pommeled by her beloved sibling—clearly the males of Virginia Stephen's world treated her too much as if she were an object, a bundle, a thing. What chance could there be for relations with men when the girl-child discovered so intensely her body's vulnerability? So

Virginia carried with her into her growing years a powerful anger and with it shame and guilt, for in the Victorian years little girls were not supposed to have such feelings or be involved in such doings.

The definitive blight of Virginia Stephen occurred when to this emotional confusion was added a kind of perpetual mourning and melancholy. She was thirteen when her mother died. The doctors said that Julia had influenza—and all of Virginia's later breakdowns were ushered in by bouts of this illness. There was no preparation for death— only a sudden summons early one morning. Leslie Stephen's grief was uncontrollable, and George Duckworth, the oldest half brother, then in his mid-twenties, assumed the father's role. "Led by George with towels wrapped round us and given each a drop of brandy in warm milk to drink, we were taken into the bedroom. I think candles were burning; and I think the sun was coming in. At any rate I remember the long looking glass; with the drawers on either side; and the washstand; and the great bed on which my mother lay." She noticed that one nurse was sobbing "and a desire to laugh came over me, and I said to myself as I have often done at moments of crisis since, 'I feel nothing whatever.' Then I stooped and kissed my mother's face. It was still warm. She had died only a moment before."

With feeling banished, Virginia Stephen could simply look at what was happening in detached sadness and silence. Someone else, shaken and grieving over the death, would be filled with too much emotion to observe. Virginia's account is both touching and intimate, as if she had coldly taken notes of the little tragic and ironic facts and physical sensations of long ago. At thirteen—that age of the *jeune fille en fleur* when all the senses tremulously listen and reach for the world—Virginia heard and sensed and touched and saw. And recorded and remembered. But she could not mourn.

The death cast a permanent pall over No. 22 Hyde Park Gate, more terrible perhaps for Virginia, given her nature and experience. Vanessa Stephen, her elder sister, then fifteen, was better prepared for life's shocks. Virginia's mercury of emotion, the stimulated nature of her sensibility, the rush of pain, hurt, rage, the sense of loss, of termination, as of the world coming to an end—all this could not be expressed and released as it might have been in other circumstances. Somewhere within, another door slammed, and Virginia immediately turned the key so that she might not *feel*. The process is carefully described in her novel *Mrs. Dalloway*. Septimus Smith can think, read, calculate; he can see with the clarity and the sharpness of immediacy. "He could add up his bill; his brain was perfect; it must be the fault of the world then—that he could not feel." Those who *can* feel find it difficult to understand this kind of dissociation. By shutting out feeling, one also shuts out pain. And that is why Virginia was able, in all her later recollections, to give us so much detail, shorn of all affect. "We were made to act parts that we did not feel; to fumble for words that we did not know."

Had Virginia been able to grieve with the rest of the family, there would not have been the formation of a kind of pool or reservoir of melancholy within her which was never fully released. It was a dead weight; she describes it in *Mrs. Dalloway* when she says, "This late age of the world's experience had bred in them all, a well of tears." Virginia Stephen left the room of death carrying her well of tears with her and returned to the nursery. She looked out of the window. She saw Dr. Seton walking up the street, his head bent and his hands clasped behind his back. Her memory had photographic sharpness. Pigeons floated and settled. She felt calm and sad. "It was a beautiful spring morning and very still. That brings back the feeling that everything had come to an end."

Thus we may see the tristimania of Virginia's life. Dissociation of grief enabled her to watch the pigeons, defensively mock the weeping nurse (she thought the nurse was pretending), see the depressed slow walk of the doctor, who had just lost his patient. Ever after, all terminations were death. This was why she was often on the verge of a breakdown when she finished a book; it represented a termination. Her own poignant mourning was shut away—and shut away also was the terrible unexpressed rage of a thirteen-year-old who experiences death in the manner of childhood, as an abandonment by the mother: the rage of being deprived, deserted, of being snatched from the warm-bodied Julia. Such rage is transformed into the eerie wailing and chanting and funeral self-immolation among primitives often described by travelers in remote lands. In the little girl perched at the window in Hyde Park Gate, in the early May morning of 1895, the rage was transformed into controlled calm. There was only a general stillness, a sad quiet, the wheeling pigeons. She could not mourn. She could not experience mourning.

On the next evening, the evening before the funeral, her half sister, Stella, took Virginia back to the chamber of death. There stood the looking glass, in which she had seen Death reflected the day before; and on the bed the same still figure, now no longer on her side but on her back, like some knight's lady in a tomb. There was only the "hollow, stern, immeasurably distant silence." Virginia kissed Julia again. It was like kissing cold iron. "Whenever I touch cold iron the feeling comes back to me —the feeling of my mother's face, iron cold and granulated." Step by step Virginia dispassionately takes us through these terrible moments. People crept in and out. Rooms were shut. Flowers were piled in the hall. For years the scent of certain flowers would bring the memories back to her. Everything seemed—as we might expect in someone to whom this death was "external"—a series of scenes, "melodramatic, histrionic and unreal." There was an unreality in the sisters' going in a cab to meet Thoby Stephen at the station when he came up from Clifton for the funeral. As Virginia had noticed the mirror by her mother's bed, so now the great glassed-in arched roof at Paddington merged with the shrouded Kensington room. The glass refracted the sun in a magnificent blaze of light "as if a burning glass had been laid over what was shaded and dormant." The train steamed into the station. Thoby embraced his sisters, amid tears. For Virginia Stephen this was "melodrama." ("Death was the glass! Death was between us!") The long looking glass of the dressing table in the bedroom, the burning glass at Paddington, came to stand for death, melting together with the mirror of childish vulnerability in the hall at St. Ives.

We know that the coalescence of the emotions, confined within, ultimately kaleidoscoped in Virginia not as mourning but as mental disorder. There were moments when Virginia Stephen identified herself with her dead mother to the extent of wanting death for herself. She was ill for many weeks. Then came the death of her second "mother"—Julia's daughter Stella —two years later. Virginia, now fifteen, still could not assimilate the idea of loss. She wrote that "just behind the surface lay the other death. Even if I were not fully conscious of what my mother's death meant, I had for two years unconsciously been absorbing it." The second blow of death struck "on my tremulous, creased self sitting with my wings still stuck together in the broken chrysalis." The image of herself as a barely hatched butterfly arrested in the spread of her wings by two deaths merged later into the image of a dying moth. She had watched the moth on her windowsill in Hyde Park Gate. One moment it seemed alive. Then she realized that she had witnessed its last flight. Its wings were folded, never to unfold again. The image of the diaphanous butterflies, on the edge of birth and on the edge of death, became one and the same. "Oh yes," she made the dying moth say as it lay on her windowsill, "death is stronger than I am." And yet Virginia would spend her life trying to be stronger than death—trying also in life to repair the damage to her selfhood, her womanhood, that made it impossible for her to be on terms of full comfort with any man.

I I

The damage to Virginia's selfhood seems by her own evidence to have been done in her childhood. There was, however, strong reinforcement of it in late adolescence. It came this time from George Duckworth, the adult half brother, whom she pictures with a certain fierceness and directness that hardly dissimulates the hatred and disgust she felt for him, until she swings to pity, telling herself that he was "a stupid good natured young man of profuse, voluable affections." Her pen is at its most bitter-ironic when she draws him as a sexually repressed Victorian, given to tears, embraces, and kisses sought from reluctant troubled sisters. Under the name of "unselfishness" he committed acts which others would have called "tyrannical"— "profoundly believing in the purity of his love, he behaved little better than a brute." He tried to get Virginia to attend parties. In one terrible scene he mocks a certain green dress in which she tried to meet his demands that she turn herself into a pretty social object. She remembered standing in front of George's Chippendale mirror seeking to make herself tidy and presentable. He made her feel, she recalled, as if she were a tramp or a gypsy. She felt shame at the parties, where she was a wallflower. She was ashamed of her clothes. She was made to feel "queer." George remained chaste until his marriage, Virginia said, but she and Vanessa paid the price for his sublimated desires. He seems to have gone as far as he could with his half sisters. "He acted in public the role of a good brother. He acted with success. How could we resist his wishes—how could we cherish other desires?" She describes him as having "the curls of a God, and the ears of a faun," but, she adds, he had "unmistakably the eyes of a pig."

This adult brother "lavished caresses, endearments, enquiries, and embraces as if, after forty years in the Australian bush, he had at last returned to the home of his youth and found an aged mother still alive to welcome him." Virginia repeated that he was "abnormally stupid." He could pass no examinations. He refused argument. He would always say, "Kiss me, kiss me, you beloved"—kisses were a substitute for all argument. "His passions increased and his desires became more vehement," so that

Virginia said she felt like "an unfortunate minnow shut up in the same tank with an unwieldy and turbulent whale."

The supreme scene is given us by Virginia, apparently with some exaggeration, as a scene of seduction. She had gone with George to one of those interminable parties in which her self-esteem suffered terribly. She describes the Holman Hunts in her brightest style. "The ladies were intense and untidy; the gentlemen had fine foreheads and short evening trousers in some cases revealing a pair of bright red Pre-Raphaelite socks. George stepped among them like a Prince in disguise. I soon attached myself to a little covey of Kensington ladies." They found the painter Holman Hunt in a long dressing gown, holding forth on the ideas that had prompted his painting *The Light of the World*. He was sipping cocoa and stroking his flowing beard. The tone of the assembly was "bright and high-minded." "At last—at last—the evening was over," wrote Virginia. When they returned to Hyde Park Gate, she went to her room, took off her satin dress, unfastened the corsage of carnations, and began to think of her Greek lessons.

"Many different things were whirling round in my mind—diamonds and countesses, copulations, the dialogues of Plato." She thought how pleasant it would be to fall asleep and forget them all. She was almost asleep when the door creaked. "Don't be frightened," George whispered. "And don't turn on the light, oh beloved. Beloved—" and he "flung himself on my bed and took me in his arms." To which Virginia added, "Yes, the old ladies of Kensington and Belgravia never knew that George Duckworth was not only father and mother, brother and sister to those poor Stephen girls; he was their lover also."

III

One important source of Virginia Stephen's will to live—in the face of her will to die—came from her father. The world has accepted Virginia's own belief, written one day into her diary, that if Leslie Stephen had lived into extreme old age, "his life would have entirely ended mine. What would have happened? No writing, no books;—inconceivable." This was but a statement of her confusion of feeling. Along with her haunted sense of her dead mother and her desire for death was her identification with the two life-giving forces in the Stephen household: her intense rivalry with her sister, which gave meaning to her life; and her wish to possess the life force of her mountain-climbing and writing father. These forces of competition and emulation fed Virginia's will to live against the destructive death forces nourished within. Vanessa remembered how in childhood Virginia pinned her down one day in the bathroom. Whom did she love more, mother or father? Vanessa had no wish to make a choice. She finally and most uncomfortably said that, as much as she loved her father, she loved her mother more. Virginia then thoughtfully replied that her love belonged to her father. The preference was stronger than she ever allowed. After Stella's death, Virginia assumed much of the care of Leslie Stephen; Vanessa was occupied with running the house. And however much Virginia found Leslie a difficult, crotchety, irritable, demanding old man, she gave proof again and again of a deep attachment. They lived in an "odd fumbling fellowship," she said; its roots lay in their common love of books and reading. She had always been given the run of the great study. "Read what you like," her father said to her when she was fifteen. She read in this big room lined with books. There stood the father's rocking chair, upholstered in American cloth, where Leslie stretched his legs and lay almost recumbent, rocking the chair like a cradle as he wrote. On the writing board he had a curious Chinese inkstand and an inkwell at one side. The Watts portrait of Sir Leslie Stephen, in its finely chiseled sadness and severity, hung over the fireplace. Some of his rusty alpenstocks stood by the side; some old trophy, a silver cup, on the mantelpiece. Through three long windows Virginia saw the roofs of Kensington. Her father remarked casually one day that he had just seen an eagle on St. Mary Abbots—an eagle in

London! Probably a refugee from the zoo. She remembered his making a special trip to the London Library to bring Hakluyt's voyages. She was enraptured by the large yellow pages. "I used to read it and dream of those obscure adventures, and no doubt practiced their style in my copybook." Leslie Stephen made his children critical. He asked them to say *why* they liked this or that storybook. The literary roots among the Stephens were strong; out of these grew the atmosphere of Virginia's prose— out of her total saturation in English literature.

Perhaps most touching, as we seek the life-giving affinities between father and daughter, was Leslie's gift to Virginia on her twenty-first birthday, just a month before he died. "Father gave me a ring—really a beautiful one, which I love—the first ring I have ever had." Leslie said that she was "a very good daughter." It was as if there were a marriage and also a laying on of hands, a literary succession. The father, who had been Thackeray's son-in-law and editor of the *Cornhill,* the man who had fashioned a great national institution, the *Dictionary of National Biography,* who had been visited by Tennyson and Browning and Henry James, performed a marriage between Virginia and the world of letters. He had been eccentric, troublesome, severe; he embodied certain forms of masculinity Virginia detested. She could blame him for her mother's hard life, and yet she wrote when he was dead, "I am happy about that ring." At moments she felt guilty. "I can't bear to think of his loneliness . . . the dreadful thing is that I never did enough for him all these years. He was so lonely, often, and I never helped him as I might have done." And then she said the opposite of what she wrote years later in her diary: "If he had only lived we could have been so happy." She helped Leslie Stephen's biographer, Frederic Maitland, prepare his book. And many years later, when she was writing *To the Lighthouse,* she recognized that she was more like her father than her mother and "therefore more critical." She added in a mood of recognition, "He was an adorable man, and somehow tremendous."

We have tangible evidence of Virginia Stephen's identification with her father. She began to smoke a pipe a few weeks after his death. Few Victorian daughters dared to take such liberties. "I find it very soothing." Having written this, she exclaimed to her friend Violet Dickinson, "Oh my Violet! I do want father so!" In her later affectionate essay on Leslie Stephen, she recalls "his taking his hat and stick, calling for his dog and his daughter," and striding off into Kensington Gardens. Now that he was dead, Virginia took to striding in solitude, shouting the odes of Pindar into the air, which caressed her "like a stern but affectionate parent."

In the end Leslie's sternness counted less than his affection. And what counted most was the image of the father writing in his rocking chair, with his pipe in his mouth, dropping books around him with a thud. Her breakdown was not long in coming after Leslie Stephen's death—the same troubling symptoms of dissociation and depression which had followed Julia's death. Violet Dickinson suggested a trip to Italy, and the sisters had their first experience of Florence and Venice. Vanessa was delighted; there was much to see, and she discovered the old schools of painting. But Quentin Bell tells us "there was practically nothing that the elder sister did not like and very little to please the younger."

They returned by way of Paris at the end of April 1904. When they reached London, Virginia completely broke down. Her usual symptoms: a swing from euphoria to silence, refusal to take food, apathy. Violet Dickinson took her into her country home. Virginia threw herself from a window. Fortunately, it was a low one. She clearly did not want to die. After that she was in the hands of the doctors. She always hated doctors. In those days of primitive psychiatry they prescribed quiet, bed rest, nourishing food. Medicine was little aware then of the nature of depression except for its classic symptoms. "All that summer she was mad," the family historian tells us.

Twenty years later, sketching *Mrs. Dalloway* in her diary,

Virginia wrote, "Mrs. Dalloway has branched into a book; and I adumbrate here a study of insanity and suicide." She added, "The world seen by the sane and the insane side by side." In the novel she invented an insane male and a dissociated female. In life, however, the two were not "side by side." They lived within the one: they were the two faces of Virginia Woolf, the frightening face of anger, shame, guilt, death; the benign face of literary experience, the heritage of Sir Leslie Stephen. In some such complex way, the madness of Virginia was metamorphosed into the asperities and sanities of her art.

WYSTAN AUDEN
AND THE SCISSORS-MAN

Wystan Auden, toward the end of his life, repeatedly criticized the writing of literary biographies. He reviewed them, and collections of literary documents such as letters, with acute interest but with a distinct strain of hostility. He felt them to be "superfluous and in bad taste." What emerged was a simple thesis: there is no way in which any biographer can do more than glimpse the mysteries of the poetic and imaginative mind. The unconscious and preconscious life of the artist is out of reach even of intimate friends, let alone serious biographers, and most certainly literary hacks. The inner world cannot be reconstructed from archives and the archives themselves are most often irrelevant. The literary work is available for critical study. All else is an invasion of privacy. Auden was never as explicit as this: but the point of view is clear in all that he said.

In his brief foreword to his commonplace book, *A Certain World,* published two years before his death in 1973, we have the full statement: "Biographies of writers, whether written by others, *or* by themselves, are always superfluous and usually in bad taste." We notice that he rules out autobiography even while recognizing that his commonplace book contained autobiographical elements. He acknowledged that all of a writer's works are "transmutations of his personal experience." Yet he insisted that no knowledge of the raw ingredients could explain "the peculiar flavor of the verbal dishes he [the artist] invites the public to taste." At the same time we can see that a certain autobiographical urge existed, for Auden proceeds to quote a passage from G. K. Chesterton:

> There is at the back of every artist's mind something like a pattern or a type of architecture. The original quality in any man of imagination is imagery. It is a thing like the landscape of his dreams; the sort of world he would like to make or in which he would wish to wander; the strange flora and fauna of his own secret planet; the sort of thing he likes to think about. This general atmosphere, and pattern or structure of growth, governs all his creations, however varied.

With this preamble Auden offered us *A Certain World,* a series of glimpses into the landscape of his dreams and memories, and their flora and fauna. He arranged his jottings and quotations under alphabetical headings; and as the spirit moved him appended certain personal reflections, many of an autobiographical nature. He said he tried to keep these at a minimum, but there are a goodly number; and he added a few enigmatic words—that it was his intention to "let others, more learned, intelligent, imaginative and witty than I, speak for me." Whom did he mean? Critics, friends, analysts?—certainly not biographers. We can only guess and wonder whether there wasn't a bit of tongue-in-cheek in this utterance.

Auden also reminded his readers in his foreword that the showing of his commonplace book was a kind of offering of his personal planet and that such planets were never "an unsullied Eden." Unpleasant facts from the world have a way of intruding into a landscape of dream, matters we sometimes think about, but against our will. He did not doubt that some of his entries would "I trust, disturb a reader as much as they disturb me."

What we observe, as we read this volume, and jump about in its alphabetized subjects, is a kind of ambiguity in the poet's mind about the facts of his life. Those he gives us are inevitably a gloss on his work. And yet he touched a goodly number of "psycho-sexual" subjects relating to himself which seemed to show an opening up rather than a concealment of his privacy. We know that in his will he enjoined his friends to burn his letters and sought, like Henry James, to clear the approaches to his privacy. Not all of his friends complied. Biographies have been written and others doubtless are on their way. The entire subject, and Auden's revelations in *A Certain World,* invite further exploration of this book; it is in reality a capital personal document and even if Auden is pulling our leg, as some might argue, the very way in which he does it tells us a great deal about his problems—the problems of the man who wrote *The Age of Anxiety.*

I will illustrate by simple examples some of the interesting glimpses Auden gives us of his personal planet. He tells us that he was both the youngest child and the youngest grandchild in his family. He was always youngest in his class. It made him feel for years younger than others—the youngest, perhaps—in any group. This opens up for biography the entire question of an artist who spent a childhood and youth not with his peers but with older persons and may have acquired as we say an old head on young shoulders. Auden in his comments remarks that he has come to see, as he walks in the street, that there are younger persons in the world, and this has finally led him to the thought that he is aging and that he will someday die. Like James Joyce, who at Clongowes was a mere babe among older boys, Auden was deprived of certain elements of his childhood and acquired an ego-structure prematurely adult. The talk he heard around him was not always within his reach. Older ideas were available, at a time when he should have been swapping boy-talk with young friends of his own age. This was a kind of forcing of experience and establishment of standards and values he should have arrived at in a maturing process. We recognize at once the extent to which Auden's few remarks have led us into a significant area of his being. When he became aware that he could no longer be young among the old, he lost what we might say was his sense of eternal youth.

He admits that music is important to him but he cannot speak authoritatively about the musical art. Moreover, music, like the artist's creativity, cannot be described. But Auden recalls with pleasure that as a boy he enjoyed band concerts and is still filled with nostalgia when he hears a band. He possessed a voice and sang as a boy in choirs, where he learned not only to sight-read but to enunciate clearly. He became conscious of meter in both speech and song, an excellent apprenticeship for a poet. Long before he took a conscious interest in poetry he was cultivating his ear.

In this way *A Certain World* is filled not only with an abundance of interesting biographical data but with the poet's memories and ideas that reflect the private world he wishes to preserve and a "certain world" he is mapping for us—or is it for himself? Auden muses that if he had gone into the church, he might now be a bishop; in politics he believes he would have been a liberal but he is inclined to conservatism in religion. He tells us the story of his patron saint, Wystan, a sort of Hamlet or Oedipus figure who objected to the uncanonical marriage of his widowed mother to his godfather. This, he tells us, led to a sad ending. The mother and her spouse simply got rid of the troublesome Wystan and as a result he was later sanctified. In this story we are given a glimpse of a destructive and murderous mother about whom we shall hear more as we pursue our alphabetical entries. What we begin to see is that on Auden's planet women are troublesome and he is uncertain of them. They appear as threatening and menacing figures, like the mother of Saint Wystan. When we come upon the alliterative "Castration Complex" among Auden's alphabetical headings, we read on with particular interest, since in Auden's time, in the Western world, the more benign Freudian view of masturbation had not yet reached the nurseries, and small boys were often threatened with violent deprivation of the precious source of their infantile pleasures, and usually by the female parent in charge of them. We find here the kind of direct use of Freudian terminology which I have criticized earlier in this book. He talks of "castration" as if it were a fact and not simply a symbolic term in the psychological therapies; and he talks of "penis envy" and uses other diagnostic and clinical terms which in literary discourse are better translated into the symbolic language to which they belong. For once in this volume I am forced to employ this "label" language, these clinical verbal shortcuts I would not ordinarily use.

Still under the heading "Castration Complex" Auden tells us that "as a child, one of my favorite books was an English translation of Dr. Hoffmann's *Struwwelpeter* and my favorite poem in the book was 'The Story of Little Suck-a-Thumb.' " We know that entire generations of boys and girls read *Struwwelpeter* and looked at the drawings in color of the terrible things that happen to naughty children. Auden selects his favorite poem, the choice of his childhood. In it Mamma announces to her little son Conrad that she must go out and leave him. Having generated what we might call a "separation anxiety," she admonishes him: "Don't suck your thumb while I'm away." The mother is still speaking—

> The great tall tailor always comes
> To little boys that suck their thumbs;
> And 'ere they dream what he's about,
> He takes his great sharp scissors out
> And cuts their thumbs clean off—and then,
> You know, they never grow again.

Small wonder that as soon as the mother turns her back, in this story, Conrad's anxious little thumb pops right into Conrad's anxious little mouth. And so we read the next verse:

> The door flew open, in he ran,
> The great, long, red-legged scissors-man.
> Oh, children, see! the tailor's come
> And caught out little Suck-a-Thumb.

> Snip! Snap! Snip! They go so fast.
> That both his thumbs are off at last.

And in the final couplet the mother's voice is heard

> I knew he'd come
> To naughty little Suck-a-thumb.

In commenting on these verses Auden supplies the psychological gloss that "of course, it's not about thumb-sucking at all, but about masturbation, which is punished by castration." Here we have an interesting omission—the punishment is not in reality castration, it is simply a *threat* of castration, which only mentally defective child-abusing parents would implement. Auden's wording is important: he speaks as if there were no other punishment because he knows the Scissors-Man in the poem is imaginary. However, the most important fact is Auden's choice of this poem as well as his designation of a punishment that is psychologically threatening. Out of the handful of verses in this popular book Auden selects the sexually forbidden one involving castration or amputation and the use of the vivid scissors-man and his surgical scissors. He had other options—the one about Cruel Frederick who kills birds and whips his dog until the enraged animal bites him; or he might have identified with the little girl Harriet, who burns herself to a small pile of ashes playing with matches, in spite of parental warnings, so that even the flood of tears from her cats can't extinguish the flames; or the very contemporary tale of the beastly boys who are dipped in ink by a social-minded antiracist giant, and are made very black indeed because they mocked and tormented a blackamoor and said "Oh Blacky, you're as black as ink." There is the one about the man who's shot at by the rabbit he tries to shoot, but the bullet destroys the coffee cup in his wife's hand; and fidgety Philip who pulls the table-cloth and all the dishes over himself—all cautionary and coercive verse designed to frighten children into good behavior. One could find castration in all of them, I believe, and learned papers have been written—or could be—on the subject. Nevertheless, it's little Conrad Suck-a-Thumb who is singled out by Wystan. He then asks the proper, the scientific, the necessary biographical question: "Why did I enjoy the poem as a child? Why was I not frightened?" His reason: well, he says, he simply wasn't a thumb-sucker; he was a nail-biter! If we ponder this, we can see a characteristic masking of reality, a rationalization to explain away genuine fright. There *was* fear, a great deal. The real fear, the real ogre in the poem, however, isn't the red-legged scissors man. Auden tells us, "I knew well that Suck-a-Thumb's fate would not be mine, because the scissors-man was a figure in a poem." There is, however, a *real* person in the poem. This is the threatening mother. And about her Auden says nothing. He adds, however, at the end of his analysis, "Very different is the fear aroused in me by spiders, crabs and octopi, which are, I suspect, symbols to me for the castrating *Vagina Dentata"* (the tooth-filled entrapping shark-vagina). So much for the fearful mother.

As we turn the book's pages we come to the D's—and Dreams. One expects Auden to be interesting and informative on this subject. What is unexpected is his dredging up an old dream of his own—a nightmare. The symbolism of dream is always suggestive even if we do not have the means of interpreting it. Here Auden seems to be adhering to his promise to give us some of the disturbing things of life. He tells us a horrible nightmare with the same coolness that little Wystan showed to the scissors-man. And since dreams cannot be interpreted *de chic,* Auden is helpful to the reader: he supplies a context.

The dream is dated August 1936, when Auden was twenty-nine. He dreams he is in a hospital for an appendectomy. A removal of an appendix—any appendage indeed—is a kind of scissors-man act. The surgeon probably doesn't say "snip-snap-snip," but the scissors is converted in dream to a surgical instrument. In the dream there was also someone with green eyes and a terrifying affection for Auden. So instead of removing the appendix, the medical scissors-man cuts off, Auden tells us, "the arm of an old lady who was going to do me an injury." He explains this to the doctors, but they aren't interested. The dream then relates an escape from the hospital and a terrified pursuit. But what's important is that we have two castrations in the dream—the threat of removal of an appendix and the amputation of a woman's arm. A later sentence supplies a context. The dreamer has "a vision of pursuit like a book illustration and I think [says Auden] related to the long red-legged Scissors Man" in *Struwwelpeter.* The dreamer thus gives us a primary association to the dream.

Let us look for a moment at the sequence we now have as supplied by Auden. He has chosen as a favorite poem of his childhood a "castration" poem, and then has talked of the vagina dentata; now he embodies, in an account of a dream, the same castration theme and "an old lady who was going to do me an injury." We may speculate that a nightmare, filled with amputations, flight and pursuit by a red-legged scissors-man (the red might even be a hint of blood, and the legs are two further appendages), suggests that the German poem did frighten little Wystan terribly. Auden furnishes a great deal of genital symbolism and expresses a horrible fear of genital-loss. But it isn't sex that's important in this material. It's the relation of the boy to a threatening figure, the woman who first leaves the little boy alone, exposed to a danger she foretells, and almost prescribes, and the little boy who is so promptly punished as she predicted. I discern in this a possible "double-bind," not unlike Raskolnikov's—though on a different level. A fear not only of the dentata—that is the terrifying shark-woman—but a fear of his own anger and aggression against the woman with whom he has also identified himself, and whom he counterattacks by dreaming that *her* arm is cut off instead of *his* appendix. By now it should be clear that Auden's planet contains a castrating mother: the scissors-man is her agent; and it is she who delivers the threat of emasculation.

It seems logical at this point, given the path we have followed, to turn to the letter P and determine what Auden wants to tell us about the penis. Here we find a passage which continues the revelations of Auden's private feelings about his private parts. He discusses "genital envy." This is pure Freud, and Auden isn't sure he agrees with Freud's insistence that women suffer from envy of the male penis. He tells us, however, that he is quite certain that "all males, without exception, whatever their age, suffer from genital rivalry" and he sees this as a threat to the future existence of the human race. "Behind every quarrel between men, whether individually or collectively, one can hear the taunt of the little urchin: My prick (or my father's) is bigger than yours (or your father's) and can pee further." The poet goes on to say that nearly all weapons, from the spear and the sword to the revolver and the rocket, are phallic symbols. And then: "Men, to be sure, also fashion traps, most forms of which are vaginal symbols, but they never take a pride in them as they do in their weapons, and, when heroes exchange gifts of friendship, weapons figure predominantly, but where, in literature can one find description of a trap, or hear of one as a precious gift."

The poet is indeed furnishing us with the flora and fauna of his landscape. Remembering that it is he who invoked the vagina dentata, we recognize that it too is a trap, a barbed trap for males; or, to read Auden's iconography directly, copulation with a woman is tantamount to castration, at least for him. The rest of this passage about the penis as weapon is devoted to the dangers of our phallic toys.

One wonders that a poet who understands the psychological meaning of human iconography so profoundly should turn the genitals into fixed symbols—the male, a weapon, the female, a trap. We know that they can take quite different forms—and reflect other feelings—in our imagination, the male an object of

ove and fertility, of warmth-giving and seed-giving, and the
emale representing warmth and nurture and also receptivity
and love. Having been given these icons, out of a poet's private
world, I would, as a biographer, have to ponder their rigidity,
and look into his poetry for clarifications. When the poet asks
vhere in literature one can find a loving description of a trap,
he answer is perhaps nowhere; but when he makes that trap
woman—for one cannot dissociate the female, as if she were a
carburetor, from her possessions—then the answer is in a thousand books, in *Lady Chatterley,* even in *Hecate County;* in all
he books which have celebrated forms of love; almost every-
vhere in Shakespeare. Think of Hamlet's fond thought of what
ies between Ophelia's legs, and yet he, more than most men,
eels trapped. And those of us, of an older generation, who once
ead the coy naughtiness of Cabell's *Jurgen* can recall that Jurgen's long sword asked insistently for a sheath, not a trap. The
experiences of love are infinite and complex. It's only when
here's some deep trouble in the relationship that women may
become traps to men, and men may become aggressors to
women *and* to each other. There are many forms of male and
emale aggression. We call it platitudinously "the war of the
exes."

Is Auden simply having fun at his reader's expense? Even if
we allow for this we still remind ourselves how revelatory the
vit and humor of the unconscious can be. His choice of subject
n each instance and his adherence to the Freudian nomencla-
ure was his and his alone. Some men would never think of the
vagina as a trap or as tooth-filled and sharklike. Their minds run
o it as a "Great Good Place." They see delicacies and softnesses
n it; and who knows what other images and symbols we might
ead given the varieties of sexual experience.

This somewhat rapid although not altogether cursory selec-
ion of Auden's subjects in this book offers ground for conjec-
ure. One way of looking at *A Certain World* is that Auden

chose this way of putting down for us a central fact of his life
—his homosexual roots. Was it on this account that he alluded
to "others, more learned, intelligent, imaginative and witty
than I" and asked that they speak for him? We no longer can
say unless some document, some letter, will one day reveal the
answer to us. But the Auden-iconography is clear enough. His
icons for the vagina are quite as clear as his icons for the penis.
His picture of a mother figure and her agent, the scissors-man,
completes the geography of perhaps the most important part of
Auden's planet. He cannot assert himself in love in the usual
ways of man and woman because in his certain world the
woman castrates the male. The only safety lies in love of his own
sex, where men make war with each other in various ways—
with their weapons—but where there is no danger of having a
scissors-man or a shark amputate the organ of delight. It is
perhaps significant that in his remarks about the phallic nature
of weapons Auden says he would prefer to leave international
relations to women: doubtless because wars are in their very
nature attempts by the warring parties to castrate one another.
But Auden adds another idea—he would leave international
relations preferably to married women. He feels safer with
them: they are no threat to him.

Beyond this speculation, we can see the mixture of innocence
and wisdom that caused Auden to inveigh against literary biography and to compile his revealing *Certain World:* for in trying
to explain to us, using Chesterton's words, the landscape of
dreams—*his* landscape, *his* dreams—he was giving proof of
artistic honesty and devotion to truth. What his innocence
refused to recognize were certain realities: that human curiosity is insatiable, that poetic mysteries are always pursued, that
biographers seek the nature of great lives in order to understand greatness. Moreover, it is impossible to attempt in the
present to legislate for the distant future—a mistake many nations make—since history is unpredictable. The last thing that
Auden could have predicted when he left his papers to hi

friend Chester Kallman and wrote his will was that Kallman would die so soon after him and the papers would end up in the hands of strangers. The lesson in Auden's case, and perhaps in others, is that the artist must live as best he can in this world and not attempt to regulate his posthumous reputation, which inevitably regulates itself. Perhaps Auden sensed this, for *A Certain World* provides many of the essential facts for the very kind of biography Auden deplored and called "vulgar and in bad taste."

A CAVE OF ONE'S OWN

There has been for many years a vigorous resistance to literary "psychologizing" and a tendency to stop one's ears the moment a psychoanalyst arrives and starts explaining that, for example, the trouble with Robert Louis Stevenson was that he had a feeding problem when he was a baby. Having as an infant been denied his mother's milk, he sought ever after to gratify his oral needs—which was why he dreamed up his story of Dr. Jekyll and Mr. Hyde and hinged the story on the swallowing of a potion; and this was why he could hold his own at the prodigious day-long luaus in Samoa and Hawaii. This, we are further told, meant that he never really became a mature person.

It so happens that the fact is right, however much the theorizing may be specious. Mama Stevenson kept a diary when Louis was an infant, and there were some infantile feeding problems. Also Stevenson no doubt, for reasons about which we can only speculate, retained certain boyish elements in his makeup and wasn't much interested in women as characters for his fiction. But we can reply that out of his eternal boyishness grew the eternally youthful *Treasure Island.* And if there was this duality in him, how well he was equipped to trace the double sides of man's nature as he did in Jekyll and his hideous counterpart! The process of applying psychiatry to literature cannot be effective if it reduces the artist to a neurosis; critics have rightly called this approach "reductive." But we are interested in how the artist triumphs over anxieties and feeding problems, all the ills of body and mind, and acquires a kind of second sight, a positive urge to create. These discussions are by no means modern: they did not originate with Freud. We have often been reminded that Charles Lamb wrote an essay "On the Sanity of True Genius" long before the advent of psychoanalysis. Men, Lamb observed, "finding in the raptures of the higher poetry a condition of exaltation, to which they have no parallel in their own experience, besides the spurious resemblance of it in dreams and fevers, impute a state of dreaminess and fever to the poet. But the true poet dreams being awake. He is not possessed by his subject but has dominion over it. . . . Where he seems most to recede from humanity, he will be found the truest to it."

Art is the result not of calm and tranquillity, however much the artist may, on occasion, experience calm in the act of writing. It springs from tension and passion, from a state of disequilibrium in the artist's being. "His art is happy, but who knows his mind?" William Butler Yeats asked in speaking of Keats. The psychologist, reading the pattern of the work, can attempt to tell us what was wrong with the artist's mental or psychic health. The biographer, reading the same pattern in the larger picture of the human condition, seeks to show how the negatives were converted into positives: how Proust translated his allergies and his withdrawal from the pain of experience into the whole world of Combray, capturing in language the very essences which seem illusory and evanescent in man's consciousness; how Virginia Woolf, on the margin of her melancholy, pinned the feeling of the moment to the printed page as the hunter of butterflies pins down the diaphanous and fluttering prize; and how James Joyce, visioning himself as Daedalus soaring over a world he had mastered, created a language for it, the word-salads of *Finnegans Wake*—but where the schizophrenic patient creates word-salads because of his madness, Joyce created them with that method in madness which Lamb was describing when he spoke of the artist's dominion over his subject. These are the victories of art over the psychic troubles which intervene at various times during our active lives.

Literature and psychology are not necessarily antagonistic, as they have been made to seem. They meet on common ground. We have for decades used psychology in criticism and in biography. When we study the motivations of Hamlet, is this not psychology? When we try to understand and speculate upon symbols in a work, are we not "psychologizing"? And in our time, when creative writers have been exposed directly to the works of Freud and Jung and use them in their writings, we must treat them for the sources that they are. How can we understand William Faulkner's *Light in August* without at least a glance at certain modern theories of conditioning and behavior? Can we deal adequately with *Finnegans Wake* without looking into Jung and his theory of the collective unconscious? What meaning can Eugene O'Neill's *Strange Interlude* and *Mourning Becomes Electra* have if they are divorced from the popular misconceptions of Freud in the 1920s? Freud himself acknowledged that Sophocles and Dostoevsky and Ibsen had the kind of glimpses into the unconscious vouchsafed him in his consulting room. The answer to the misguided use of psychoanalysis is not to close our ears but to ask ourselves: How are we to deal with this difficult material while remaining true to our own disciplines—and avoid making complete fools of ourselves?

It is fairly obvious that we can handle it only after we have studied and mastered that part of psychology useful to us, as we must master any learning. Our success will depend entirely on the extent to which we know what we are about and the way in which we learn to use this intricate discipline. We must not run amuck; above all, we must beware of the terminology and jargon of the psychoanalysts. What we must try to do is to translate the terms in a meaningful way and into language proper to literary discipline. Critics who babble of the Oedipus complex and who plant psychoanalytical clichés higgledy-piggledy in their writings perform a disservice both to literature and to psychoanalysis. Biographers who take certain arbitrary symbols, and apply them rigidly to the wholly volatile human personality, inevitably arrive at gross and ludicrous distortions. These are matters highly complex and difficult to explain. I have accordingly sought an illustrative problem to demonstrate what I would deem to be the use—and the abuse—of psychology in the writing of biography and literary criticism.

I

My text is a novel by the American elegiac novelist Willa Cather, published in 1925 by Alfred Knopf. It fell to my lot in the early 1950s to complete a biography of Cather left unfinished by an old friend, who had died in the midst of his work. To complete the work of another is one of the most difficult tasks a writer can undertake. One has in effect to do the entire job all over again in order to seize all the invisible threads which exist in those portions already completed. My friend, Edward K. Brown, a companion of my Paris years, had written nine chapters. I found that three more were required, and in the course of my work I came on much interesting material relating to Cather's novel *The Professor's House.* This is the novel I propose to deal with. It is not a fully realized work, although it has been influential on other writers. My first and prime goal was to discover what significance the professor's house has in the story, since it is the dwelling which was given the primary place in the title.

The Professor's House is the story of a professor in a midwestern university who has achieved success but derives no particular pleasure from it. The novel is a record of his mental depression. With the money received from a prize he has won for a monumental historical work, Professor St. Peter has built a new house to please his wife and daughters. He would prefer to remain in the rented house in which he has shaped his career for thirty years. Indeed, he cannot bring himself to move out of his old study, located in the attic, where still stand the wire forms on which a dressmaker fitted the clothes for his wife and

growing daughters. The attic sewing room is lit by an oil lamp.
It is heated by a stove. Professor St. Peter has scorned cushion
comforts. He had a "show" study downstairs and has one in the
new house. But the attic room, with its silent dummies, is comfort enough for him. He clings to the old place even after the
rest of the house has been emptied and the moving is over.
Since the lease still has some months to run, he decides he will
keep his former workroom until he has to surrender it.

His elder daughter is Rosamond, an attractive girl who has
married a suave, fast-talking, pretentious, but cultivated young
man named Louie Marsellus. Marsellus has, with great practicality, turned to commercial use in aviation a certain discovery
made by one of the professor's former students, Tom Outland,
who was Rosamond's fiancé but who was killed during the First
World War. Outland bequeathed his patent to Rosamond, and
since her marriage to Marsellus it has become a source of
wealth. The professor loves his daughter very much, but intensely dislikes the upstart qualities of her husband, and accordingly feels a certain alienation from her. The professor's wife,
however, is extremely fond of her son-in-law and his European
affectations. She feels that her husband, in his withdrawal from
the entire family, does not sufficiently recognize how materially
its fortunes are being altered by Louie Marsellus's business acu-
men. There is a second daughter who is married to a newspaper
columnist named McGregor. They tend to side with the father
against the somewhat vulgar *nouveau riche* world of Louie and
Rosamond. The latter are also building a house—in the style of
a Norwegian manor, set incongruously in this midwestern com-
munity.

The first part of the book, titled "The Family," sketches for
us the professor's alienation from those closest to him because
of his feeling that his wife and daughters do not really understand his deeper emotional life, and his rebellion against the
materialism of the college town. He has set himself apart successfully over the years. He has made for himself a French

garden in this prairie setting; he has cultivated his love for French wines and delicate sauces; he has a beach house on the lake and spends long lonely hours by the water. He is a Gallic epicure isolated, like his garden, in surroundings to which he cannot ever wholly belong. He has had only one student in all the years of his teaching for whom he could feel affection: Tom Outland. He dislikes the new generation of students. He dislikes college politics. He has no real friends among his colleagues. He feels himself oppressed by the prosaic, mediocre world of the town of which his wife and daughters are so much a part. Commercial values have been exalted here over those he cherishes: the rich fabric of art related to the rich fabric of the old religion in which great cathedrals and the drama of Good and Evil exalted men to a high creativity.

The second part of the book is called "Tom Outland's Story." Here Willa Cather attempts a risky technical device, which is nevertheless time-honored in fiction. In the manner of Cervantes or Smollett she interpolates a story within a story: she gives us an autobiographical fragment written by Tom Outland and confided to Professor St. Peter. It describes a crucial episode in the young man's life. Cather explained that in writing this part of the novel she had in mind those Dutch paintings in which interiors are scrupulously rendered; in many of these there was "a square window, open, through which one saw the masts of ships, or a stretch of gray sea"; the effect is that of an inset, a picture within a picture. Having given us the interior of the professor's family life, she directs our attention to the one important window in it—the one that looks out upon Tom Outland's adventure.

The crucial episode has been his discovery of a Cliff Dwellers' village tucked into a wall of rock high in a New Mexico canyon. Here was beauty at once primitive and sophisticated. Here were houses that let in wind and sun and yet sheltered an unfathomable past. Here also was a great tower: "It was still as sculpture. . . . The tower was the fine thing that held all the

jumble of houses together and made them mean something.
. . . That village sat looking down into the cañon with the
calmness of eternity." The Cliff Dwellers' houses are never
overtly contrasted with the houses in the professor's town, but
they invite contrast. In the modern town the emphasis, as my
friend Edward Brown observed, is on the individual buildings.
In the ancient village it is on the architectural as well as the
social unity.

Tom has made his discovery with the aid of a fellow cow-
puncher, Roddy. He travels to Washington in great excitement
to inform the Department of the Interior, taking with him
samples of the ancient pottery he found in the long-deserted
houses. In the capital he is promptly wrapped up in heedless
red tape; he sits in impersonal outer offices; he is met with
general indifference. Civil servants seem to him strange modern cave dwellers living in rows of apartments as if in rabbit
warrens; and their careerism and arrogance blot out all his
hopes. He turns his back on Washington, disillusioned; he feels
he has done the proper thing as a citizen, but the petty officials
do not share his interest in his country's distant past. However,
a still greater disappointment awaits him. Roddy, during his
prolonged absence, has profited by the arrival of a German
anthropologist to sell the entire contents of the cliff town. The
ancient relics have been packed and shipped to Europe, and
Roddy has deposited the money for Tom in a bank, thinking he
has driven a good bargain. Tom, in anger at what he considers
a betrayal, breaks with Roddy and then returns to the cliff town
to spend a few days in magnificent solitude, hiding in the high
tower his notes and records of the entire adventure. Then,
descending again, he withdraws the money from the bank and
uses it to go to college, there meeting the professor who
becomes his guide and mentor.

The final part of the novel is a mere sketch. Titled "The
Professor," it returns to the dilemma of St. Peter's isolation in
his attic. Lonely and depressed, he remains there while his

family is away during the summer, living a monastic dream life, with the old sewing woman turning up to act as charwoman. One day, on awakening from a nap, he discovers the room is filled with fumes from the stove, but he is incapable of making the effort to arouse himself and to throw open the window. He has lost the will to live. The fortuitous arrival of the sewing woman saves him, and there the novel ends. We can only speculate that the professor will go on living in isolation amid his family.

I I

What are we to make of this novel—if we can call it a novel? It is a stitching together of two inconclusive fragments about a professor, his family, and his wish for death and the adventures of a young man alone with the past on a mesa and briefly in touch with the modern urban life of Washington. The two episodes relating to the professor hardly constitute a novel; they convey a picture of his deep depression, which nothing in the book really explains. Why does he wish for death at a time when his life has been crowned with success and when his family flourishes as never before; when indeed there is the promise of a grandchild, for Rosamond expects a baby as the book ends? The Tom Outland story fills in the background of Rosamond's wealth and gives us the strange story of the intense young man who alters the whole course of the professor's life; this does not illuminate, however, the professor's final state of mind. His wish to die is at no point sufficiently motivated by the facts of the small-town life, the general hopelessness of the Philistine surroundings. To believe so intensely in art and the religion of art, and to have created so fully, and yet at the same time to be overpowered by a sense of futility and ineffectuality—these are the contradictions we discern within the professor.

Professor Brown found an inner unity which he explained in terms of the symbolism of houses within the book. It is a striking passage. There are, he points out, the two houses of the professor, and of these the old house is the significant one. The new house is wrong for him. The Marsellus-Rosamond Norwegian manor house is also wrong. It is a product of pretension and materialism, without regard for the style of the town and the essential dignity of human dwellings. The homes of the Cliff Dwellers—for these are houses also, primitive and wind-swept on their mountainous height—possessed that dignity. In the third portion of the book, the link between these houses is established. Brown continued, speaking of this final part:

> The first and second parts of the book which have seemed so boldly unrelated are brought into a profound unity. It is in this third part of the novel that the large background of emotion, which demands rhythmic expression if we are to respond to it as it deserves, becomes predominant. In the first part it was plain that the professor did not wish to live in his new house, and did not wish to enter into the sere phase of his life correlative with it. At the beginning of the third part it becomes plain that he cannot indefinitely continue to make the old attic study the theatre of his life, that he cannot go on prolonging, or attempting to prolong his prime, the phase of his life correlative with that. The personality of his mature years—the personality that had expressed itself powerfully and in the main happily in his teaching, his scholarship, his love for his wife, his domesticity—is now quickly receding, and nothing new is flowing in. What begins to dominate St. Peter is something akin to the Cliff Dwellers, something primitive which had ruled him long ago when he was a boy on a pioneer farm in the rough Solomon valley in northwestern Kansas. To this primitive being not many things were real; . . . what counted was nature, and nature seen as a web of life, and finally of death.

The professor remembers an old poem he has read, Longfellow's translation of the Anglo-Saxon *Grave*. He doesn't recall it quite accurately (that is, Miss Cather didn't), but this is what is given in the novel:

> For thee a house was built
> Ere thou wast born;

> For thee a mould was made
> Ere thou of woman camest.

And Brown concluded:

> All that had seemed a hanging back from the future—the clinging
> to the old attic study, the absorption in Tom Outland and the civili-
> zation of the Cliff Dwellers, the revival of interest in the occupations
> of his childhood and its pleasures—was something very unlike what
> it had seemed. It was profound, unconscious preparation for death,
> for the last house of the professor.

This seems to me quite admirable literary criticism. The critic
has seen the unity of the book created by the central symbol;
he has penetrated to the professor's state of mind and grasped
that his interest in the occupations of childhood is a stepping
backward—or forward—to old age and death. But the story, as
told by Cather, in reality leaves the critic helpless in one respect: There is no way to explain why the professor should at
this moment of his middle years lose his will to live. We are
given no clue. Cather records merely the professor's melancholy.

I I I

And now let us examine this ingeniously constructed novel.
I have always suspected that Virginia Woolf was influenced by
its structure in writing *To the Lighthouse,* a novel with a similar
tripartite story, set in different moments of time, in which
houses (including the lighthouse) also provide the organizing
symbol. Let us look at Cather's novel, first through the understanding of symbolic statement offered us by Sigmund Freud in
his book on dreams, before the development of ego psychology,
and by the American psychiatrist Harry Stack Sullivan, whose
theories place emphasis on personal relations.

The striking element in the story is the professor's strange
attachment to his attic room, high up, old, and cramped, but
safely distant from the family life in the house below. Now,

people do form attachments to rooms and to houses, but the professor's attachment here verges upon the eccentric. He clearly thinks of his attic as a place of—and Cather's words express it—"insulation from the engaging drama of domestic life . . . only a vague sense, generally pleasant, of what went on below came up the narrow stairway." And later he thinks that "on that perilous journey down through the human house, he might lose his mood, his enthusiasm, even his temper."

This is much more than a professor seeking a quiet corner for his working hours. The room is "insulation." The professor withdraws from his family and at the same time makes demands on it, for care, food, attention. There is decidedly something infantile here, the security a baby feels in its possession of the mother and the breast for which it need make no return. In this attic room, tiny and snug as a womb, cradled in a warm and alive household but safe from any direct contact with the world outside, Professor St. Peter can feel taken care of and as undisturbed as an embryo.

The room, furthermore, is used by one other person—the motherly sewing woman, Augusta. Adjuncts to this mother figure are the two dressmaker's dummies. Seen as part of the sewing woman, the mother figure, these two dummies express opposite experiences of the mother: one is described as matronly, of a bulk suggesting warm flesh and reassuring physical possession; the other is of sophisticated line, suggesting spirit and sexual awareness and interest. So the professor has in his secluded place the beloved mother, who cares for and protects him but is also of some sexual interest to him. He wants his mother to be both a mother and an erotic stimulus, and above all he wants to possess her exclusively.

Willa Cather now weaves a second story, but it is in reality a repetition of the same theme. Her hero, again a man, yearns for a high mesa, a sun-beaten plateau, and when he conquers it he finds a cave city. Caves are often feminine sexual symbols.

These caves are for him inviolate and untouched, like a seem-ingly virginal mother preserved from others, a mother of long ago, of the infant years, who belonged only to the child greedy at her breast. There is also beautiful pottery. Pottery is again often a feminine symbol. One has only to recall some of Picasso's paintings, and how often he transforms pottery into women.

The hero cherishes these artifacts and comes to regret that he has a male companion with whom he must share them. The disinclination to share might be seen as sibling jealousy for the mother, or the kind of rivalry a boy, in his Oedipal phase, has for the father, who possesses the mother in the sexual way the boy aspires to have her. The hero is disillusioned first when his mother country, symbolized by Washington, is not interested in his discoveries and, in effect, rejects him, and then when his male friend puts the pottery to some practical use: so that we might say the boy is disillusioned when he first learns that in reality his mother is not a virgin and that his father is the cause of her having been thus despoiled. The hero angrily drives the male friend, father or sibling, away and spends a period among the caves—that is, with his mother—as blissful as a babe. He preserves a record of his narcissistic-infantile paradise, the para-dise of life in the womb, of possessing the mother physically, in a notebook which he carefully secretes in the tower. Like the professor's attic room, the tower is still higher and more se-cluded than the dwellings, where the mother can be preserved, if not in actuality (the pottery), at least in the diary describing his intimate life with her (Outland's detailed account of the caves and their contents as he first found them). Life, its rude events and passage of time, its insistence on moving forward and routing the infant from the womb and from its mothering, also disrupts the hero's blissful eternity on his hidden mesa, in his caves, with his pottery. He has been disturbed. He seeks stubbornly at least to preserve the memory of days with his mother (the mesa, etc.), even as the professor cannot leave his cubbyhole study and would not want the dressmaker's dummies removed.

But life does move on, and in moving on it demands that we follow. The professor seeks a solution to this problem. The family which sustained him in the house below, while he took attic refuge, moves to the new house. If he follows he must accept a new room, a modern room, a room on a lower floor; he must take his place in the family on a different basis: his daughters are now married; they will have children. He must change and grow too, accept his new role as father-in-law and eventually as grandfather. He must, in other words, meet life in an adult way and recognize the demands which are being made on him to take a more active part in the lives of his grown-up children.

But the professor clings as long as he can to the old attic room, and with the life gone from the house beneath he is actually threatened with greater isolation than ever before. He has a choice: he can maintain this state of alienation from his family or he can emerge from his passive dependency and assume the active life expected of him. Appropriately enough, Willa Cather ends her story with the professor nearly suffocating in his room. To remain in the womb beyond one's time is indeed to suffocate. The tenacity of the professor's—and the writer's—determination to maintain this *status quo ante,* if only in fantasy, is illustrated in the ending of the story. It is the sewing woman— who, by the way, was sensibly eager to move to her new, bigger sewing room, to a new life, a new relationship, and cannot understand the professor's infantile attachment to the old room, the old relationship—it is the sewing woman who rescues the professor from suffocation. A mother figure has once more appeared upon the scene for the professor, who thus hangs on to his fixation even though it has brought him an immense threat. The book ends with the professor's problem unresolved, save in the sense that ultimately Mother Earth will enclose him in her womb.

IV

Psychoanalytic theory, by singling out certain primal elements in the picture, has illuminated our story and offered rather crude answers to some of our questions. The professor's death wish, undefined by the author, would appear to be due in part to lingering infantile needs, so strong that this successful adult teacher and writer, otherwise a figure of dignity and maturity, adheres to a pattern of behavior which belongs to his childhood. This he masks by rationalizations: a love for the past, a dislike of the present. But how are we to handle this material, so heavy with Freud's ideas about infantile sexuality—its insistence upon the attic as a womb symbol, its incestuous fantasies and Oedipal situation—a kind of "psychologizing" which can have meaning only to those who have worked with these concepts on a clinical level? And does this interpretation, fascinating and incredible though some of it is, tell us anything about the novel as novel? Or are we being offered a virtually meaningless diagram, highly speculative, of the unconscious fantasies of the professor, derived though it may be from the manifest material placed in the book by the author?

We all live in some form of house; and doubtless for some of us, on some unconscious level, caves and attics may be wombs and houses mothers, and the smooth curves of pottery may suggest the curves of women. But houses, and the rooms within them, are also universal facts and a universal reality. They testify to man's need for shelter and warmth. It is true that we are thrust out of the womb into the world and must inevitably acquire some shelter, by stages that start with the basket and the cradle and end in adult dwellings. And it is true that there are certain individuals who, instead of welcoming the shelters of this world, long for the unattainable state of the embryo where one was sheltered from everything. Wombs are for bliss-ful embryos; houses for growing children and adults. We juggle, so to speak, with the obvious when we invoke such universal symbols.

And what has become of the fine social criticism in the novel? In tracing such a diagram of the professor's neurosis, it is de-scribed as a compulsive desire to cling to the past for infantile or infantile-sexual reasons. Yet the social criticism is perhaps the best part of Willa Cather's novels. They record the protest of a gifted woman against the ever increasing conformities and clichés of American life. Her voice is never more appealing than when she shows how the capital of the pioneers was con-verted into the small change of standardization; and that while the original settlers wrested from the land the glory of America, the sons of the settlers became real-estate agents, parceling this land out and dealing in mortgages, or front-office men—like Louie Marsellus. The anguish of Tom Outland in Washington (whatever neurotic traits he may thereby reveal) is still the genuine anguish of someone who wants government to meet its responsibilities to the past, to history.

And what of criticism of the novel itself? To label the symbols within it in terms of the clinic, or to describe the "interper-sonal" relations between the professor and his family after the manner of Sullivan, gives us no help in assessing the book as work of art. We have merely used psychoanalytic ideas as in-struments of quasi-clinical diagnosis. Has Cather successfully carried out her general intention? What is the explanation of the professor's happiness in the past? Why does he experience malaise in the present—a present in which, even without neu-rotic motivation, the malaise of aging can certainly be held to be genuine?

I have given the point of view of one critic about this novel, and a Freudian approach to the material. It is my contention that the method used in this approach leads us to a "diagnosis" which can have little meaning unless it is translated into different terms. And I hold that this translation is possible only by calling upon the resources of criticism *and* biography. Let us therefore pursue our inquiry on this third level.

Psychoanalysis is concerned with what goes on in the unconscious and how this is reflected in conscious thoughts and actions. It deals always with a given consciousness. A dream cannot be truly interpreted, as we have seen, unless it is attached to the dreamer, although it may be a pretty story and have distinct meanings for someone to whom it is narrated. These meanings, however, are not necessarily those of the dreamer, who has put into the dream personal life-symbols. The personal symbols can be understood only after a close study of their recurrent use in the weaving of that person's dream structures. As with dreams, so with the work of art. Ernest Jones has significantly said:

> A work of art is too often regarded as a finished thing-in-itself, something almost independent of the creator's personality, as if little would be learned about the one or the other by connecting the two studies. Informed criticism, however, shows that a correlated study of the two sheds light in both directions, on the inner nature of the composition and on the creative impulse of its author. The two can be separated only at the expense of diminished appreciation, whereas to increase our knowledge of either automatically deepens our understanding of the other.

It is true that sometimes we have no alternative but to cling to our shreds of evidence and to speculate as best we can. But with a writer who lived earlier in our own century, we have abundant data relating to actual experience. We can attempt to determine how this experience—which she at best may have only glimpsed—was incorporated into the imaginative act.

V

Our data are derived from Brown's biography of Willa Cather and from the valuable memoir written by her friend of four decades, Edith Lewis. In these works we discover how intensely Willa Cather suffered as a little girl from an initial displacement. She was born in Virginia and lived in a large house. At ten she was taken west to the Divide, to a new house. Here she discovered also the sod houses of the early settlers, even as she was later to observe the cave houses of the Cliff Dwellers in the Southwest. We note that the professor in her novel was "dragged" to Kansas from the East when he was eight and that he "nearly died of it."

In Nebraska, Willa Cather found that nearly all the inhabitants were displaced from somewhere else, and some had been involved in a transatlantic displacement. Her later novels were to depict with deep emotion the meaning of displacement for the pioneers—from Europe and civilization to the rugged prairie. Willa Cather in her own way had shared in this experience; their anguish was hers. Then, in Red Cloud, Nebraska, where the adolescent girl began to discover the life of the frontier, there was a neighboring house in which lived a childless couple. In her own house there was the clash of temperaments and the rivalries of a large family of boys and girls; in their midst was a refined Southern-bred mother, a gentlewoman, somehow strangely aloof and exhausted by repeated pregnancies. And so this other house became a retreat; the cultivated Mrs. Wiener from France served as a kind of second mother to Willa Cather. She provided books and quiet surroundings; the future author could lie for hours on the parlor rug, reading and dreaming. A fairly circumstantial account of the two houses may be found in Cather's late story, "Old Mrs. Harris." From the small town Willa Cather went to Lincoln, Nebraska, to attend the university, and here she discovered still another house. It was filled with robust young men, over whom there presided an Old World mother. Willa Cather had again found a home, this time as an escape from the dreariness of a furnished room. The house was that of the Westermann family, and the late William Lynn Westermann of Columbia University, a distinguished Egyptologist, testified to the accuracy of Cather's picture of life in his early home as portrayed in her novel *One of Ours.*

In 1895 Willa Cather went to Pittsburgh and worked on a newspaper. She lived in a series of depressing boardinghouses. The way in which she escaped from these into the world of the theater and music is reflected in her ever-popular short story, "Paul's Case." After five years of drab existence she met a young woman who changed the course of her life. This was Isabelle McClung, the daughter of a prominent and wealthy Pittsburgh judge, a strikingly handsome woman interested in the arts. So attached did she become to Willa Cather, the radiance of her personality, and the promise of her art, that she invited her to come and live in the McClung family mansion. The gesture might be described as protective and motherly or sisterly, and Isabelle became, indeed, during these years, a patron of Willa Cather's art. Her house was many times more elegant and spacious than the Wiener house or the house of the Westermanns. Here Cather put together her first book of verse, began to publish short stories, and finally her first volume of tales. She was given a quiet room to work in at the rear of the McClung mansion. It had been a sewing room. Still standing in it were some dressmaker's dummies.

Willa Cather remained deeply attached to this house, and to her friend. The house represented security and peace. From it she was able to face the world and build her career. Even after she had moved to New York and taken up a new abode in Greenwich Village—thus establishing her own home—and was the successful managing editor of *McClure's Magazine,* she would return to Pittsburgh for periodic visits with Isabelle McClung and uninterrupted work in her favorite room. Whether the relationship was actively or latently lesbian may not be particularly relevant here. It is clear that a deep affection and love existed between the two.

In the midst of the First World War there came a break. It followed Isabelle McClung's decision to marry a violinist she had known for some years, Jan Hambourg, who with his father and brother had a school of music in Toronto. This happened in 1917 when the writer was in her late forties. Isabelle too was no longer young. Thus a significant change was introduced into the fixed pattern of the years. And it is from this moment that the biographer can date a change in Willa Cather's works. They reflect an increasing tension and deep uneasiness. She had lost a beloved friend, an intimate companion—and who can now measure the passion and grief that came to her in middle life with this sense of loss? Her novel *One of Ours*, written in the early twenties, is an anxious book; on the surface the anxiety is related to the disillusion that followed the war and to a strong sense of betrayal by the new generation in Nebraska, which was watering down the achievements of the pioneers. For all its defects it won a Pulitzer Prize. The title of the next novel clearly conveys the state of mind of the author: it is *A Lost Lady* —and it tells of a woman who clings to a vanished past in a changing world. After this, Cather wrote *The Professor's House.*

But just before she set to work on this novel, before she had even had the idea for it, she had gone to France to visit Isabelle and Jan Hambourg. Isabelle, in her French home at Ville-D'Avray, had set aside a study for her friend. The new house would incorporate in it this essential feature of the Pittsburgh mansion. Edith Lewis testifies, "The Hambourgs had hoped that she would make Ville-D'Avray her permanent home. But although the little study was charming, and all the surroundings were attractive, and the Hambourgs themselves devoted and solicitous, she found herself unable to work at Ville-D'Avray. She felt indeed that she would never be able to work there."

Why? Miss Lewis does not tell us. But she does tell us what we have already surmised: that there are some traits of Jan Hambourg in the character of Louie Marsellus. Hambourg was a cultivated musician, widely read in French literature, and apparently as good a conversationalist as Marsellus. Willa Cather had dedicated *A Lost Lady,* one of her most popular books, to him and by this act welcomed him to the circle of her intimates. The curious thing is that she dedicated *The Professor's House* to him as well. As we compare the somewhat glib and pretentious Louie with the real-life musician, we recover similarities or exaggerations at so many points that we are prompted to conjecture whether the novelist did not find it necessary to write this flattering dedication—"For Jan, because he likes narrative"—to overcome her guilt over the unflattering portrait she had painted, or to disguise what she had done. Behind the ambiguous compliment to a man who had taken her loved one from her, we may read a considerable infusion—and confusion—of emotion: jealousy, guilt, anguish, and downright hatred. A dedication is, by its nature, so friendly an act that it is perhaps difficult to think of it as masking an animus. But two dedications plead too much: and in this instance they are not symptoms of Cather's affection for Jan. The dedications, we may guess, are really a further salute to Isabelle McClung, to whom Willa Cather had dedicated an earlier book. In later revisions, the novelist removed the Hambourg dedication from *A Lost Lady*. However much she found Jan Hambourg a civilized and cultured being, she would have preferred to have him as her friend rather than as the consort and husband of Isabelle-Rosamond.

We can now see what profound adult emotion contributed to *The Professor's House*. Willa Cather's early uprootings have only a partial meaning in explaining her attachment to a fixed abode; her mother's aloofness and her search for substitute homes readily fit into the emotional backgrounds of the novel. The Pittsburgh house with its sewing room has been transposed into the professor's frame house on the prairie. Like the professor of her fiction, Cather won a prize during her middle years; like him she achieved considerable success. The house at Ville-D'Avray becomes the new house built by the professor's family. It is no substitute for the old one, and the professor can no more share it with the newcomer to his family than Willa Cather could share the French home with both Isabelle and Jan. Isabelle was no longer a beloved figure exclusively possessed by her; she must be shared as Willa had to share her mother with her brothers, as the professor must share his daughter with Louie, and as Tom Outland shares his caves and pottery with Roddy—who betrays him.

Here we touch the heart of our psychological analysis. We can see what brought on the depression of Willa Cather's middle years in the very midst of her success, and we can understand why she wrote that "the world broke in two in 1922 or thereabouts," for we know that to her search for inner security, going back to childhood, was added the deeper sense—hardly irrational from an adult point of view—that she had been cast off, that her beloved had turned from her to another. The reality was that Isabelle had moved forward in life and had married. Willa Cather had been unable to move forward; for her there had been a "divorce," and this represented a regression. In her novel, Cather is so identified with her professor that she is unable to supply a "rejection motif" for his despair. All she could say was that the world was out of joint for him—as it was for her. This depression is described in the first part, in the account of the professor who doesn't want to keep pace with his family, although his work has been crowned with success. The professor grieves not for a lost love; he is simply alienated.

Such is the nature of our inner fantasies that they persist in seeking expression. Emotion only partly expressed continues to "want out." In the first part of the novel which emerged from these fantasies, the professor is at an impasse.

Willa Cather's fancy takes a second try—she opens a window on a further landscape, as in a Dutch painting, and here she is able to release her deepest feelings, those which tell the fuller truth. The Tom Outland story is linked to Isabelle in a curious way. It would seem that in Willa Cather's consciousness the Pittsburgh house, standing on high ground, could be identified with the mesa and the tower. For, some years earlier, when she

published *The Song of the Lark,* her first novel to draw upon
the Southwest, she dedicated it to Isabelle McClung with the
following verses:

> On uplands,
> At morning,
> The world was young, the winds were free;
> A garden fair
> In that blue desert air,
> Its guest invited me to be.

Uplands had become Outland. The world in the "blue desert
air" of the mesa is a re-creation of the feeling of freedom Willa
Cather had experienced in her life with Isabelle, patron of the
arts, and in the sewing-room sanctuary of the Pittsburgh mansion. But Tom Outland is betrayed twice: the maternal-paternal
government rejects him; and when he returns home he finds
that Roddy, his boon companion, his "loyal" buddy has denuded
his cliff sanctuary of all that was precious to him. The fantasy of
rejection and loss is thus incorporated into the novel.

The Tom Outland story is complete. That of the professor is
not. By merging the insights gained from psychology with the
biographical data that give us clues to the workings of the author's imagination, we are enabled to render a critical evalua-
tion: we can see the crack in the façade of *The Professor's House.*
The professor lives for us as a man who has given up his good
fight and takes the world as preparation for the grave. Suddenly
we recall his name: Professor St. Peter. He has retreated into a
vale of misanthropy and despair. He has everything to live for;
and for reasons unexplained and unresolved he does not want
to live. The materialism of an age, the marrying off of one's
children to persons we may like or dislike, the process of growing old—these are not sufficient explanation for a depression as
deep and as consuming as the professor's. The world is never
all that we would want it to be, and lives are lived in a constant
process of change and of loves lost and won. The novel is incom-

plete because in the original fantasy Cather could not admit to
herself that she felt deceived and cast aside; and we may conjecture that it was difficult for her to accept the triangular relationship Isabelle had in mind when she prepared a study for the
writer in her French home. Moreover, Cather was in no position to state openly her feeling that Jan Hambourg was a
usurper who had taken her place in the life of her dearest
friend. She expressed it by creating the unpleasant Louie Marsellus and then glossed the portrait with an implicit semblance
of affection in the dedications. If we wanted to pursue our
psychological speculation, we might find that, to a woman as
driving and masculine and as bold as Cather, the loss of Isabelle
McClung brought to the surface older defeats and awakened
hurts received in her younger days. The story of the professor,
with which she began the novel, was too close to herself. By
creating a second story she obtained the necessary distance.
This does not alter the strangely childish moments in Tom Outland's behavior, suggested in the more clinical psychological
interpretation. In times of trauma there are regressions. Cather
had to work her way out of her broken world. Writing *The
Professor's House* was one way of doing this; and the substance
of the story suggests to us that the break with Isabelle had
sickened her almost to death—certainly to a wish for death.

Willa Cather's later work can be read in the light of certain
hesitations and misgivings within her strong stance in the
world: her pride as an artist and as a "self-made" individual. Her
choice of the rock as a symbol of endurance and survival in her
novel *Shadows on the Rock,* her rigidity in the face of her
nation's growth and change, her gradual return in her writings
to childhood situations: these spring from the same overpowering isolation, the same death wish—yet struggle to live—acted
out in the suffocating attic by the professor. I could find other
episodes in her life to amplify what I have said. Not least is the
one in which she had to uproot herself from her Bank Street
apartment in Greenwich Village because a subway was being

run through the area. She took refuge for a few days in a lower Fifth Avenue hotel and remained there for years. Whatever rationalizations might be offered, it was clearly difficult for her to move, and a sheltering hotel, ministering to her needs, seems to have made her reluctant to search out an apartment and reestablish a home. I am told that Cather intensely disliked being in the hotel—all the more reason, we might suppose, for her to have left it sooner than she did. The world did break in two for her. One part of it moved on; she remained stranded in the other. And *The Professor's House,* in its very structure, contained this break. It is an unsymmetrical and unrealized novel because Willa Cather could not bring the two parts of her broken world together again.

And yet this novel, however much we may fault it, reveals a strong creative imagination. Its defects illustrate the imagination's gropings to fuller expression. We know that in dream we often tell ourselves a story, and as our unconscious continues to be teased by the unresolved stuff of life, we redream the dream and tell ourselves a totally different story—which, however, on examination proves to be the same story artfully disguised and metamorphosed. Tom Outland enabled the novelist to get outside herself. His sufferings could be made explicit; she was hiding from her own. And his retreat into his past, his reliving the experience high in the mountains where he had found his treasure—and a cave of his own—becomes an act of catharsis. In this way Cather's imagination, in taking the deeper plunge, carried out a self-rescue. She was able to say, through Outland, "I was robbed, robbed, robbed! My friend betrayed me! I have suffered a terrible loss. I must mourn for it and live through it and I wish I were dead." This inner statement which I extrapolate from the evidence completes the story of Tom Outland and of his creator but at the same time leaves the story of the professor incomplete.

In engaging in this kind of creative process, that of endless making and finding, the artist not only discovers intensities and relief from stress but invents new forms out of the beauties of the imaginative life. The stuff of sleep and dreams is far from inchoate and chaotic. Somewhere within we not only choose precise symbols, we find an organic structure for our parable— for ourselves.

THE CRITIC

AS WOUND-DRESSER

They might have peopled a play by Chekhov or a Russian novel —young Edmund Wilson, Jr., an only child, reaching out to a brilliant, moody, melancholy father, often "in eclipse in some sanatorium for what were then called 'neurasthenics,'" and to a deaf and strong-willed mother. They lived in a self-contained world like the Bolkonskys or the Karenins, in relative affluence but without the aristocratic trappings, an assortment of aunts and uncles and cousins who came and went in their particular exclusive corner of New Jersey, soon overrun by suburbs. The ancestry had been Presbyterian; the Calvinism lingered. There were distinctions of caste and a sense, however powerless, of being "gentry" in a private universe. Edmund Wilson painted them with candor and vividness in *A Prelude* (1967): the gentility of the upper middle class, marriages within closed circles ("because there was no one else"), tensions, terrors, explosions. Wilson would write, "I had known almost no one but the members of my own family." This was before he went off to prep school. And when he emerged from college, he was "unable to get on with ordinary people." Riding a bicycle at thirteen or fourteen, he said to himself suddenly, "I'll eventually have friends with whom I'll have something in common."

He had many friends and the admiration of the world when he died in 1972 at seventy-seven, but there was to the end something aloof and shut in, as if he were still reaching out from behind obsolete invisible barriers, using the full force of his intellect to establish a truce with mankind. Between the lines of his remembrances one can see the walled-in childhood, a life of solitary discoveries, of self-help and early resource, in a situation that, in a less robust and tenacious child, might have led to collapse. It led instead to a kind of forcing of observation and expression. Perhaps Edmund Wilson's tenacity and his drive to strength came from the assertion of a young spirit unwilling to capitulate as his father recurrently did.

He learned early how to be independent in his confining environment. His father, Edmund Wilson, Sr., was a lawyer and, in middle life, attorney general of the state of New Jersey, first under a Republican and then under the Democrat Woodrow Wilson (no relation). The younger Edmund always had mixed memories of Red Bank, New Jersey, where he was born May 8, 1895. The atmosphere of his home, when he reached the age of recognition, was "oppressive." His father's relapses into apathy, his mother's deafness, which had come early, were the central facts; but Edmund Wilson told himself later that even if his mother had been able to hear, he doubted whether they would have had much to say to one another. He remembered in his teens making methodical notes on the train home from school—"notes of topics about which I could communicate to her." On the day she took him to the Hill School, in Pottstown, Pennsylvania (*aetat* thirteen), she called him "Bunny" in front of the boys. The vigorous, slim, good-looking youth found himself reduced then and there to "Bunny"—and for a lifetime. He fought the jeering boys; then he accepted the reality and ultimately signed himself Bunny to his intimates. His being Edmund Jr. bothered him less, perhaps because his father was so often absent from the family scene.

He was not so much an alienated child as one in whom there had been certain rechannelings of emotion, a development of strong defenses; such was the effect upon the male child, mentally alert and possessing acute senses, trained in coping with strange obstacles. Wilson's own way of expressing this (in his major essay on Dickens) was that "lasting depressions and terrors may be caused by such cuttings-short of the natural development of childhood." Whole areas of being could be clamped off, large energies had to find new outlets. In some such way, extraordinary lives compose themselves out of extraordinary circumstances. Edmund Wilson's chapters on "family" in *A Prelude,* his earlier sketch of his father, his tributes to his old masters Rolfe and Gauss, provide hints of his quest for solutions. Books, language, the world of imaginative reconstruction, established some kind of communion with the remote "outside." He seems to have developed a particular meticulosity of mind, cultivated doubtless against chaos, and yet somehow escaping the inevitable rigidities that might have frozen Wilson and made him a functionary, or a specialist, or a lawyer like his father. Instead, he pursued his obsessions and compulsions in literature, a wide quest for many languages, esoteric meanings, dictionaries—an almost Balzacian catholicity, but with much greater exactitude, if less talent, than Balzac. Later he would pursue sex in the same way. He had so little knowledge of women and of how a man should relate to them (as readers of *A Prelude* will remember) that he went to consult a doctor at Princeton when he had a spontaneous emission while reading a book. The dammed-up sexual drive was but one of many dammed-up drives, and Wilson learned the secret of "conversion"—into a fascination with the macabre, for example, or sleight of hand. He was always interested in monsters and became a very good magician and puppeteer. He tells us occasional dreams. They suggest some of the benign and morbid traits acquired in dealing with frustration. A dream of sleeping with his mother may have been "Oedipal," as Wilson mused, but we might interpose that it was one way for a little boy to attempt, at least in sleep, to cross the barrier that stood between him and his sphinx-like female parent. He dreamed also (an early nightmare) that his father was sharpening a knife in the kitchen to kill the entire family. This he also thought was "Oedi-pal." Yet we might equally see Wilson, in dream displacement, putting his father into the role he himself would have liked to have. There must have been times when a little boy so circum-stanced would have nourished, in his deeper fantasies, the childish wish to wipe out his difficult parents—and with the flourish of a carving knife or cutlass.

The evidence of the early years clearly leads to the conclusion that Edmund Wilson reached in his old age: that his boyish self had been starved of human intercourse, except through ave-nues of the world's wonder, the comfort of storybooks and the "reality" of people in those books. Perhaps his insatiable curios-ity, which remained to the end and had in it a buoyant youthful-ness, stemmed from this childhood filled with unanswered rid-dles, the *Why?* the *What does it mean?* of a juvenile facing an impassive sphinx. In the family annals we discover certain friendly aunts who helped more than they perhaps knew: Aunt Laura Kimball, "I learned a good deal about books from her"; Cousin Helen Stillwell, who drew pictures of dragons and imag-inary monsters, nourishing the macabre and a latent interest in sadism. She also sang English music-hall songs, read him Mrs. Gamp and Uncle Remus, played by ear the entire score of a musical comedy she had just seen. This amazed and delighted him. Another cousin, fifteen months older, provided male com-panionship. "Sandy" gave Edmund Havelock Ellis, and thus at least printed knowledge of sex. Exuberant, lively (they were much together during an early trip abroad), Sandy turned out to have *dementia praecox,* as schizophrenia was then described: and when Wilson returned from the war he found his favorite cousin locked away—for life. His regular visits to Sandy re-ported in the notebooks show both compassion and malaise. There is a living recall of the way his father was so often locked away from him; perhaps Wilson had a latent fear that he too might have in him the strain of mental illness that haunted the family.

I

To understand Edmund Wilson's particular talents as writer and critic we must look closely at his father. *A Piece of My Mind* (1956) ends with an essay called "The Author at Sixty." Yet the essay is not about the author; it is about his father, who died at sixty-one. This suggests an ambivalent identification. The account of his father shows that the senior Wilson was a highly gifted freewheeling lawyer, always able to keep his family in comparative affluence. He practiced law with resource and skill and had great successes; he lost only one case and was careful thereafter to take cases he was sure of winning. His method of handling a jury, as described by his son, could be applied to the way in which the son composed one of his own literary essays. The father attacked the jury "with a mixture of learning, logic, dramatic imagination and eloquence which he knew would prove irresistible. He would cause them to live through the events of the crime or the supposed crime, he would take them through the steps of the transaction, whatever this was, and he would lodge in their heads a picture that it was difficult for the opposing attorney to expel." Wilson, later describing the effect that reading Taine had on him, paid the same kind of tribute. Taine "created the creators [in his history of English literature] as characters in a larger drama of cultural and social history, and writing about literature, for me, has always meant narrative and drama." Behind Taine and Michelet, there was the figure of his father and his courtroom dramas. And the son was impressed "by the intense concentration" that the feats of persuasion cost his father. "They could not be allowed to fail"—on the occasions when he prepared a brief at home.

A legal personality so erratic, compulsive, and uncompromising could find no permanent berth. He was invited to join large New York legal firms but declined. He took cases for corporations and won them; he also fought the corporations; he hated the railroads and sought litigation with them at the drop of a hat: a package of books and sweets shipped to his son at school was damaged in transit; the father sued the railroad and won the price of the damaged goods. The father was deeply versed in the law—and Wilson's cultivation of "literary arcana" may have stemmed from Edmund Sr.'s way of digging into legal obscurities. Challenged by Governor Woodrow Wilson to get rid of the Atlantic City bosses, Edmund Sr. (then attorney general) told himself he could never get a convicting jury in that politics-ridden city. So he found an old law that permitted importation of jurors when a change of venue was impossible— and sent the Atlantic City politicos and many of their henchmen to jail. It was a great success. But the father shook his head. He knew that there would be new political bosses and a new system of patronage as soon as the storm blew over. He had demonstrated, however, what research and resourcefulness could do. When Woodrow Wilson became President he offered the senior Wilson a seat on the Supreme Court as soon as one should fall vacant. The father said it might be "interesting." No vacancy occurred, however, and he never achieved this highest office. In spite of success, he had great periods of apathy. He cared nothing for atmosphere. He seems to have modeled himself a little on the ruggedness of Abraham Lincoln, another moody man of law. The son remembered his father's dreary office, always the same one, an uncomfortable room over a liquor dealer's store, "rather pleasantly permeated by a casky vinous smell." Even this was lost on the father. He never drank.

In his professionalism and commitment, the father set an example the son would always follow. He was without snobbery or racial bias, but he showed always the innate pride and aristocratic stance of a member of the gentry. His son said "he dealt with people strictly on their merits" yet always "to some extent *de haut en bas.*" Wilson too looked at life and art—and his fellow writers—from a higher plane. It was a part of his individualism. He never joined writers' organizations; he refused honors—save those that carried money awards. He worked most of his life like his father, distinctly alone and with great concentration and thoroughness when he became genuinely involved in a subject. The senior Edmund's private methods of inquiry were also those of his junior. The lawyer liked to travel, and "from the moment he arrived in a city he began asking people questions, beginning with the driver of his cab." Those who knew Edmund Wilson remember how relentlessly he could cross-examine in private talk; how on entering a room he instantly came to the point, either delivering himself of recondite material he had discovered or seeking the total satisfaction —it could never be satisfied—of his curiosity. The son's intellectual process, his ability to sort, organize, and use literary evidence, his sense of drama, had its origins in the example of this gifted and unhappy parent; and perhaps the senior Edmund's greatest gift to his son was the gift of intellectual sympathy. "I was always surprised," Wilson wrote in his portrait of his father, "by the sympathy, or rather perhaps by the judicial detachment, with which, in important decisions, he treated my point of view." No better description could be given of Edmund Wilson's finest writings.

This then was perhaps the deepest emotional experience in Wilson's early life, and one that it must have been difficult for him to recognize and face: to have so attractive and magnetic a father, and yet to be shut away from him, was a painful mixture of possession and loss of which Edmund Wilson's later card tricks and sleight of hand may have been a caricatured expression. "Now you see it and now you don't." Young Edmund loved his father, and yet there could be no expression of that love. The photographs in *A Prelude* of the senior Wilson show a handsome man with fine mustaches, distinctly a "personality," and yet something veiled and mysterious, with depths of depression, in his eyes. His father and his cousin Sandy represented an element of "loss" in Edmund's experience, of ache and yearning, a feeling for masculine strength and tenacity that contrasted with the motherly presence that was not in the least "motherly." Mrs. Wilson, the former Helen Mather Kimball, was a woman of limited intelligence, prosaic, self-confident, and self-assured. One who knew her in her later years said "her criterion of success was making money and the status that money gave—which both her husband and son despised." She would much sooner have had her son be an athlete; even when a very old lady she continued to attend the Princeton football games. She never read Edmund's writings. Her feelings were directed into the simplicities of her gardens, and she enjoyed the brightness and variety of the flowers and no doubt the smell of the tractable earth. Her soundless world could touch the soundlessness of bulbs and flower patterns, and she could show love and sympathy and a kind of spontaneous creativity in her feeling for the plants. In all his adult years Edmund kept only one picture of his mother, taken in a group of relatives when she was young. But he always kept around him pictures of his mother's gardens at Talcottville and Red Bank.

She provided, in her fixedness, a kind of stability that Edmund's early-learned rage for order could not find in the paternal self-abandonment. The sphinx was frustrating; she didn't even ask riddles. She was obdurate, pleasure-loving, often openly hostile to her ailing husband. Her deafness may have been partly psychological. She had taken Edmund Sr. to see a great specialist in England; the specialist pronounced him "mad" and the wife during the voyage home suddenly became totally deaf. As it turned out, her husband was far from mad; he simply dropped into despondency for long periods. But the mother had walled herself in, and she was impregnable. She seemed masculine in areas in which the father tended to be feminine. Edmund Sr. vowed, when his son was naughty, that he would whip him within an inch of his life—but he never did. Mrs. Wilson spanked effectively, using a metal hairbrush, and complained that the proceeding dented the metal. The image of a woman, of women, modified for Edmund by less punitive and impregnable aunts and cousins, nevertheless remained;

they could inspire fear. It is perhaps no accident that in *I Thought of Daisy* and "The Princess with the Golden Hair" the contrasting women define Edmund's problems in wooing and courtship. Women could be elusive—as Edna St. Vincent Millay was, brilliant, intellectual, independent in love—and therefore unattainable; or they could be down-to-earth creatures, with whom one went to Coney Island and played games. The "democratic earthy woman" pitted against the woman of mystery, the socially attractive aloof princess with the golden hair, an idealized version of Wilson's mother. She is a dream, not flesh, when he finally is able to bed with her. But the little dance-hall girl who becomes the narrator's mistress and tells her stories of low life is a lively human partner. (The record of this affair fills many pages of his journal.) Perhaps Wilson was most at his ease in earlier years with waitresses, dance-hall girls, and hookers. He could relate to them in a fundamental physical way; they were below his social level and therefore outside his early experience. Men tended to be easier and more accessible; and Edmund Wilson's school world was then wholly a man's world.

With so much ambiguous masculinity in his childhood—that is, a weak father and a strong mother—it was inevitable that this should create a certain amount of sexual confusion in Wilson's makeup. We might conjecture that his unconscious identification and preference was male. But his conscious anxiety, and fear, was that he would not be male enough; and one way to prove his masculinity was to woo and chase women, which he did with a goodly amount of success. This was reassuring. But his successes in bed did not diminish his fundamental distaste for women even though he sought them into old age—and could be very tender and caressing with them. "Womanizing" protected Wilson from being homosexual—and he was invariably contemptuous of gays. His own lovemaking, as he describes it in his journals, tended to be artificial and mechanical, as if he were standing in a corner of the room, a voyeur of himself in bed.

The words Wilson uses about his mother can be applied to the less attractive side of himself. She was "brusque and gruff." She was also, and these became benign traits in Wilson, "positive, self-confident, determined." By the time the boy was thirteen he had achieved discipline and self-assurance; he had conformed and been imaginative enough to find his own solutions and escapes within that conformity. Edmund Wilson realized, when he grew older, that there had been little "in the way of human relations" that could afford his mother happiness. Yet his mother's harsh stability was more acceptable to an outgoing and life-seeking boy than his father's self-defeat. This must have fortified Edmund's will to persevere and to conquer.

I I

Enlargement of his world and escape came at thirteen—his prep school and later Princeton flowed together as a continuous experience. The "Bunny" Wilson who was escorted to the Hill School in 1908 by his mother was singularly prepared—as few boys are—for the rougher discipline of school away from home. He brought to this Presbyterian institution his orderly mind and the carapace derived from his mother. The school itself was run (as he later said) with all the efficiency of an industry or a corporation. It was well organized, well staffed, well equipped. It made the boys aware of duties and responsibilities. It stimulated individuality (strange as this may seem to modern American eyes) by its refusal to be permissive. "Our whole life was regulated by bells"—but it *was* regulated. The students were drilled, and they were well drilled. Every moment was put to use for work or play. As a result, Hill students were rarely turned down by the Ivy League colleges. In the remorseless paternalism of the school, Edmund at first found "the suffocating repressive effect of the Pennsylvania mill town." But a later essay and later memories show an awareness that Hill had given him solid foundations on which to build his life and diminished the wear-and-tear of life in his family. He disliked intensely the first weeks. He was not accustomed to being with crowds of boys and to rushing about on the double. How little "suffocating" the school ultimately was may be found in Wilson's implication that "home" was even more suffocating. He hated going home for holidays. His precocious tales and verses were published when he was a freshman in the Hill School *Record.* He was a serious yet fun-loving boy, in a puritanical straitjacket. There was, moreover, a master of Greek named Alfred Rolfe who gave him a standard, a focus, a sense of personality; Wilson has described him in a finely written essay (in *The Triple Thinkers*) with the same affection he later bestowed on Christian Gauss of Princeton. Rolfe had the maternal assurance and firmness; Gauss was a highly literary but healthy version of the paternal brilliance. At Hill, Rolfe, tall, well dressed, with blond mustaches that hid his lips and masked expression, was merciless in his demands; his gentlemanly sarcasm was without ambiguities. He taught Homer and made the students "translate every word into an English not unworthy of the original." Wilson was forced to scan every line, to understand every form. Of Rolfe he said, "The first time that you heard him read aloud a passage of Homer in class you knew what Homer was as poetry." Later the master would take a personal interest in his gifted student, give him access to his library, share Wilson's admiration for Bernard Shaw. And if he imparted a soaring feeling about ancient Athens, he spoke for an American Athens as well—Rolfe came from New England and was Wilson's "only personal contact with the Concord of the great period, and I feel that if I had not known him, I should never really have known what it was, and what a high civilization it represented." Hill School and Rolfe—and Homer; but he studied also routine subjects and—at last—had friends of his own age to make up for the lonely years. In *A Prelude* he describes these friends in some detail; they made him aware of other families, other worlds, showed him that life was not necessarily composed of Wilsons, Kimballs, Knoxes. They offered also a further resource;

he paid visits during his summers, another way of prolonging his absences from Red Bank.

Wilson entered Princeton in 1912. The story of his four years at college has often been told in the lives of other members of the brilliant group of young men who graduated just before America's entry into the 1914–18 war. F. Scott Fitzgerald was "the first educated Catholic I had ever known," and John Peale Bishop, who became his close friend, was a handsome West Virginian, a Southern aristocrat who quoted Shelley and Swinburne when he appeared on the college scene. In Wilson's day it was the old Princeton, "between the pressures of narrow Presbyterianism and a rich man's suburbanism." The young adult could dedicate himself to his vocation—poetry, fiction, style, form, verbal elegance, a reaching out to grasp the universality of the human imagination. Behind this passion there was a profound interest in ideas, in essences. In art, and in life, Wilson was a product of an aristocratic ideal. The eighteenth century had lingered in his family, and Wilson seemed to be a distillation of it as he moved out into larger experience. His point of attachment, besides his devotion to the *Nassau Lit.,* was Christian Gauss, who illustrated "man's divine pride of reason and imagination." Gauss had "shuttered" eyes, but when he looked they were "clear green" and "as hard and as fine as gems." Gauss's preceptorials—his informal seminars for half a dozen students—seemed in the end like a conversation begun in youth which was continued into maturity and old age, for in later years Wilson never lost touch with him. He was "the most accessible of talkers." Wilson would himself be quite as accessible—when he was interested. He also knew how to listen. He admired Gauss's precision of thought, his unhurried pace, the way in which he opened for students the two great literatures of the Latin world. At the pinnacle was Dante, and in more immediate times he was a votary of Flaubert, exemplar of style achieved through tremendous will. One can discern how many Old World values were implanted by Gauss in the young man;

he gave him a feeling, never lost, for the interrelation of literatures; this led him to an extraordinary mastery of French and
Russian and to studies in Hebrew and Hungarian. If Rolfe was
a link to Concord, Gauss was a link to the 1890s, in his anecdote
of his coming upon Oscar Wilde (after the *débâcle*) sitting in
melancholy exile before piles of unpaid saucers. Gauss had
bought him drinks and talked with him. Rolfe opened the ancient world to Wilson; Gauss opened the modern—opened we
might say the way to Axel's Castle and the highway to the
Finland Station. Wilson would travel the first at the end of the
1920s, the second at the end of the 1930s.

The young Princeton student was still virginal, still afraid of
women, still rigidly puritanical. He did not drink—he would
never smoke—and he was shy and distant in the presence of
young females. Today he might be dubbed a square, yet this
would be mitigated by the effect of his lively hedonism; he
wrote a Princeton Triangle Show; he made friends with the
frivolous playboy students and was always ready for fun, and
even those who thought him priggish and arrogant admitted his
force, his clarity, and his integrity; he refused very early to
accept the commonplaces of college life and expressed forth-
right opposition to the war. When he graduated, he asked himself what he could do to be closer to the society of his time, to
descend from the clouds of intellect and literary expression. His
life had been spent in books, fancies, writing, learning. His
immediate solution might seem strange, given his hostility to
the war. He went to a military training camp at Plattsburgh,
which had been set up in preparedness for possible American
entry. He was looking, he said, for "something more active,
something closer to contemporary reality." He may have simply followed certain friends into this camp, as a way of spending
another summer away from home. If he sought information
about the Army, he found out soon enough. He was bored; he
was completely convinced "that I could never be an officer."
And at this juncture he made his rueful remark about not being

able to get on with "ordinary people." Plattsburgh did not help, for he found college and Hill friends and life went on as before, only it was under canvas. He read a great many books and was a miserable failure at the rifle range.

His second attempt to move out into the world was made that autumn of 1916. He got a job as a reporter on the New York *Evening Sun.* He did not, however, have the push required of fledglings, and his shyness prevented him from invading privacies to get a story. He preferred to write about the arts, and did some descriptive reporting. He lived comfortably on his $15 a week, with an occasional supplement from his father, in a shared apartment on West Eighth Street; by pooling resources, he and his two friends could afford a Chinese servant and they gave pleasant dinner parties. Scott Fitzgerald had a memory of Wilson at this time—glimpsing him from a taxi. He was wearing a tan raincoat over his brown getup. "I noted with a shock that he was carrying a light cane." He seemed to Fitzgerald "no longer the shy little scholar of Holder Court; he walked with confidence, wrapped in his thoughts and looking straight ahead, and it was obvious that his new background was entirely sufficient to him." Fitzgerald added, "That night in Bunny's apartment life was mellow and safe, a finer distillation of all that I had come to love at Princeton. The gentle playing of the oboe [by Wilson's friend Morris Belknap] mingled with the city noises from the street outside, which penetrated into the room with difficulty through a great barricade of books."

III

Such pleasures, still collegiate, did not endure. America entered the war in 1917, and Edmund Wilson experienced the first crisis of his ordered, organized, and outwardly placid life. His dedication was to civilization and to letters. "I did not know what to do," Wilson wrote. He reminded himself of Plattsburgh. How deep his anxiety was, we may judge by his saying (and he would repeat this more than a decade later when he had a nervous breakdown), "I usually know exactly what I want to do, and it has been only when I could not make up my mind that I have really gone to pieces." He did not go to pieces. In August 1917 he found a solution. In this he followed the dictates of his humanitarianism. He did not want to be drafted; he accordingly enlisted—and asked for duty in Base Hospital 36, which went into camp in September. He was on his way to France in November. Shortly after landing, he wrote to F. Scott Fitzgerald, "I feel that the door of the house of mirth, and in fact any normal human occupation, is shut till the war is over." And he added, "Remember me to Gauss; I think of him often in France. In spite of the fact that I had been here before, years ago, it was chiefly because of what he taught me that I felt so little a stranger when I arrived here a couple of weeks ago."

Edmund Wilson's fragmentary army notes and the two vivid Maupassant-like tales he reprints in *A Prelude* ("Death of a Soldier" and "Lieutenant Franklin") reflect the depths of his experience abroad. Hill and Princeton had been Arcadia—out of which Wilson stepped into regimentation and then horror. If he was not a stranger to France, he was a stranger to death. At first the student of Homer and Dante went through the usual indignities. "I feel a fool, a cipher," he wrote to a friend. By its very nature, the Army forced on Wilson a lower valuation of himself—lower, he mused, than any he had had in prep school. He surrendered the direction of his life: a painful thing for someone as independent as he was. He received orders blindly, when all his faculties had been trained to examine and to question. The only element he welcomed in his new life was the fellowship of a host of Americans from all parts of his land. It opened democratic vistas. The Army broke some of his shyness, helped him to feel a bit closer (though inwardly still aloof) to persons outside his narrow world. Death soon became routine, and he learned to live with it. This was an abrupt end of his youth, a sudden sealing off of an earlier existence during his twenty-third and twenty-fourth years. Stationed at Vittel, the

French watering place, where the luxury hotels had been turned into hospitals, he was first a stretcher-bearer. There were few ambulances then; the great age of the motor was yet to come and the stretchers met the wounded as they arrived by train in the thin gray dawn or in the midst of snowstorms. Wilson remembered the screams of mustard-gas victims, their swollen membranes and genitals; his passage on chemical warfare in *The Cold War and the Income Tax* derives its vigor in part from that terrible memory. He also would remember piling the bodies of dead American soldiers as if they were logs during the flu epidemic of 1918. He saw victims of shell shock and also of syphilis, and after a season in the charnel house appealed to his father to get him moved to another part of the Army. His endurance of horror apparently had given out. The elder Wilson did manage to pull strings in Washington, and just before the Armistice, Edmund was made a sergeant and assigned to military intelligence. In Chaumont briefly he translated documents from French into English; he then got a glimpse of Trier and the occupation (the scene of the story "Lieutenant Franklin") and finally shipped back to be demobilized. A passage in this short story suggests the essence of his feelings after his exposure to war—and its byways—during the previous twenty-four months:

> All about them outside this room, the desolation of Europe opened: the starved fatigue of the living, the abyss—one could not look into it!—of the dead; that world had been cursed for four years with the indictment of every natural instinct, the abortion of every kindly impulse. And tonight in this bright-lit room, where still the wine from Moselle grapes was yellow, where still Schubert music swam in sun, the fellowship of men was reviving.

His war notes list some two hundred books read between August 1917 and the time of the Armistice, little more than a year later. It is a formidable list. It includes the then unknown Joyce *(Dubliners),* the posthumous novels of Henry James, just published, Edith Wharton, Edna Millay, whom he had not yet met, Kipling, Rebecca West, Lytton Strachey, Renan, Rémy de Gourmont, Compton Mackenzie, Walt Whitman *(Leaves of Grass* and *Democratic Vistas)*, Zola, Chesterton. He returned to New York with the letdown that comes after a routinized life devoid of everything but simple army responsibilities. He said he could "never go back to the falseness and dullness of my prewar life again. I swore to myself that when the war was over I should stand outside society altogether."

We know that Edmund Wilson did not stand outside society "altogether." The words were spoken in disillusion, yet they reflect also that part of the writer which had always stood outside (and always would). To be sure, he had fled an enclosing family, an inhibiting clan; and his conscious energies were clearly directed toward as much "involvement" as possible. He was less aware, however, of the stratagems, defenses, subterfuges he had developed during many years to placate the family sphinx. They were by now his second nature, even when he was in the heart of the Village, drinking bad gin. His novel, written at the end of the twenties, is highly documentary. His protagonist thinks of "the terror, the terror mastered by the mind, and clutched and wrenched into beauty," and again "what a gulf between the self which experiences and the self which describes experience." By the time Edmund Wilson wrote *I Thought of Daisy,* he was aware that he carried within himself a subversive *persona,* a kind of chronic presence, or call it a wound, which at times negated his highest impulses, his naturally expansive and generous feelings. Familial attitudes and residual Puritanism imposed constraints, hesitations, guilts, and caused him to use guile and indirection. These in turn created subterranean distress. To reach for warm human companionship and love—a part of the natural order of things—required unremitting effort; in Wilson it was self-conscious, sometimes "bunny" shy, sometimes the activity of the satyr. The conflict is expressed in the title of his novel; he *thinks* of Daisy, the good down-to-earth girl with whom he can go to Coney Island, an idealized version of his down-to-earth mother. But he loves Rita, the poet, and "her terrific images of the commonplace." And he sees in her "the fierceness with which only a woman, when woman's narrow concentration has been displaced from its ordinary objects, can concern itself with art."

His character Hugo embodies this dichotomy of the spirit. Wilson describes himself when he writes, "Hugo was on close terms with no one. As soon as he had sampled a conversation and caught the social flavor of a household or a group, he would simply go straight away and bottle a specimen for his books." Hugo regards women "as the most dangerous representatives of those forces of conservatism and inertia against which his whole life was a protest." These thoughts, applied to various characters in the novel, show moods, doubts, conflicts, a tug-of-war *within*, which progressively led to depression and a brief period of panic breakdown. He came to see that he was wounded—a wounded would-be artist—who struggled to practice his craft *against* attitudes formed in his early experience. There is a reference in *Daisy* to Philoctetes, the Greek archer, whose suppurating wound prevented him from using his unique skill. In the pages devoted in these notebooks and in his novel to literature as "fraud" and "imposture," Wilson seems to be mulling over Freud's early theories of art and neurosis, the classic disabling which both intensifies creation and undermines it. We find here the seeds of the influential essay he would write ten years later entitled "The Wound and the Bow." Edmund Wilson's interests were scattered, and his initiation into methods of psychotherapy during his breakdown in the 1920s made him an early experimenter in literary psychology. He did not have the single-mindedness of his successful peers, F. Scott Fitzgerald or John Dos Passos. Wilson's struggle was between beauty and outrage, between the life he wanted to live and the life his primary self imposed on him. This guided his writings, dictated his alienation, made him look at people as if they were detached personages on a printed page. His greatest strength lay in his intellect: he had extraordinary critical acuity. But there was something coarse-fibered and blunt in him that deprived him of sufficient feeling for human beings to write about their lives as the great English novelists had done, or the Russians, whom he closely read.

If we look between the lines of his journals, which he kept for almost fifty years, we gain some measure of the stresses under which Wilson carried on his fertile work in the literary magazines. When the stresses became too great, he lapsed into depression; and then he always took refuge in drink. At one period during his breakdown he briefly became addicted to a drug, paraldehyde, but he had sufficient strength to overcome the addiction. He worked his way out of his 1920s depression by studying the subjective worlds of the moderns; and this was strange, for they were in reality not his sort. He was himself very concrete and Defoesque; he could never understand Kafka, but James Joyce and Gertrude Stein were literary puzzles to be solved; he could empathize with T. S. Eliot's melancholy, and he could grasp the symbolism in the work of these writers, so that his *Axel's Castle* was a ground-breaking book. But when he had completed it he had some doubts whether the job had been worth doing. In dealing with the struggle of modern writers to express themselves and their worlds, and in trying to be an artist himself, which he could not entirely be, he was led to Philoctetes and his wound, for he was intensely aware of his own difficult nature, his misanthropic alienated side, his indelicacy, his irascibility, his often overbearing and subjugating temper. With distinct areas of human feeling closed to him, he still could show moments of gentleness and tenderness, and could turn on this kind of feeling in his pursuit of women, or if he were with a congenial male colleague. His second wife, who loved him, could say to him, "You're a cold fishy leprous person, Bunny Wilson," and he recorded her words in his journal in a matter-of-fact way without comment.

IV

The myth of Philoctetes and his terrible wound, which prevents him from using his god-given skill, is rooted in the mental and moral history of man. Aeschylus and Euripides had treated it; but only incomplete accounts remain of their plays on this theme. The extant play of Sophocles served Edmund Wilson as the basis for his essay "Philoctetes: The Wound and the Bow" which he first published in *The New Republic* and then made the title essay of a volume containing "Seven Studies in Literature" published in 1941. As epigraph he used lines from a poem by James Joyce, one of the most wounded artists of our time: "I bleed by the black stream, For my torn bough." Philoctetes, with his enchanted bow, his poisoned arrows, his supreme archery, not only bleeds, but his wound (originally a snakebite) is an offense to the nostrils of society. He has been set aside like a leper; exile has forced upon him the life of an *isolato,* on an island, itself a symbol of disconnectedness from mainlands. Alone, he staunches the painful and foul-smelling injury which will not heal. However, the Greeks—the world—need his great bow. Troy cannot be conquered without it. The crafty Odysseus seeks ways to use—to exploit—the weapon. He plots to steal it from this unapproachable pariah.

Edmund Wilson tells the story with characteristic sobriety and leisure, in his most matter-of-fact way, so that he makes the myth speak with the simplicity and directness of a parable. The second part of the play allows us to trace the fuller drama of Wilson's mind as he rewove the drama of Sophocles into a modern commentary. In the ancient play, Odysseus sends Neoptolemus, the son of Achilles, a mere youth, to steal the magic bow of Philoctetes. The youth approaches the wounded man with understandable caution and diffidence; the stench is overpowering. And yet he is eager to accomplish his mission. What he discovers, with the quick empathy of his years, is a suffering human being—whom he has been asked to rob. Something holds him back. He endures the horror of the wound; he nurses Philoctetes through delirium; he sees the blister break and drain and experiences the agony of his prey. Out of his sympathy comes recognition: the guile of Odysseus has overlooked a fundamental fact. The unique bow needs its unique bowman. Neoptolemus cannot bring himself to cheat or to steal. He faces the wrath of the suffering man by confessing his proposed treachery. The better solution, he feels, is to help the archer instead of stealing the instrument of his craft. Wilson writes, "It is in the nature of the things of this world where the divine and the human fuse, that they cannot have the irresistible weapon without its loathsome owner, who upsets the processes of normal life by his curses and his cries, and who in any case refuses to work for men who have exiled him from their fellowship."

We must recognize the delicate question of "identification." It is not easy to identify with Philoctetes; he is a creature of pitiable suffering; he is ill, ostracized, turned in on himself. A spectator's identification tends to be with health, not sickness. The wound is physical and symbolic. Wilson's particular wound was psychological. We may hazard a guess that the former stretcher-bearer and stauncher of soldiers' wounds, the caretaker of the dead and the dying, felt a profound link with Neoptolemus, even while his intellect focused on the craft and dilemma of Philoctetes. The passage that ends the essay is devoted entirely to the role of the young man in the Sophoclean drama:

> Only by the intervention of one who is guileless enough and human enough to treat [Philoctetes] not as a monster, nor yet as a mere magical property which is wanted for accomplishing some end, but simply as another man whose sufferings elicit his sympathy and whose courage and pride he admires. When this human relation has been realized, it seems at first that it is to have the consequence of frustrating the purpose of the expedition and ruining the Greek campaign. Instead of winning over the outlaw, Neoptolemus has

outlawed himself as well, at a time when both the boy and the cripple are desperately needed by the Greeks.

We can look even more deeply into the identifications between Wilson and the young Neoptolemus. If, in his allegory, Philoctetes was cast in the role of the archetypal wounded artist, then we can say that Neoptolemus becomes the archetypal wound-dressing critic. He is Walt Whitman dressing the wounds of soldiers in the hospitals of the Civil War; he is Edmund Wilson dressing the wounds of American soldiers on the Western Front. The critic, in his many roles, can be cast in this role, even as Henry James cast him as "the real helper of the artist, a torch-bearing out-rider, the interpreter, the brother." André Gide, in his version of the Sophocles play, to which Edmund Wilson briefly alludes, had had in mind the deeper homoerotic feelings between Philoctetes and Neoptolemus; and Wilson, with his latent homosexual feelings so carefully hidden from himself, goes far enough to say that, in Gide, Neoptolemus "forgets his patriotic obligations for those of a personal attachment." A critic, too, selects his subjects most often through personal attachment. One might say that the deeper and hidden side of Wilson's interest in "The Wound and the Bow" resides in the attachment of male to male, and that this gives us a common tie between two such different figures as Walt Whitman and our modern critic. In his book on the Civil War, *Patriotic Gore,* Wilson pays rather scant attention to Whitman—one supposes again that he tended always to look away from homosexual feeling out of some inner anxiety about it. But in the book he brings himself and Walt together in one sentence, as wound-dressers. He writes, "Like everyone who in any war is thrown with the rank and file and is brought to realize their helplessness and the pathos of our common humanity," Whitman resented those who manipulate or condemn this rank and file. Here we have a glimmer of recognition; it goes back to the young Edmund Wilson, Jr., of 1918 for the Walt of the

Civil War. In his future criticism, Wilson's long list of essays shows him alert psychologically, and in a distinctly original way, to the psychic wounds of art. In defining Neoptolemus, Wilson defined himself and made himself one with a poet like Whitman and his concern for the "common humanity" of art and society.

V

The vision came to Edmund Wilson by degrees. He would gradually make himself mediator between the cunning of men like Odysseus, who "use" art for governmental or military or commercial purposes, and those who, like Neoptolemus, seek to understand and be a brother to the artist. Wilson had tested the arts and tried his hand at poem, story, play. He moved from the high-flying life of the 1920s to the "proletarian" era of the Depression. And at the beginning of the new World War, with heightened vision, he was able to merge his diverse weapons into the single power-bow of humane criticism: he accepted himself at last for the literary journalist he was and entered into the role with a renewed vigor and all his acquired authority. No other of our critics had served quite so long in preparing himself; beside Wilson, the much-respected Desmond MacCarthy in England, with his fineness of mind and delicacy of spirit, seemed a gentleman amateur; the brilliant V. S. Pritchett came closer, but he was more specialized and much more refined. Van Wyck Brooks was more historian than critic; and then he disliked the moderns. Brooks's wound—vividly described in his memoirs—had taken him backward to Concord instead of forward; he seemed to move with Emerson and Thoreau; he studied the "wound" of Mark Twain. The far-ranging criticism of Wilson was his proper instrument, created by the necessities of his particular life experience. He could lend himself in a true humanistic spirit to the literary arts in America and, with his extraordinary skills of reportage, to politics and society as well. He could practice the "sympathy and judicial detachment" he described in his father. He could offer himself—even if it made him an outlaw—as a "general touchstone" and be neither judge, schoolmaster, nor dilettante, but a helper, a brother of the artist. More than intermediary, such a critic partakes of the law of the healer as well as the philosopher. He becomes the enemy of the deceivers and the entrepreneurs. To be such a truth-bearer it was necessary to be open to language, psychology, history: he must understand the strivings even of the little men of art, a Harold Frederic or a Henry Blake Fuller, or the travail of a John Jay Chapman—quite as much as the protean artists who transcend place and time and speak to the entire world. Art, an obstinate record of man's imagination, far from being a magician's sleight of hand, becomes in this light the fullest expression of the artist's being, his despair, and his serenity; it was the duty of criticism to see the grand lines, the sweep of a great work, its impact upon society and its time, and on posterity.

And criticism had to explain, elucidate, give insight into the complexities of art. Wilson had more in common with the universal minds of the eighteenth century than with the hurt lyricists of the nineteenth. He could never prevent himself from ranging far afield. He was based in literature but he wrote of the Zuñi and the Iroquois; he journeyed to Israel to learn about the Dead Sea scrolls. He was an adventurous traveler. He had to master languages. "I always find a pleasure almost sensual," he wrote, "in attacking a new language." He annexed Russia as a large province of his intelligence and sensibility. And he was never satisfied with his conquests. One day at Harvard he suddenly said to me, "You have never taken me to the grave of Henry James." I had thought he had long ago visited that quiet spot in Cambridge. So there was an afternoon's pilgrimage, a long ramble in Cambridge cemetery, with pauses and discourse before the resting places of the Howellses and the Jameses, and of many Cambridge worthies who lie on that hill within view of Soldiers' Field. Wilson seemed always to have more ideas than he could use, more arrows than he could shoot. It would take him years to synchronize and unify his hyperactive talents.

With time he created the series of books by which we know him, extraordinary gatherings-in of the fruit of his thrusting mind and his unappeased curiosity. He came to recognize in the end that he had a mastery of "the short." His training as literary journalist, the necessity of publishing in the magazines, made the briefer forms convenient, even mandatory. And then he brought the whole of himself to such a powerful focus and concentration on any problem—a given career, a movement of ideas, a social phenomenon, the character of Casanova, the perversities of Sade—that tension could not be long sustained. He was incapable of writing a long and meditated work; perhaps he was too impatient.

As a result, some of his writings are labored, careless, badly researched—like his book on Canada—and contain all kinds of little slips of fact and bias of judgment. His best writings are consummately organized scenes and pictures, miniatures and portraits. His masters were Taine and Michelet: and he associated to them the insights gained from the Greeks and classical psychology. A series of essays on modern writers became *Axel's Castle,* his seminal work on symbolism; a further series "in the writing and acting of history," dealing with Marxism, ended as *To the Finland Station.* By the same method he brought into being his "literary chronicles."

What characterized Wilson's criticism was his probity, his search for the truths of a given problem, his interest in curious byways which illuminated the whole, and his refusal to compromise with the commonplace. He refused also to use criticism as an instrument of power—or as an expression of his personality, a common failing among dictators of public taste. He remained aloof, detached, objective, sometimes stern, and even when he dealt with certain types of mediocrity it was in a spirit of enlightened inquiry. Knowing himself a critic, he remained always attached to his works of the imagination. I remember his saying to me with some vehemence (one day in Princeton), "Why do you speak to me always of my criticism? I have written plays, poems, stories, light verse, novels. I am a writer—a writer of many things." Nevertheless, the world knew him best as explorer of faraway regions of the mind. In the pages of *The New Yorker* he was the analytical traveler, the student of Russian literature, the vigorous questioner of races and cultures, the incorruptible reviewer. Fulfillment came, and belated fame. His whole life is a study in re-creation, writing, revision, the continuing self-discovery and self-renewal within which a troubled and alienated being was able to retain an overview of the world; and with this there remained his compassion for the sufferings out of which art is born. It was in part a compassion for himself that he could extend to others.

I remember an evening in Princeton in Edmund Wilson's house, in 1953. He was spending the winter there. Elizabeth Bowen, the novelist, was visiting, and John Berryman and I called after dinner. Berryman was writing his "Homage to Mistress Bradstreet." The poem had filled him to repletion, so that he seemed constantly to overflow, and he had brought some pages he had just written. We sat in the big room in its pools of light, within the outer chiaroscuro, Miss Bowen with her controlled stutter and natural charm, Elena Wilson, warm and sympathetic, and Wilson, large, expansive, magisterial. He asked Berryman to read from his work in progress.

The poet had then—before he cultivated his Whitmanesque beard—a hard-seamed face, and his voice was tightly drawn. He mumbled his lines, he dropped his words, he drowned in his personal anguish, pushing on blindly and only half coherently. Edmund Wilson, sitting beside him, listened with all the intentness of which he was capable. After a bit, he began quietly to feed some of the lines back to Berryman—and by the same token to us. He fell into this quietly, tenderly, with a voice that was almost a caress. The suffering poet hardly heard him. He plunged ahead, and I felt as if I were listening to a discordant Gregorian chant, in which Berryman's splutter of words was followed by a modulated and repetitive response. It was the poetry of reiteration, a vocal embrace, an administration of aid: Neoptolemus and Philoctetes, Walt Whitman and one of his young men. I felt myself in the presence of a high form of sympathetic criticism—the critic as helpmate, as explicator, as friend, not only of the common reader but of the artist himself. This was the most endearing side of Edmund Wilson.

I V

The James Family

The Killer and the Slain

Kipling's American Double

THE JAMES FAMILY

Father and Children

It is impossible to write of so idiosyncratic and eccentric a character as the elder Henry James without speaking of three of his
children who carried his family name into history: of William,
the psychologist and philosopher, of Henry Jr., the novelist, and
of Alice, the diarist. Without them we would remember the
father as a salty quaint character, an old-fashioned worthy, in
the sense that he had a marked personality, who had emerged
from a pioneering and homespun America and written a book
called *The Secret of Swedenborg.*

I

His friend William Dean Howells said he kept the secret very
well. Santayana characterized the elder James as "one of those
somewhat obscure sages whom early America produced: mys-
tics of independent mind, hermits in the desert of business, and
heretics in the churches." We would think of him in this homely
way were it not that he lives also—in the fullest sense in which
parents create posterity—in the writings of his celebrated sons
and in the memories of his gifted daughter. We can find him,
in Alice James's diary, as a distinct paternal image, whose affections, in the presence of his progeny when they were small,
melted into the universe, and who devotedly gave them a kind
of all-embracing but ambiguous love when they reached maturity. We would probably call him today an excessively "permissive" father; permissive enough to have quietly undermined
Christmas by showing his children—after solemnly pledging
them not to tell their mother—the heaped-up gifts sequestered
in a closet to await Santa Claus; who left his family to go on a

journey but returned almost immediately, unable to endure the anxiety of separation. And when he did manage to break away for some necessary trip, a letter from his daughter, then thirteen, mirrors his feelings: "My dear Father: We have had two dear letters from you and find you are the same dear old good-for-nothing home-sick papa as ever."

It is doubtful whether the discipline of genius, which we discover in the careers of both William and Henry James, would have been achieved with the aid of so relaxed and volatile a parent. Other forces must have been present. The disciplinary force seems to have been incarnated in the mother, Mary Walsh James. The role of the two parents in the lives of their children is best described, I think, in the words used by the novelist son to characterize Mr. and Mrs. Touchett in *The Portrait of a Lady*. His father, the son in that novel often said to himself, "was the more motherly; his mother, on the other hand, was paternal, and even, according to the slang of the day, gubernatorial."

The sons thus owed a distinct part of the order of their existence to their mother. But she had, as is often the case with active and practical people, little feeling for words and less for ideas. She left words and ideas, and the life of the dream, to her husband. Life was strenuous enough when one had to use a gubernatorial hand; the governing intelligence lay elsewhere. "Your father's ideas!" she might exclaim to her sons; and if we cannot recapture the tone, and if this was perhaps a family joke, it was symbolic nevertheless of the difference between the paternal and maternal worlds. The elder Henry had a lifelong desire to say things out. Yet rare and vivid though his language was, and playful and teasing his mind, he never fully communicated his message. "Oh, that I might thunder it out in a single interjection that would tell the *whole* of it, and never speak a word again." Since he did not succeed in thundering it out, he spoke many words, again and again. And this was perhaps fortunate, for it is in what he said that we can trace the influence of the father on the children and discern that William and Henry were, in reality, the image of two sides of his being. It was they who in the end—without the thunder—were able to express a great part of "the whole" of their father's ideas and feelings, the things in particular which the elder Henry James concealed from himself, in his search for a way of life and for spiritual comfort. In the process they rechanneled and toned into art and science much of the picturesqueness and rudeness of his language and thought.

There were, in the elder Henry James, two qualities which stood out in his intercourse with his fellows. He was filled with a yearning for logic and metaphysics in his search for a system in the universe and an understanding of God's relation to man and man's relation to God. But his mind was the reverse of logical. It was erratic, argumentative, mercurial, a leaping, somersaulting kind of intelligence. He suffered from a constant glow of words and a constant confusion of feeling. Certainly some part of this derived from the Irishness of his nature and the streak of poetry and paradox in him, which he sought constantly to profane by an incompatible logic. His imagery could be vigorous and hearty, with a fund of aggression in it. He depicted enemies and friends as sausages frying in their own grease; he likened their discourse to the quacking of ducks; but he also invoked the sun's radiance to picture the qualities he liked in men, and he drew easily upon nature for many of his homeliest examples. The poet in him was capricious, savage, witty. The would-be logician in him was an easy rationalist who liked the optimistic side of things, but it was an optimism shadowed by a deep sense of evil as an extra-human and baleful thing. Tolstoy is said to have cherished one of the elder Henry James's books; like Tolstoy, he was intent upon seeing the universe whole. But also like the Russian he was constantly distracted by the richness and variousness of the world. Another gifted man of similar temperament, Bernard Shaw, once told me in his quixotic and paradoxical way that he thought the elder Henry was worth his sons put together. Shaw used to tease the novelist son in saying this, but the latter took pride in his father. Tolstoy, Shaw, James the elder—a strange trio—and they had this in common: all three were gifted artistic individuals who tended to deny the artist in themselves. We know how Tolstoy repudiated art for religion; Shaw proclaimed himself a didact and a socialist preacher; the elder Henry constantly reminded his sons that art was "narrowing."

II

I do not think that the elder Henry was ever aware that he was unable to accept the poet within himself. His ancestral Calvinism was too strongly present in all that he did even though he had repudiated it. It remained a kind of habit of mind; it also made him an individual constantly at war with himself. Art seemed to him one of man's playthings. He could rejoice in poetry; he even edited an edition of Blake—to be sure, choosing a visionary poet—but he referred poetry not to his emotions but to his intellect and to his ever-present cosmic sense. The novelist son who shrank from the cosmos and preferred a well-defined and well-tilled artistic garden, found it wonderful to contemplate "things, persons, objects and aspects." But these, he said, were doubtless all "frivolities" in his father's world. The novelist would accept "a state of faith and a conviction of the Divine, an interpretation of the universe" if only it had supplied him, as he said, with more features and more appearances. He tugged, as realistic writers do, at the particular; his father always answered with the general.

Thoreau shrewdly observed that the elder Henry James was too easily satisfied with broad and comfortable generalizations, especially about society and the social order. He offered, as he said, "quasi-philanthropic doctrines in a metaphysical dress." Austin Warren, in his biography of the father, observed that he "steadfastly chose to regard heart [rather than head] as the primary fount of knowledge." A parent who was a bundle of contradictions, quick, inconsistent, explicit in his criticisms of his fellows, and yet always broad and general about everything; who dragged his children about Europe in the days of the stage-coach in search of an education, surrounded them with tutors and governesses, and seemed to find none good enough to meet his erratic standards; who was large-hearted and generous, but easygoing to a fault and wholly without awareness of what he did to his children by giving them a vagabond existence, may be interesting for us to contemplate—racy, vivid, amusing in his idiosyncrasy—but he was clearly a great problem for his sons. In their movement from school to school and city to city, life assumed the effect of aspects and varieties, a passing show; and the father, seeking an ideal education for them, inveighed against "the over-education of the scholarly class." In religion he showed them always the passion of his feeling for God and his creation, and an open dislike for the man-made Church. But the family, as Henry remarked, was "pewless." Which may account for the novelist's investigation, in more mature years, of the churches of all faiths, which he visited and contemplated with secular eyes, as social institutions as well as scenes and places of worship. And it explains perhaps the quest that led his brother William to write the inspired work we know as *The Varieties of Religious Experience.*

I have said enough, I think, to suggest the air of contradiction and ambiguity and uprooted drift in which the two gifted sons of this curiously gifted man grew up. If the father had no theory of education—or too much theory—we can at least say that whatever it was, it seems to have worked. For what apparently happened, in the circumambient vagueness in which the sons moved, was that they grasped for the tangibles of existence and sought what they could find that was concrete in their parent. With the directness of childhood they could cut through his repudiation of art and learning and social custom and perceive the failed artist and scholar submerged in him. The buried artist in the elder Henry was the accessible, the friendly, certainly the most charming part of him. They seized on what was pictorial, vivid, searching, paradoxical, in his view of the world. But then, instead of looking away again at the transcendent, and converting reality into the abstruse, Henry the novelist wholly took possession of the aesthetic side; and William of that side which leaned toward hard reason and logical inquiry—but to which he could bring scientific method. Henry, through observation and analysis, went in search of essence: to see life and sum it up, in picture and scene, in the wit of words, in tale and novel—this became for him the beginning and the end of his existence. To feel beauty, having perceived it, and to live beauty, was Henry's religion, and there were voices in the air which helped, the voice of Pater, of Arnold, the lyrical voice of Tennyson, the psychological penetration of Browning seeking to place himself in the very consciousness of his fellow creatures—as Henry James would ultimately do. Experience for the novelist was something to be looked at intently and converted into words: to be reimagined and altered at will—as artists do, refashioning the world into a world of their own, and which—for such is the ineluctable law of art—they then make us accept as part of ours.

III

William, the oldest son, had the same large grasp of life as did his younger brother, but he looked upon it with scientific rather than aesthetic eyes. He had the same rich verbal endowment; but his need was not to see how he could refashion the world into words and grow ever more cunning in language and style. To be sure, he had his particular art of saying—he was one of the few men of science who was brilliantly articulate. His language was quick, spontaneous, lucid; metaphor came to him as easily as breathing. The varieties of any experience fascinated him, whether he was trying to capture and describe moments of consciousness or endlessly attending spiritualistic seances and seeking to discover the nature of extrasensory perception. "He could see most cunningly out of the corner of his eye," said Ralph Barton Perry. The collection of varieties of experience was not all; he collected them in order to do something about them. He had a kind of restless impatience as he contemplated his materials: one had to translate thought into action. In his brother Henry there was the explorer of life with a large sense of the past, of history, of civilization, of art; William was an explorer who tried to shake off the past; he had a need beyond exploration to test his discoveries, to test them for truth. He remains one of the great pioneers in the exploration of the relation between mind and body—as distinct from his father, who discoursed on the relation between body and soul.

It seems to me that we are on reasonably safe ground in our speculation: the unrealized artist and the unrealized scientist in the father became the artist Henry and the scientist William. The hidden messages were revealed to them. Henry, the pursuer of beauty and the concretions of existence, brought his father's poetry into the art of the novel. William, by choosing scientific method to explore the very truths his father felt but did not understand, gave us first his psychology and later his philosophy of pragmatism, written in a style rare in science, the style of the artist. In seeing this, we can see the essential being of the brothers. In my biography of the novelist, I have set down this contrast, describing the steps by which William and Henry, faced with their vague and volatile father and their demanding mother, facing each other as siblings and rivals, sought to assert their egos in characteristic ways, as genius must. Behind the intensities and passions of his imaginative life, Henry James was patient, persistent, calculating, secretive. He had in him his mother's fixedness of purpose in dealing with practical matters, as well as his father's artistic sense. William's nature was directly opposed to this. He was openly assertive. For all his periods of morbid introspection, he was capable always of reaching into the warm sunlight of human intercourse. He discovered himself in teaching the young, in founding the first psychological laboratory in America, in communicating with scholars in many lands. Henry remained solitary, subterranean, in spite of an outwardly strenuous social life and his continual passage through the great cities of the Western world and among the great artists of his time. He remained a recluse of the writing desk; he harbored and built up his resources. The drive to power from his inner fortress was from the first compelling. William on his side prodigally expended his gifts in immediate action. Henry remained celibate. William married and had children. William's literary style, as I have observed, was direct, easy, bubbling inventively into lucidity. Henry's had in it much more art, and much cultivated literary power, but also, as he grew older, much more indirection. William was all idea and intellect, suffused with feeling. Henry was all feeling and passion—intellectualized.

To the scientist brother, the aesthetic Henry was a problem. There was an artistic hedonism in him and a touch of the feminine that suggested a possible homoeroticism; William James, with his masculine drive, feared this and disliked it. In 1889, the year the philosopher achieved fame, he wrote to his wife, "Harry is extremely easy and genial, but his whole way of taking life has so little in common with mine that that too is innutritive in the respect for which I came abroad." He always tended to back away from his brother and travel on to his next destination. Decidedly, William and Henry could not spend much time together comfortably in any one room. William fled, and more often than has been recorded. And it has also been recorded that to a complete stranger he referred to him as "my younger and shallower and vainer brother."

Thus each son of the elder Henry achieved his originality and lived out—with the Atlantic between them—his genius. Henry the novelist forged an inimitable style and created his empire of letters; and in combining the rare qualities of creator and critic he combined qualities that had existed in a father in whom creator and critic were at war with each other. William became one of the rare philosophers of this world, who could meditate on the conduct of life as his father had done, but in the words of the human spirit. In his sons the talkative father found his truest voices. They completed what he had been unable to build. What was originality and idiosyncrasy in him was translated by them into creative energy.

I V

I should like to add a few words about the articulate daughter. Alice James's legacy, in this family of feeling—as much a family of feeling as a family of minds—is a comparatively brief diary kept in a sickroom toward the end of her abbreviated life, reflecting the closed-in world of the invalid and written not so much for an audience as through some powerful desire to give expression to herself, as her elder brothers were able to do. In our age, when women have found a place in the world, she might have achieved a fuller life and a happier one. But in the James family of four boys and herself, she remained largely the voice of a certain kind of noble courage, reflecting some of the moments of serenity which she had captured from the father's temperament. "In our family group," her novelist brother once wrote, "girls seem scarcely to have had a chance." And Alice became, indeed, a classical Victorian spinster invalid. She did not allow this to defeat her; she had her own wit, and style— a high individuality and sense of her feminist being. She must accordingly have an individual portrait.

In the history of this family it seems to me there is no moment more remarkable than that which I have told in one of my chapters, describing the novelist son's first visit to the newly cut grave in the Cambridge cemetery where his father was buried close to the mother in December of 1882. The philosopher had written a farewell letter to his father, saluting him on the threshold of the new and the unknown, a remarkable letter telling him how much his—William's—life, his being, his consciousness, had been derived from his parent. We have no witnesses of the solitary and mystical act Henry performed. All we know is that on a cold clear day before the year ended, he stood amid the snowdrifts, where the view is that of Soldiers' Field and the river Charles, and read into the frosty air and over the fresh grave his brother's words of farewell to their father.

The *ave atque vale* of the oldest son, delivered in the voice of the second son, was a kind of symbolic act of unity. In that moment it was as if the three were one—the two Henrys and the William—a single voice of articulate American thought and feeling, the eloquent and humane language of the heritage of genius.

The Anguish of Alice

Alice James began to keep a commonplace book at the end of her second year in England. She had crossed the Atlantic in November 1884, and the first entries are dated *"December 1886."* Into this book she copied verses, aphorisms, passages from novels, sentences culled from her wide and ever-curious readings. We encounter at the outset lines from the *Rubáiyát* —"the wine of life keeps oozing drop by drop, the leaves of life keep falling one by one." On the next page she sets down Hamlet's "I do not set my life at a pin's fee." Carlyle's "Everlasting Yea" follows—her father might have written it—"There is in a man a HIGHER than Love of Happiness: he can do without Happiness, and instead thereof find Blessedness," and immediately after this she copies (in the French in which she read *War and Peace*) Tolstoy's account of Prince Andrei at Austerlitz— the vivid moment when the wounded prince, falling backward, discovers above him the blue immensity of the heavens and experiences, in the very midst of battle, a sense of exquisite peace. The pages of the commonplace book are filled with the words of famous writers. They seem to speak for Alice. In 1887 she is quoting Howells and Loti, La Bruyère, Flaubert, Edgar

Quinet, George Sand, and again Tolstoy. In the following year Renan, Maupassant, her brothers William and Henry, Auguste Comte, George Eliot. But when she writes down the year 1889 it is to announce, in effect, that she will henceforth deal with her life in her own words: "I think that if I get into the habit of writing a bit about what happens, or rather doesn't happen, I may lose a little of the sense of loneliness and desolation which abides with me."

She kept her diary faithfully thereafter, save on days when she was too ill; and she persisted even when she lost the strength to write. During the last months of her terminal illness, she dictated. Apparently the diary came to be much more than a substitute for loneliness and desolation. On one of the pages she set down words from Cotton Mather, "so the character of his daily conversation was a trembling walk with God." In a certain sense Alice's diary, with its mixture of stoicism and doubt, its laughter at death—and its fear of death—its renunciation and its protest, represented her particular and frequent "trembling walk with God."

I

Alice James was born in New York City on August 7, 1848, the fifth and last child of Henry and Mary James. The father, who came from Albany, was a man of leisure in a country where leisure was almost unknown; while his fellow Americans were pushing farther westward in their conquest of the continent, the elder Henry James dreamed of utopias and of a Swedenborgian heaven on earth. With a comfortable income inherited from his Irish immigrant father, and a large house at 58 West Fourteenth Street, he provided his four sons and his daughter with a wide, far-ranging, and deeply troubled childhood. There were long stays in Europe, pensions, experimental private schools, a train of tutors and governesses. The elder Henry was a dreamer in his library and a maker of paradoxes on the lecture platform. A friend of Emerson, Carlyle, Thackeray, and most of the Boston Brahmins, he limped through life (he had lost a leg in a boyhood accident), cheerfully and gregariously, but also, his children were to feel, with a certain ineffectuality and vagueness. His wife, a plain, unimaginative woman (considerably transfigured in the imaginative prose of her novelist son), provided the practical down-to-earth management required in a household otherwise volatile. Her children in later years spoke of her "self-effacement." This masked a strong will and a vigorous guiding hand. Not the least of the family's paradoxes thus was a father who was in reality maternal, and a mother inclined to be gubernatorial, as Henry James implied and Alice's recollections in her diary suggest.

Alice grew up in a family circle almost entirely masculine, save for the hovering figures of her mother and her mother's sister, Catherine Walsh, the "Aunt Kate" of the family. Five men—the father and the two older sons (who were half a dozen years older than Alice), and the younger brothers of her own age, Garth and Robertson—dominated her early years. Her elder brothers cultivated a courtliness with her that was really a form of self-display and teasing, and her younger brothers, when they did not ignore her, heaped the usual petty indignities small boys have in reserve for baby sisters—"the anguish," Alice remembers (recalling a childhood outing), "greater even than usual of Wilky's and Bob's heels grinding into my shins." The "greater even than usual" sums up chapters of childhood history. Even the great Thackeray teased, when he joined the family at dinner in Paris. From his towering height he looked down on the eight-year-old Alice, in her pretty frock, and in a high, shocked voice said "Crinoline—I was suspecting it! So young and so depraved!"

Alice may not have known what the word "depraved" meant, but she knew she was the butt of laughter—as she was in countless family episodes. She found ways of defending herself; her mother's letters record that she often effectively "sassed" her father and brothers. A family friend in Newport later spoke of the "unhappy" James children, fighting "like cats and dogs"; and if Alice was not in the thick of the battles, she constantly sought to raise her feminine voice among the stronger male voices around her, which means she learned how to be aggressive, like them, with words.

Alice's education seems to have been as casual as that of her brothers: a modicum of home learning; French taught by the same governess who taught her brother Henry; certain struggles with arithmetic, when the family was in Geneva and the boys had been farmed out to various schools. "Our Alice is still under discipline," writes the father to a friend, "preparing to fulfil some high destiny or other in the future by reducing decimal fractions to their least possible rate of subsistence." The European experiences of the young William and Henry, which played so large a role in their development, touched Alice much less, perhaps because she was only seven when the family went abroad in 1855. The Jameses were constantly on the move; and later the sons and daughter complained they had had a "hotel" childhood. They were swept from Geneva to London, London to Paris, Paris to Boulogne-sur-Mer, a sweep across the Atlantic for a brief stay in Newport, and, just as they were restoring their American roots, a sweep eastward again to schools and pensions in Geneva and later in Germany. Small wonder that Alice, in adult life, warned William against repeating the same pattern with his children. "What enrichment of mind and memory can children have without continuity and if they are torn up by the roots every little while as we were? Of all things don't make the mistake which brought about our rootless and accidental childhood." Europe should be left for his children "until they are old enough to have the Grand Emotion, undiluted by vague memories."

On the eve of the Civil War, the Jameses finally ended their wanderings and settled in Newport. Here Alice passed the early years of adolescence. Her younger brothers disappeared from her life; they became soldiers—but then they had always disappeared to play games not for girls. Her older brothers remained at home, but went through a long period of self-absorption and invalidism, suffering deeply from the fratricidal war. Alice was much alone. She describes in her diary how she took gloomy walks around Newport, "absorbing into the bone that the better part is to clothe oneself in neutral tints, walk by still waters and possess one's soul in silence." That was woman's place in the genteel society of her time; but neutrality was impossible: there remained in Alice the long-formed need to assert herself. The old articulateness could not, in reality, be silenced. "The only thing which survives," she concluded, "is the resistance we bring to life, and not the strain life brings to us."

Alice brought a full measure of defense rather than resistance. Increasingly it took the form of a struggle between body and mind. When she was fifteen there were attacks of "neuralgia," and William James writes in a letter that he hopes Alice is "back at school instead of languishing and lolling about the house." At this school Alice remembered a struggle between doing her lessons and "shrieking or wiggling through the most impossible sensations of upheaval."

By the time the family moved to Cambridge at the end of the Civil War, the upheavals took serious form. When a conversation proved too exciting, Alice had a fainting spell. At the moment of falling asleep she experienced terror. And the house in Cambridge provided a melancholy environment. In one of his letters Henry speaks of their home as being "as lively as an inner sepulchre." And the backward glance of an eyewitness, Lilla Cabot Perry, who married a boyhood friend of the Jameses, is eloquent. Recalling various households in Cambridge, she speaks of "the poky banality of the James house, ruled by Mrs. James, where Henry James's father used to limp in and out and never seemed really to 'belong' to his wife or Miss Walsh [Aunt Kate], large florid stupid-seeming ladies, or to his clever but coldly self-absorbed daughter, who was his youngest child. . . . Henry James's mother (even to my own perception as a child) was the very incarnation of *banality* and his aunt, Miss Walsh, who lived with them, not much better. His father always seemed to me genial and delightful . . . but he seemed to me out of place in that stiff stupid house in Cambridge."

We must allow for possible limitations of a Cabot-eye view of the James household in Cambridge, so at variance with most of the pictures offered by the Jameses themselves. There is much in it, however, that corresponds to the content of the mother's letters to her children. The truth was that 20 Quincy Street harbored during the late 1860s three disturbed young adults: the two older brothers and Alice, with her illnesses which set the stage for her invalidism. Her breakdowns, particularly that of 1868, when she was in her twentieth year, are documented in letters written by her parents to the youngest son, Robertson, who was living in the West. She had "violent turns of hysteria." "Alice," the father wrote, "is half the time, indeed much more than half, on the verge of insanity and suicide." During this period she had violent impulses to "knock off the head of the benignant pater." The controlling of such impulses imposed upon her a burden which she described with insight: that of being "doctor, nurse and straitjacket, all in one." And by being ill, she rendered herself powerless to execute the violence. At the same time she could hold those around her in bondage. "Father is bearing Alice's calls upon him in a most miraculous way," the mother writes. Alice demanded indeed that he be at her bedside day and night. During certain of these hours she told him of her wish to commit suicide. Was it a sin? The elder Henry coped with this in a shrewd, self-exalting way. He did not recognize that Alice was reaching out for love and some expression of being wanted. No, he replied, suicide wasn't a sin. It was absurd to believe it sinful if Alice wished release from her suffer-

ing. He gave her his fatherly permission to end her life whenever she wished, asking her only to do it in such a way as not
to distress her friends.

In subsequent conversations Alice rationalized her assertive
and attention-getting threat and saw it had a deeper purpose:
it had been a way of saying that she was free. "Now she could
perceive it to be her *right* to dispose of her own body when life
had become intolerable, she could never do it." Alice later told
her father she was still "strongly tempted," but she never took
the final step that would have brought her peace. She lived to
pursue her career as an invalid and to exact from her brothers
and friends the love she had failed to receive when young in the
heavily masculine James family. To his youngest son the father
wrote:

> Never have I had such deep tranquil joy in thinking of the Divine
> name revealed in Christ as in these profoundly trying experiences
> with Alice. I certainly never before saw such a believer in the truth
> of a better world as she is, when her suffering is most acute; and
> when she comes out of it I never saw one so fitted by her grace and
> playfulness of wit to adorn this life. But I really think she is gradually
> getting better, though she is opposed to doing so herself, and evi-
> dently desires to go into the spiritual world at once, if it were possi-
> ble.

His optimism reveals his failure in empathy and his characteristic egotism. He "spiritualized" his children.

Between illnesses there were forays into activity. For a while
she attempted charitable work in Boston and New York. She
belonged to a sewing circle and went to parties. She indulged,
when she could, in the minor sociabilities of Quincy and Kirk-
land streets in Cambridge. In 1872 she traveled abroad with her
brother Henry and their Aunt Kate. All the remedies of the
time were attempted—massage, visits to specialists in Manhattan for ice and electric therapy, special "blistering" baths, so-
journs in the "Adams Nervine Asylum" near Boston—but they

proved ineffective. She was to speak in her diary of "the ignorant asininity of the medical profession in its treatment of nervous disorders" and of "these doctors who tell you that you will
die or *recover.*" To which she grimly added she had been at
these alternatives since she was nineteen "and I am neither
dead nor recovered."

The doctors diagnosed her illnesses as "rheumatic gout" or
"spinal neurosis." When she had palpitations they spoke of "car-
diac complications" and "nervous hyperaesthesia." They
seemed to find Alice's heart strong, and most of the treatments
prescribed seem to have been for "nerves." We may speculate
that at least some part of her condition was the common one of
Victorian restrictions on women. Elizabeth Barrett offers a
record of an analogous kind of bedridden life and of her escape
from it. But no Robert Browning came to carry Alice off to some
Italy of her own, as in the drama of Wimpole Street. What we
read in her diary is a sense of early frustration, that of an originally strong-limbed healthy girl who never found an opportunity to be active. In our time she would have played tennis,
swam, or jogged. In earlier New England she wore long dresses,
sat decorously at dull teas and parties—and had periodic prostrations.

Years later Henry James was to understand this. He wrote to
Mary James Vaux, his niece, as we have seen earlier, that "in our
family group girls seem scarcely to have had a chance." And he
concluded, having been the closest witness of her final decline,
that Alice's "tragic health was, in a manner, the only solution
for her of the practical problem of life."

In the early 1880s, Alice James demonstrated that she could
meet responsibilities with courage, strength, and resolution.
Her mother's death in 1882 found her active in ministering to
her father. They sold the Quincy Street house and moved into
a smaller residence in Boston, in Mount Vernon Street. Here,
during the greater part of a year, "haunted by the terror that

I should fail him, as I watched the poor old man fade, day by day," she nursed her father and presided over the household. She and her Aunt Kate were with him during his last hours; the sons were away, and when Henry arrived after rushing across the December seas, the funeral had already taken place. Her father left her ample means; and to her $3,500 a year Henry added his share of the Syracuse rents, $1,200 a year, since he was earning much more by his pen. Henry remained with Alice in the house on Beacon Hill for several months. The bachelor son and the spinster daughter seem to have found much peace and harmony in being together. The novelist slept in his father's room and settled the family affairs. Alice kept house. "My sister and I make an harmonious little *ménage,* and I feel a good deal as if I were married," the novelist wrote to his London publisher. They had always felt an intimate kinship that transcended ties of family, a strong emotional compatibility reaching back to their early years. The novelist now could replace the father in his relation to Alice, and his bestowing of his income on her was in itself a fatherly act. He felt for her a peculiar and intense affection, such as he was to describe in some notes for a story he never wrote—"two lives, two beings and *one* experience," an intensity of feeling "in relation to the *past,* the parents, the beloved mother, the beloved father—of those who have suffered before them and *for* them and whose blood is in their veins." The brother and sister of James's unwritten tale were to experience "the pain of sympathy" and "a deep, participating devotion of one to the other. . . . The brother suffers, has the experience, and the effect of the experience, is carried along by fate, etc., and the sister understands, perceives, shares, with every pulse of her being." When the novelist set down these quasi-incestuous words, Alice had been dead three years; but some part of his emotion seemed to go back to this period of their life together, during a winter and a summer in Boston.

Henry remained with Alice for the better part of a year and then returned to London to resume his own life. Alice seemed well established and comfortable in Mount Vernon Street. Although their Aunt Kate lived in New York, she could be relied upon to visit her niece regularly. William James and his family were easily accessible in Cambridge. And Alice had a new friend. Henry James had seen her sufficiently to recognize the beginning for his sister of a close and, as it proved, an abiding attachment.

II

Katharine Peabody Loring and Alice James met during 1873. Alice was then twenty-five and Miss Loring twenty-four. The frail Alice had been promptly attracted to the energetic young woman from Beverly, Massachusetts, who was identified with various social and charitable enterprises in Boston. To a friend (Sara Darwin) she described her as having "all the mere brute superiority which distinguishes man from woman combined with all the distinctively feminine virtues. There is nothing she cannot do from hewing wood and drawing water to driving runaway horses and educating all the women in North America." Miss Loring, shortly after their meeting, took Alice with her to New Hampshire. To the astonishment of the James family, Alice went willingly instead of begging off, as was her custom, from any new experience. "I hope her experiment has been happy to the end—if the end has come, as I trust not," Henry James wrote to his mother. He added, "I trust she built a monument somewhere of forest leaves (or rather of New Hampshire granite) to the divine Miss Loring, who appears to unite the wisdom of the serpent with the gentleness of the dove."

To Alice, her brother expressed delight in Miss Loring's "strength of wind and limb, to say nothing of her nobler qualities." During the summer of 1881, Alice and Miss Loring traveled abroad, visiting England and Scotland. Henry James saw them briefly and was delighted with the "precious Miss Loring," who wore high collars, with pince-nez attached to a ribbon, and was a distinctive Bostonian bluestocking. He wrote his mother that she was "the most perfect" companion Alice could have found. "Alice seems so extraordinarily fond of Miss Loring that a third person is rather a superfluous appendage." During his two visits to America (1881–82 and 1882–83), he became better acquainted with his sister's friend. She seemed to know how to cope with Alice's nervousness; she was a good nurse; she attended her with loving attention. Sometimes she took her under her own roof at Beverly to care for her during her prostrations. But Miss Loring could not give all her time to her Cambridge friend. She had a sickly sister, Louisa, to care for as well. And in 1884 she took Louisa to Europe, in the hope that this change would effect a cure.

Left behind, Alice seems to have been seized by a kind of inner panic. In her diary she speaks of "these ghastly days" and of longing "to flee in to the firemen next door and escape from the 'Alone, Alone' that echoed through the house, rustled down the stairs, whispered from the walls, and confronted me like a material presence." Beyond a normal need for friendship, the little girl lurking in Alice out of earlier years craved undivided attention as well as the center of the stage. Alice issued an appeal to Miss Loring, who generously recrossed the Atlantic to escort Alice abroad; the latter would visit her brother Henry in London while Katharine was occupied with Louisa. And Louisa, in turn, became Alice's rival for Katharine's attention. Alice sailed with no thought of remaining abroad. But it proved a decisive step.

It was November; the sea was calm, yet Alice never left her cabin. She had one of her nervous attacks shortly after the ship sailed, and Miss Loring spent the voyage attending her two invalids. Henry James, boarding the vessel at Liverpool when it was still out in the stream, was astonished at Alice's feebleness. Two stout sailors carried her ashore, and she spent a week recuperating in a Liverpool hotel, attended by a maid Henry had brought along and a nurse. Then the novelist took her to London. Miss Loring, meanwhile, had taken her sister—whose health was much less precarious than Alice's—to Bournemouth. By the time Henry had installed Alice in lodgings off Piccadilly, near his own rooms, the situation seemed clear to him. Alice was bitterly jealous of Miss Loring's sister, Louisa; she wanted to have Katharine to herself. And something else became increasingly clear. "I may be wrong in the matter," the novelist reported to his brother, "but it rather strikes me as an effect that Katharine Loring has upon her—that as soon as they get together Alice takes to her bed. This was the case as soon as Katharine came to London to see her (she had been up before) and she has now been recumbent (as a consequence of her little four-hour journey) ever since she reached Bournemouth." The British doctors gave Alice a thorough examination. Their verdict coincided with that of their American confreres. They could find no sign of organic illness and they too ended by treating her as neurasthenic.

The trip to Europe proved beneficial for Louisa Loring. As she recovered, Katharine was increasingly free to be with Alice. When she was not, Henry James, reinforced by servants and a nurse, took charge. Whatever her ailments, if any, it became clear to the novelist that his sister was involved in an inextricable human relationship which had to take its own course. As he explained to his Aunt Kate (many months had by this time elapsed and Louisa had been pronounced cured), "Katharine comes back to Alice for a permanency. Her being with her may be interrupted by absences, but evidently it is the beginning of a living together, for the rest of such time as Alice's life may last." There was evidently, said Henry, "a kind of definite understanding between them." He added that "we must accept it with gratitude." He observed that also "there is about as much possibility of Alice's giving Katharine up as of giving her legs to be sawed off." Alice had told him that "if she could have Katharine *quietly* and *uninterruptedly* for a year 'to relieve her of all responsibility' she would get well." James could only say to this, "Amen! She will get well, or she won't, but, either way, it lies between themselves." He could hardly cease his career as novelist and set himself up as his sister's nurse. When his Aunt Kate offered to come to England to help, he urged her not to; Alice "would then have *five* people under contribution, really, to take care of her, and she has quite enough now." Miss Loring, on her side, told Henry it was her desire "quite as strongly as Alice's, to be with her to the end." Henry James observed to his aunt that "a devotion so perfect and so generous" as Miss Loring's was "a gift of providence so rare and little-to-be-looked-for in this hard world that to brush it aside would be almost an act of impiety. Not to take it would be to get something much worse." What this meant to Alice may be judged from a brief allusion in a letter to William James of 1891. "This year has been the happiest I have ever known, surrounded by such affection and devotion, but I won't enter into details, as I see the blush mantle the elderly cheek of my scribe." In Miss Loring Alice had found not only a companion but a friend whom she could love.

If Alice was too ill to be an active lesbian, she was nevertheless finding fulfillment by being *chronically* ill and so having her loved one near her. There was a distinctive underlying sexuality in the relationship: but it would probably be equally true to say the relationship was symbiotic and involved a double power play. Alice James got her sense of power and gratification in manipulating her friend, and her friend experienced a conjunctive power in controlling Alice. Both enjoyed their roles. The situation would evolve into the central subject of Henry James's novel *The Bostonians,* which he wrote while he was observing the power-drama in his own family.

The novelist discovered on his side that he was tied by a kind of delicate moral bondage to his sister's sickbed, very much as his father had been before him. He kept in close touch with her when he traveled on the Continent; he could go only when Miss

Loring was fully available; and on at least two occasions he rushed back to London in answer to urgent telegraphic summons. Alice never recrossed the Atlantic. She feared the voyage, and she was never again sufficiently strong. She lived periodically in London, and part of the time at Leamington. When she was better, she held a semblance of a salon, receiving, while on her couch, certain of her brother's friends: Mr. Lowell, Mrs. Humphry Ward, Mrs. Matthew Arnold, the aged Fanny Kemble, who, in spite of a bad heart, came puffing up the stairs to pay her a call. After a longish residence in Leamington, she settled in Kensington and finally in a little house at 41 Argyll Road, on Campden Hill. She began to keep her diary in May of 1889. It tells the remainder of her story. Little more than a year before the end, the doctors finally discovered an organic symptom. Alice developed cancer of the breast.

III

How she faced this final verdict of the hitherto baffled doctors is told in the diary, and between the lines we can read Alice's confusion of feeling—relief that the eternal ambiguity of her life was to be ended, awe and fear before the unknown, "the great mortuary moment," as she characteristically put it. When William received word of the definitive diagnosis, he wrote a gentle and consoling letter to his sister (on July 6, 1891) that did not altogether conceal his deep anxiety. Alice would now know, he said, "a finite length of days, and then goodbye to neurasthenia and neuralgia and headache, and weariness and palpitation and disgust all at one stroke—I should think you would be reconciled to the prospect with all its pluses and minuses!" He went on to speak of immortality and the "explosion of liberated force and life" that would come "when that which is *you* passes out of the body." It might seem odd, he said, "for me to talk to you in this cool way about your end; but my dear little sister, if one has things present to one's mind . . . why not speak them out?"

Alice's reply, dated July 30, 1891, had in it some of the same coolness—at least on the surface. She would have felt wounded and misunderstood, she said, if William had "walked round and not up to my demise." Her letter is of a piece with her diary:

It is the most supremely interesting moment in life, the only one in fact when living seems life, and I count it the greatest good fortune to have these few months so full of interest and instruction in the knowledge of my approaching death. It is as simple in one's own person as any fact of nature, the fall of a leaf or the blooming of a rose, and I have a delicious consciousness, ever present, of wide spaces close at hand, and whisperings of release in the air.

Like Tolstoy's Prince Andrei, she was now looking at the blue immensity of the sky. She told William he greatly exaggerated the tragic element "in my commonplace little journey."

You must also remember that a woman, by nature, needs much less to feed upon than a man, a few emotions and she is satisfied; so when I am gone, pray don't think of me simply as a creature who might have been something else, had neurotic science been born. Notwith-standing the poverty of my outside experience, I have always had a significance for myself, and every chance to stumble along my straight and narrow little path, and to worship at the feet of my Deity, and what more can a human soul ask for?

William, speaking both as a doctor and a psychologist, advised Alice to accept all possible relief from pain. "Take all the morphia (or other forms of opium if that disagrees) you want, and don't be afraid of becoming an opium drunkard. What was opium created for except for such times as this?" Alice, how-ever, did not take well to drugs; and William, who had seen the great Charcot use hypnotism at the Salpêtrière, advised Alice to resort to this when sedation did not help. Dr. Lloyd Tuckey, an eminent British alienist, was summoned and he taught Miss Loring to use a modified hypnosis, on the theory that Alice should not be put wholly to sleep in this way. This induced a calming of the nerves, and she was able to drop off "without the sensations of terror which have accompanied that process for so many years."

What is striking in the diary is the quantity of cheerfulness in Alice's dying. She follows with great excitement her brother's first nights in the provinces and in London when he dramatizes *The American.* He brings her his anecdotes regularly; and Alice occupies herself with "the grim shoving of the hours behind me." She came to recognize that her diary was "an outlet to that geyser of emotions, sensations, speculations, and reflections which ferments perpetually within my poor old carcass for its sins."

The end came with great rapidity on March 6, 1892, and there is preserved among the family papers Henry's minute account of the last painful hours written for his brother William, with all the precision and power habitual to the novelist's pen. Alice had a troubled dream just before her death. She saw certain of her dead friends in a boat, on a stormy sea, beckoning to her as the boat moved into the shadows. She dictated her journal to within a few hours of her death and took the trouble to rephrase a sentence that bothered her. Before she lost consciousness she dictated a cable to her brother and his family in Cambridge, "Tenderest love to all. Farewell. Am going soon." Katharine and Henry sought to create an intense stillness in the house in which she lay; and before sinking into her last sleep she told Henry that "she *couldn't* oh she COULDN'T, and begged it mightn't be exacted of her, live *another* day." If she wished for death, she nevertheless died reluctantly. She remained unconscious for twenty-four hours. It was the next afternoon—a Sunday—that Alice's breathing finally ceased while her brother was raising the blind to let a little more light into the room. Three days later, Katharine and Henry accompanied her body to Woking, where cremation took place. The ashes were taken back by Miss Loring to America: and were laid in the family plot in Cambridge cemetery.

The claim of life against the claim of death—this is the assertion of every page of Alice's diary. Even when her strength failed her, she brought a resistance to death that was all the stronger for her having decided long before that she would not take her own life. In her final entry she says she had "almost asked for Katharine's lethal dose," but added that "one steps hesitatingly along such unaccustomed ways and endures from second to second." The need to endure beyond the grave was reflected in her worries, even in the final hours, about her prose. This prose had in it many echoes from her father—his quickness to seize on the paradoxical and the contradictory, his double-play between man's glory as a creature of God and man's mundane stupidity. However much she might be exhausted and depressed, Alice's aggressive intellectual strength, her ability to exclaim and to complain—literally to fight disability and the cruelty of her fate—revealed itself in all that she set down. Life is reduced in the diary largely to the simple existential fact—as it was for her. "He didn't fear Death, but he feared dying," she had written in her commonplace book, long before the doctors gave her the final verdict. Yet she chose the act of dying rather than the immediacy of death, even as she had chosen illness, and to this act she addressed herself in her pages.

For the rest she had her string of daily facts, her comments on British manners, the crass egotism of the gentry, the misery of the masses, the heroic qualities she saw in Parnell. Her expatriation aided her. One cannot imagine her keeping quite this kind of diary in Mount Vernon Street: she needed something alien on which to discharge her anger. Her British surroundings made her even more American than she was. Only an American, living abroad, could ridicule "the British constitution of things" quite as pointedly as Alice does—the monarchy and "its tinsel capacity," the "boneless church," the "hysterical legislation over a dog with a broken leg whilst Society is engaged making bags of 4,000 pheasants or gloating over foxes torn to pieces by a pack of hounds!" The docility of classes enslaved by respectability, whatever the "good form" of the moment may be; and finally the supine masses,

> the passivity with which the working man allows himself to be patted and legislated out of all independence; thus the profound ineradicables in the bone and sinew conviction that outlying regions are their preserves, that they alone of human races massacre savages out of pure virtue. It would ill-become an American to reflect upon the treatment of aboriginal races; but I never heard it suggested that our hideous dealings with the Indians *was* brotherly love masquerading under the disguise of pure "cussedness."

That was the bite in Alice's prose, as she looked at the British world through the newspapers; and doubtless there was within it an unpleasant, overly aggressive side, which her brother caught when he was creating Rosie, the little working-class invalid, in *The Princess Casamassima.* Alice could seize on one of her brother's amusing anecdotes—say, his remarks about some individual—and spend a full page tearing the poor man to pieces. Life had to answer for a great deal to her; and when she could discharge her resentments nowhere else she attached them to a mere bit of gossip, a humble paragraph in the *Standard* or the *Times.* She possessed a vigorous and often belligerent democratic feeling. "She was really an Irishwoman!" Henry exclaimed as he read her, "transplanted, transfigured—but none the less fundamentally natural—in spite of her so much larger and finer than Irish intelligence. She felt the Home Rule question absolutely as only an Irishwoman (not anglicized) could. It was a tremendous emotion with her—inexplicable in any other way—but perfectly explicable by 'atavism.' What a pity she wasn't born there—and had her health for it. She would have been . . . a national glory!"

Henry's tribute to Alice's diary was contained in a long letter written to his brother from Rome on May 28, 1894. The first part expressed his concern at the printing of four copies by Katharine Loring (one for each of the brothers and one for herself), and the failure to disguise names and persons, the danger this represented to his privacy and the privacy of others. Then, turning away from his misgivings, he launched into an appreciation of his sister's power as a writer, and here there were few reservations, save in his feeling quite accurately that the diary reflected Alice's confined state. As he put it, "she simplified too much, shut up in her sick room, exercised her wondrous vigour of judgment on too small a scrap of what really surrounded her." He felt her opinion of the English might have been modified

> if she had *lived* with them more—seen more of the men, etc. But doubtless it is fortunate for the fun and humour of the thing that it wasn't modified—as surely the critical emotion [about them], the essence of much of their nature, was never more beautifully expressed. . . .
>
> As regards the life, the power, the temper, the humour and beauty and expressiveness of the Diary in itself—these things were partly "discounted" to me in advance by so much of Alice's talk during her last years—and my constant association with her—which led me often to reflect about her extraordinary force of mind and character, her whole way of taking life—and death—in very much the manner in which the book does. I find in its pages, for instance, many things I heard her say. None the less I have been immensely impressed with the thing as a revelation of a moral and personal picture. It is heroic in its individuality, its independence—its face-to-face with the universe for-and-by herself—and the beauty and eloquence with which she often expresses this, let alone the rich irony and humour, constitute (I wholly agree with you) a new claim for the family renown. This last element—her style, her power to write—are indeed to me a delight—for I never had many letters from her. Also it brings back to me all sorts of things I am glad to keep—I mean things that happened, hours, occasions, conversations—brings them back with a strange, living richness. But it also puts before me what I was tremendously conscious of in her lifetime—that the extraordinary intensity of her will and personality really would have made the equal, the reciprocal life of a "well" person—in the usual world

—almost impossible to her—so that her disastrous, her tragic health was, in a manner, the only solution for her of the practical problem of life—as it suppressed the element of equality, reciprocity, etc. . . . As for her allusions to H.—they fill me with tears and cover me with blushes. What I should LIKE to do *en temps et lieu* would be should no catastrophe meanwhile occur—or even if it should!—to edit the volume with a few eliminations of text and dissimulations of names, give it to the world and then carefully burn with fire our own four copies.

Alice would have agreed with her novelist brother's view that she had been exposed to too little of the world, for she speaks of "my centimeter of observation" and "the poverty of my outside experience." Henry's eloquent appraisal expresses the essence of his sister's life and the strength and weakness of the book she left to the world. His is the testimony of an artist as well as of a brother—one who, next to Miss Loring, had been the most intimate witness of his sister's painful end, in her restricted alien world. That world did not know her; she remained an intensely private memory in the lives of her distinguished brothers and her few surviving friends. It was only years after they had all disappeared from the scene that the contents of the diary became known.

Alice James's record is a particular page of personal history, in an otherwise obscure life, as well as a page in the annals of a family of intellectuals. There are few such documents in American or English literature. Its "facts," as Henry James warned us, are suspect; it is filled with gossip and exaggeration; it seems to be, at times, little more than a series of exclamations. Yet it is an intensely human document. One thinks of Marie Bashkirtseff's journal—the young Russian woman who died of tuberculosis at a much earlier age than Alice. She, however, had been out in the world and had led a precarious life as a painter; she had "lived" in a way that Alice never could. Yet one analogy is possible, for what is to be found in both these nineteenth-century diaries—although they are worlds apart—is the spirit that moved the diarists: their supreme need to perpetuate themselves and the intensity of this need. Alice's diary was her way of conquering time, as Proust might say; it was also her way of asking for a hearing beyond the grave. Not her pages but the spirit residing in them gives the diary its unique place in literature and testifies to its continuing appeal, not least as a passionate document for "literary psychology" but as a feminist manifesto.

The Terror of the Usual

To understand how the author of "The Turn of the Screw" created his apparitions, we must look first at certain elements of his personal history. A ghostly event had colored all the days of Henry James's childhood and youth. It occurred when he was just emerging from the cradle. His father, Henry James, Sr., had taken his family abroad, and in the spring of 1844 they were living in a house on the edge of Windsor Park in England. The elder Henry was an amateur theologian who liked to study the scriptures; he was a busy, sociable, contradictory man, very active in spite of a wooden leg, the result of a childhood accident. He had a lively temperament, an Irish wit, a fund of aggressive eloquence. In his later years, in a book called *Society the Redeemed Form of Man* (and in a chapter titled "My Moral Death and Burial"), he described how one day, in his house at Windsor, he ate a good meal and sat gazing idly at the embers, "thinking of nothing, and feeling only the exhilaration incident to good digestion." His mind was unfocused; he was delivered up to day-thought and day-dream. Suddenly he experienced that "fear and trembling" described in the Psalms, recorded by many visionaries and saints. He had a horrible sense of panic. "To all appearance," the elder Henry wrote, "it was a perfectly insane and abject terror, without ostensible cause." He saw nothing. The room was filled with the light of common day; the embers in the grate glowed; the table was before him, with the remnants of the meal upon it. Yet he had the certitude that there was "some damned shape squatting invisible to me within the precincts of the room, and raying out from his fetid personality influences fatal to life." Within ten seconds the elder Henry felt himself "a wreck," reduced, as he put it, "from a state of firm, vigorous, joyful manhood to one of almost helpless infancy." He remained frozen in his seat. He remembered he wanted to call for help. He wanted to run to the roadside, to ask passersby to shield him from his vision of damnation. But he controlled his "frenzied impulses." How much time passed he could not say. It seemed like an hour, during which he was "beat upon by an ever-growing tempest of doubt, anxiety and despair, with absolutely no relief from any truth I had ever encountered save a most pale and distant glimmer of divine existence." Finally he found the strength to abandon the struggle and call his wife to help him.

The sequel to this moment of the supernatural was often told in the family annals: how for the next two years the elder Henry suffered from a "ghastly condition of mind"; how doctors recommended rest, sleep, "cures" at watering places. Nothing helped, until a lady recommended the writings of Emmanuel Swedenborg, the Swedish visionary. In his books and teachings, the novelist's father found calm and solace. Swedenborg gave him a picture of man as having the divine aspect of God and capable of converse with angels. He helped him overcome his fear of the Calvinist deity of wrath. As might be expected, this "vastation"—for so the Swedenborgians called his moment of fear and trembling—remained a profound family memory. Henry James was put in possession, from the first, of a sense of extra-human evil, the idea that man could be haunted—as his father had been—by daylight ghosts.

In his early years, William James, elder brother of the novelist, who would be the founder of psychological study in America, had an experience that seemed almost a recall of his father's, save that he materialized the invisible shape of evil. In recording the event, he notes that he had been in a state of "philosophical pessimism and general depression of spirits." One evening he stepped into a dressing room in his home to procure some article—"when suddenly there fell upon me without any warning, just as if it came out of the darkness, a horrible fear of my own existence." The fear was embodied in the memory of an epileptic patient he had seen during his medical studies in the asylum, "a black-haired youth with greenish skin, entirely idiotic, who used to sit all day on one of the benches, or rather shelves, against the wall, with his knees drawn up against his chin, and the coarse gray undershirt, which was his only garment, drawn over them enclosing his entire figure. He sat there like a sort of sculptured Egyptian cat or Peruvian mummy, moving nothing but his black eyes and looking absolutely non-human." "That shape am I," William James told himself—"at least potentially," and he became "a mass of quivering fear." Like his father he awoke for days after with "a sense of the insecurity of life." He had never known such insecurity before, and he never felt it afterward. "It was like a revelation," he said. William James pursued his inquiries into the occult all his life in the margin of his psychological and philosophical studies. He attended séances, studied mediums, investigated every manifestation of the "spirit world" reported to him. Ultimately he wrote his inspired book, *The Varieties of Religious Experience.*

The younger Henry James had no waking experiences comparable to those of his father or brother. But he recorded in his autobiographies the memory of a nightmare which he described as "appalling" while at the same time calling it "admirable" and a "dream-adventure." Fear and delight were mingled in it. He dreamed that he was defending himself in abject terror against an invader, fighting to keep him from bursting through the closed door of his room. Then suddenly the tables were turned. The door was open. However, instead of the monster entering he saw that it was racing away down a great corridor filled with works of art amid thunder and lightning. He recognized the place: it was the grand Galerie d'Apollon in the Louvre. What had begun as a nightmare of confrontation ended in total victory. Unlike his father and brother, Henry James seemed to be saying with Dr. Johnson, "I, sir, should have frightened the ghost." Particularly interesting was Henry James's revelation that this dream was dreamed late in life. It seems to belong to a period later than that in which he wrote most of his ghost stories, and it suggests that he discovered in some strange way the means by which he could both dream of terror and find the control and the defense to banish it. He seems to have had to fight this kind of battle repeatedly, for there are records of other and similar dreams with this recurrent theme. Lady Ottoline Morrell's memoirs record Henry James's telling her a dream, how "he found himself in a house or shop full of furniture, huge rooms of beautiful cabinets and chairs and tables. He wandered all over the house feeling a vague mysterious presence. At last, arriving upstairs, he found himself in a room in which an old man was sitting in a chair. He called out to the man, 'You're afraid of me, you coward.' The man said, 'No.' Henry James replied, 'But you are, I know it. I see the sweat on your brow.' "

There is an extraordinary dream "maneuver" in these nightmares. James begins with a strong sense of terror or anxiety; then in the same dream he proceeds to an action which defeats this anxiety. Threatened, he turns the tables and becomes the threatener. This is expressed in the account of the dream of the Louvre as "I, in my appalled state, was probably still more appalling than the awful agent, creature, or presence." He would never forget this: that a haunted person's fright can also prove frightening. This is clearly suggested to us in "The Turn of the Screw." It is also the theme of his unfinished ghost novel, *The Sense of the Past,* in which a man from the present wanders into the past and then is terrified that he will remain imprisoned in it. In his fear he at the same time creates fear in all the other personages. The dreams of confrontation take the shape of a confronting "me" and "not-me," as in his ultimate supernatural tale of "The Jolly Corner."

Out of this kind of family experience, and his own occult dreams and imaginings, came Henry James's ghost stories—out of the novelist's sense that man somehow is in some relation with impenetrable and mysterious forces, outside himself, outside of human control—as they had been outside of his father's or of William's. This led James to write not only stories in which there are materialized ghosts, but another kind he described as "gruesome" and "quasi-supernatural." His earliest tales, those of the 1860s, are sufficiently conventional. The second group, including "The Turn of the Screw," belongs to his middle age, when he was in a state of great anxiety and depression. It is in these that he established his "daylight ghost," the ghost that walks without benefit of white sheet, bloodstains, shrieks, unearthly noises, and other Gothic elements. The last batch, written in the new century, contain some of his most interesting phantoms and anti-phantoms, some demonic and frightening, others benign and even occasionally comic. James's finest tales often are without phantoms at all, but are wrought with an ambiance of "the strange and sinister embroidered on the very type of the normal and easy." As with his father's "vastation," James sought to create what might be described as "the terror of the usual."

His masterwork of the gruesome and ghostly is the tale he wrote late in 1897—his story of a haunted governess and some children—which from the first captured the public imagination and has since been turned into a play, an opera, and a film, as well as a television drama. Critics have not been able to agree in their interpretations of "The Turn of the Screw," but they are in full agreement that, of its kind, it is a masterpiece. James said that in this tale he wanted to make the air "reek" with evil.

The story is told by a young governess in a manuscript she has left behind after her death. What is at stake is the credibility of this young woman as a witness. James gives us a hint when he speaks in his preface of his having had to keep her record "crystalline" because she was describing so many ambiguities and anomalies. However, he promptly adds these significant words: "by which I don't of course mean her explanation of them, a different matter." There is no question that the young woman sees the ghosts of Peter Quint and of Miss Jessel. We recognize also that she is making an extraordinary effort to keep calm in the face of the evil she fears. The evil, however, is in her own mind; when she has the "certitude" that her ghosts have come for the children, the reader must decide whether she is stating a fact or enunciating a theory. Looking back over her story, we discover that her circumstantial account of the behavior of the children establishes them as "normal." Little Miles wants to know when he is going back to school; little Flora's escapade with the boat is perfectly in character for an eight-year-old. Yet the governess makes the behavior of the children seem sinister. The real "turn of the screw"—the particular twist of pain in the tale—resides in what the governess is doing to the children. They, on their side, try constantly to accommodate themselves to her unearthly vision.

James said he wanted to convey the "communication to the children of the most infernal imaginable evil and danger—the condition, on their part, of being as *exposed* as we can humanly conceive children to be." Exposed, we may judge, not to the ghosts, which they do not even see, but to the governess, who does see them. In the final scene, horrible in its intensity and violence, the governess wins a strange victory. She believes she has succeeded in driving the evil spirit out of little Miles; she has saved his soul. But, as in tales of demonic possession, "his little heart, dispossessed, had stopped." "The Turn of the Screw" is a powerful tale of possession, as in the old fables of demons and dybbuks; and it is the governess who is possessed. Her demoniacal and malevolent imagination converts her anxieties and guilts, her romantic-sexual imaginings, which she considers "sinful," into demons and damned spirits. In seeking to cope with her own demons she infects those around her—as Hitler, raving and ranting, infected an entire nation with his hysteria. The contagion, indeed the epidemic quality of the malevolent imagination, is the ultimate horror of James's tale. This is perhaps why many have experienced it as the most frightening ghost story they have ever read.

Its effects are derived from James's theories of the supernatural. "So long as the events are veiled," James once explained, "the imagination will run riot and depict all sorts of horrors, but as soon as the veil is lifted, all mystery disappears." Everything in James's tale is mysterious; every part of "The Turn of the Screw" seems to be concrete, and yet there is always a refusal on his part to specify. The story itself, we are told, is a printed version of a copy of an old manuscript. The governess has no name. She doesn't describe herself. We do not know what kind of clothes she wears. We have only the barest details of her background. We know only her daydreams. These are abundant and fanciful. In his preface, written ten years after publishing the story, James is explicit about what he has done. He tells us he has given each reader a blank check—told him to draw all the funds he needs out of his private bank of horror. "Only make the reader's general vision of evil intense enough . . . and his own experience, his own imagination . . . will supply him quite sufficiently with all the particulars. Make him *think* the evil, make him think it for himself, and you are released from weak specifications."

James spoke of the ghosts of Miss Jessel and Peter Quint as not being ghosts at all, in the usual sense, but "goblins, elves, imps, demons, as loosely constructed as those of the old trials for witchcraft." They represent any of the forms taken by the good and bad fairies of the mind—the witches bent on violence or the fairies "of legendary order, wooing their victims forth to see them dance under the moon." For James the ghostly tale was "the most possible form of the fairy-tale." In the fairy tale, great wonders are made real to children; ogres and giants are encountered; Cinderella finds her prince; carpets fly. So the wonders of the imagination in the ghost story—the goblins and demons of man's inner world—take their shape and are spun into the wonders of the storyteller's art.

He expressed this in another way in the great theatrical scene of *The Golden Bowl,* his last novel, when the heroine watches a game of bridge in which her unfaithful husband and his mistress are partners. She thinks of "the horror of finding evil seated, all at its ease, where she had dreamed only of good; the horror of the thing hideously *behind,* behind so much trusted, so much pretended, nobleness, cleverness, tenderness." This was the first "sharp falsity" she had ever encountered, and James images the falsity as if it were a ghost: "it had met her like some bad-faced stranger surprised in one of the thick-carpeted corridors of a house of quiet on a Sunday afternoon."

This is the most horrible kind of fright—a house of quiet, a Sunday afternoon, and suddenly an ugly presence, the horror of the thing behind the calm surface. The known things of life present no problem; it is the mysterious, the unknown, the imagined horror, the thing *behind* which shakes heart and mind. In his artist's way, James refuses to deal with rationalizations. He isn't going to explain his father's vastation. The terrible ghost was invisible; yet his father's fright was genuine, his haunted state had been horrible. James sought to capture this kind of reality in occult experience. That is why his ghost stories, even those written mechanically for the Christmas issues of magazines, have in them a sense of strangeness, an evocation of an impalpable world, of private phantoms. The novelist added few new situations to the supernatural; he invented no new haunting apparitions. Yet he took the worn ghost story and left it immeasurably enriched. He showed us how the unreal and phantasmagoric are attached at a hundred points to daily existence; and he drew his readers into the mysterious world of daylight ghosts by a subtle grasp of what a storyteller can do for his listeners, like the narrator of the *Arabian Nights.* He knew, uncannily, how to make us walk in his company, in the broad daylight of our own lives—with our own ghosts.

THE KILLER AND THE SLAIN

The starting point for this inquiry is a dedication. The last novel written by Hugh Walpole, the popular English novelist who died in 1941, was entitled *The Killer and the Slain*. He left behind the completed manuscript, marked as follows: "This macabre is dedicated in loving memory and humble admiration to the great author of *The Turning of the Screw*." The British edition adhered to this wording. The American edition corrected Walpole's slip; Henry James's famous "macabre" is titled "The Turn of the Screw."

Dedications reveal certain things: they originate in some form of personal relationship; they reflect certain wishes or intentions on the part of the author. We have seen this in the way in which Willa Cather, motivated both by dislike and guilt, dedicated two of her novels to the same man. The form of the Walpole dedication is distinctly affectionate. However, it doesn't mention Henry James by name. He is admired as the author of a specific work. It is the work that is essentially in question: the author of a macabre dedicates his story to a master of the occult. But in his dedication—James had been dead for a quarter of a century—Walpole gets the title wrong. On investigation, I found that Walpole had also dedicated an earlier book, a limited edition of certain of his reminiscences, to James: "For Henry James As He Knows With Love." This intimate tribute to the novelist was published in 1932, when James had been dead sixteen years. Thus both of Walpole's dedications were posthumous. The more public tribute in *The Killer and*

the Slain was, as I have said, in Walpole's last book. The dedication, when it finally appeared, was an offering from the dead to
the dead.

The problem of the dedication was first brought to my attention by Rupert Hart-Davis, my British publisher, in 1950. He
had been Walpole's editor and friend and was his literary executor. He had decided to write a biography of the novelist, and he
asked me what I could make of the dedication: its posthumous
character, its homage, and the slip of the pen. Could this have
significance? I said I would try to see what the story itself told
me; later I would look at any data Hart-Davis could furnish. He
accordingly sent me a copy of the English edition and wrote in
it, "in hope of a diagnosis."

I

I read the absorbing macabre in one sitting. It was what we
today call a page-turner. The story dealt with a murderer who
becomes the man he murders. I noticed Walpole subtitled it "A
Strange Story," but with time it had lost some of its strangeness
because we have become accustomed in the media to Jekyll-
and-Hyde tales of doubles and Conradian "secret sharers." This
seemed indeed dream stuff, as if Walpole wrote off the top of
his head. His use of relevant detail, his general way of sketching
a character, his skilled pacing suggested that the author's pen
couldn't keep up with the speed of his fancy.

In literary psychology one looks carefully at the names chosen by an author for his characters. The narrator, who is also the
killer, is John Ozias Talbot; his double is James Oliphant Tunstall. John and James—like Joyce's Shaun and Shem—are common enough, but the choice of James at once gives us a link to
the dedication. The character doesn't begin to resemble the
author of "The Turn of the Screw." Still, both characters are
given the same initials, which is appropriate, since they are
doubles. I thought the names Tunstall and Ozias a bit out of the
way until I discovered there had been an Ozias Humphrey

among Horace Walpole's friends—but Horace was no ancestor of Hugh's. The Tunstall (a name that occurs in Walter Scott) I found was also the name of Bishop Cuthbert Tunstall (1474), and this might have some connection because Hugh Walpole's father was in his later years the Bishop of Edinburgh. I could find no associations for Oliphant, except that it crops up in literary history and the novelist Mrs. Oliphant had been an acquaintance of Henry James's. A name exploration is always amusing, but it can lead us into a dead end. We never know whether the names have the same meaning to the writer as they do to us. So for the moment I pigeonholed them. Perhaps later they might shed some light.

I was struck, however, by one fairly tangible association. It is well known that persons using disguised forms of their name very often retain some resemblance. In naming his principal character John Ozias Talbot, and making him a writer, the novelist selected a name partly like Walpole: the *albo* in Talbot is pretty close to the *alpo* in Walpole. John Talbot is described as a sensitive young man who has been raised in a small English seaside town, the son of the local antiquarian. However, he dislikes his corpulent and doting father and finds his affectionate embraces suffocating. He worships his mother. Walpole describes Talbot in some detail as an artistic youth. He is effeminate in build, afraid of the world, afraid of his playmates, shy at school, bookish, fearful of swearing and drink, certainly not a "man's man"—and for that matter, scarcely a woman's, either. At school, the passive Talbot encounters James Oliphant Tunstall, who is the opposite of himself, active, masculine, athletic, with skill in drawing (mainly bawdy pictures), and occupied with the sensual things of life. "I'm the other side of yourself, the side you're not very proud of," he says to Talbot, whom he often treats roughly and humiliates—once by snatching off his bathing trunks so as to expose his genitals. Between them there is a certain attachment, difficult to define.

They go their separate ways after they leave school. Talbot

succeeds to his father's antique shop, writes a minor unsuccessful novel, marries a young woman even though she tells him she respects him but doesn't love him. The marriage speedily deteriorates. Talbot leads a passive self-absorbed life and allows his wife to run the business. They change roles. In effect she becomes the man of the family.

Then Tunstall returns to town. He is more macho than ever. An artist of sorts, heavy, dissipated, he spends much of his time in the local tavern; and he resumes his old aggressive manner toward his former schoolmate. He confides in him, gives him all the details of his affair with a woman in the town, urges Talbot to drink with him. The latter shrinks from him as always and is filled with a certain loathing. Yet Tunstall continues to remind him they have much in common. Talbot rejects this vehemently.

Walpole makes a special point of endowing Tunstall with what are regarded as masculine physical characteristics—he is big, hairy, gross, compared with the hairless, thin-skinned Talbot. Tunstall is filled with sexual swagger and even begins to show an interest in Talbot's wife and his little son. It is when Tunstall begins to pay attention to the boy that Talbot decides he must act. He knows from Tunstall when the latter will be on the cliffs, waiting for a signal light to appear in the house of his mistress. With great care he goes to see a movie (he chooses *David Copperfield,* for which Walpole wrote the script in Hollywood) but immediately leaves the theater through a side entrance. His alibi established, he waits for Tunstall and with a tremendous show of energy has no difficulty catching him by surprise and pushing him over the cliff into the sea.

I I

Suddenly John Talbot feels himself more masculine than he has ever been. He goes home and makes love to his wife; for the first time since his marriage he shows a power of assertion. After a while he begins to put on weight; hair begins to grow on his body. He starts to drink. Tunstall's friends become his friends; he even takes over Tunstall's mistress. The body is ultimately found in the sea, but Talbot is not even suspected and a verdict of accidental death is returned by the coroner. Tunstall's widow, whose name is Leila, becomes friendly and gives Talbot her husband's ring, as if she were marrying him. The killer gladly wears it. He has become the slain.

But he finds something holding him back from the widow. He doesn't attempt to make love to her; he treats her as if she were his mother. He has become the man he killed but he cannot become the husband of the widow. He also finds himself rejecting his own wife, and he becomes suspicious of Leila's brother, a man as modest and reticent as Talbot had been. It occurs to him that this man may kill him, as he had killed Tunstall. Tunstall-Talbot now lives out the classic Jekyll-Hyde nightmare. He determines to shoot the Tunstall brother-in-law; and Tunstall's widow begins to see that Talbot acts as one possessed. In her presence, and in a scene she later describes vividly, the killer is finally purged of the slain. Instead of shooting the man who resembles him, he shoots himself. In a sense the slain has now killed the killer. But the Satanic forces—the essential Evil—have been banished.

Here the connection between Henry James's "Turn of the Screw" and Walpole's fantasy becomes clear. In James's story two children have been confided to a governess who believes the boy, little Miles, is being corrupted by a dead man, a former servant named Peter Quint. At the end of the story the governess confronts the ghost of Quint (which she sees, though the boy doesn't) in an attempt to exorcise the evil she feels has taken possession of the little boy. The last words of the story, as little Miles dies, are "and his little heart, dispossessed, had stopped." The final scene of *The Killer and the Slain* draws on the James story, and the entire idea of one individual becoming possessed by the evil of another seems to have been suggested by Walpole's reading of "The Turn of the Screw." We remind ourselves that Walpole had used Talbot's little son very much as if he were little Miles being corrupted by an evil man. Tunstall had shown lewd drawings to the boy. Hugh Walpole could well appreciate the rectitude of the governess, who had come out of a Hampshire vicarage; he was, after all, the son of an Anglican bishop. What, we may now ask, was Walpole trying to express in this fantasy? It is the inner story, the story behind the story, that will lead us back to the dedication.

III

What was Hugh Walpole really trying to tell us? What does his story of a killer who becomes the slain express as a fantasy which sprang full-blown from Walpole's unconscious and was set down by him with such urgency? It is a tale of a man lacking masculinity who is fighting the idea of becoming masculine; and in trying to kill the masculinity he is possessed by those very macho qualities he hated in his double. Only by suppressing the masculine side can he feel masculine—that seems to be the essence of the matter. He can become the slain man in all respects but one: he cannot sleep with his widow. We seem here very close to the Freudian idea of the Oedipus complex, with the difference that Oedipus committed unwittingly the incest which Tunstall-Talbot cannot commit since he regards the widow as a mother. And this suggests that Tunstall has been a kind of father figure—strong, powerful, masculine. And the fact that he *becomes* the father seems important, for it suggests that although the fantasy was Oedipal, its principal component was homosexual. In the end, the murderer, having had the strength to intraject his double, is overcome by guilt—and by the fear that he too will be a victim of what he has done. He must punish himself, but not so much for the crime he has committed as out of fear of the masculinity he has won at such a price. What we begin to see is that Walpole identified Tunstall's kind of masculinity with evil. The conflict in the author reflected in his story is between deficient manhood and overcompensation for the

THE KILLER AND THE SLAIN 315

lack of it. In other words he can accept himself neither as the weak Talbot nor as the strong and evil Tunstall. And since he can only integrate the two in a fantasy, he must annihilate both. One part of the divided self destroys the other.

It is now possible to look back at Walpole's slip of the pen. He wrote *turning* instead of *turn*. This is the difference between a continuum and an accomplished act. A *turn* of the thumb-screw inflicts pain; constant *turning* inflicts continuous pain. The dedication, we may now surmise, seems to speak for an unresolved and continuous conflict in Hugh Walpole—something that was "turning" during all the years of Walpole's life.

IV

I have told the story of the friendship between Henry James and Hugh Walpole in the final volume of my life of James, *The Master,* and I will only briefly summarize it here. (Walpole was among the first to call James "Master"—a name used also by Conrad and others for Henry James's mastery of the novel form and his life achievement.) Walpole was twenty-four when he met the sixty-six-year-old James in 1908. He had come to London to make his way as a writer. James was then beginning to experience the depression of aging. He had an enormous reputation, but his books did not sell. He felt rejected by his admiring public and very lonely. Young Walpole came to him in admiration and worship. James allowed Walpole to write to him as "dearest Master," and James on his side wrote "dearest, dearest darlingest Hugh." Shortly after they met, James wrote to a friend that he had been touched by "Walpole's beautiful candour of appreciation of my 'feeble efforts' etc. I feel for him the tenderest sympathy and an absolute affection." James gave this affection to the end and remembered Walpole in his will. But he was very critical: he endowed Walpole with his own artistic drive, his own demands for perfection. The result was that he was, as he himself said, "damned critical" of Walpole's writings.

By the time James met Walpole, the American novelist had

discovered and recognized—late in life—his homoerotic feelings and accepted his unlived homosexual life, although we have no way of knowing how much he "lived" out the late awakening of his passions. In James's stories about writers there always is a young devoted acolyte in the foreground. It was almost as if James had invented Hugh before their friendship. There was a story, spread by Somerset Maugham, that Hugh offered himself to James, who reacted with "I can't, I can't, I can't!" (Maugham disliked Hugh and mocked him later in *Cakes and Ale.*) The James-Walpole relation increasingly became that of father and son, and Walpole on one occasion signed himself "your loving *fils.*" The friendship lasted into the 1914–18 war; Hugh was on the Russian front in an ambulance corps when he got the news of James's death in 1916.

V

It is therefore understandable that at the very beginning of the Second World War, in 1939, Hugh's mind went back to the beginning of the earlier war and he wrote a reminiscence of Henry James. In the second paragraph he says, "What wars can do to extend horizons! James died in the middle of the 1914–1918 War and now in the 1939—? he seems a mythical figure, like one of the Blake presences in *The Book of Job.*" That spring Hugh began to write *The Killer and the Slain,* although the idea had been in his notebook for almost ten years. In September 1937 he wrote that "the theme has obsessed me as no idea for a book ever has before." He added that "it will undoubtedly write itself and should be my *best* macabre and one of the very best ever *if* it comes out right."

The First World War had been a troubled time for Hugh. Disqualified from the army by bad eyesight, he was uncertain what to do, and yet not to be a soldier was to fail to assert his masculinity. When James had met him, the young writer still had a reputation to make. James had encouraged him, but not without his characteristic mix of warmth and condescension. He wrote of Walpole's first novels that they were "juvenility reacting in the presence of everything." Since Walpole was by that time thirty, he may have winced at the word "juvenility." James also said that the novels reflected a "primitive predicament" and were written on "more or less virgin snow," upon which he looked forward to "the imprint of a process." To have his work, however youthful, characterized by a master of the novel in this way—and from whom he sought appreciation—could be both flattering and painful. James on his side carried out one of his characteristically evasive tactics. Unable to say much in praise of the work and yet not wishing to hurt, he praised Hugh himself, and clearly hurt him very much.

In his 1940 reminiscence, Walpole remembered that he was welcomed by James's friends "because of my vitality. They all hoped that in time I might mature and learn some taste, discretion, wisdom. What they most of them lacked was this same physical vitality. If only I might combine it with a few brains! they murmured." He was still, as late as this, seeing himself in Tunstall terms; but he wanted to be like Henry James, whose personality was strong, creative, and power-wielding. Walpole was proud of his own physical vigor and his athletic abilities. At the same time he felt himself the immature and weak aspirant to "taste, discretion, wisdom." He could thus, in writing *The Killer and the Slain,* consciously or unconsciously (I suspect largely unconsciously) put some of his feelings about James into the super-masculine character to whom he gave the name of James—James Oliphant Tunstall.

The choice by Walpole of the name James may seem rather obvious. But we must remember that with the entire alphabet to choose from, Walpole had selected the letter J. The name James inevitably had strong associations. We now ask ourselves what made him put Oliphant beside it?

We think at once of Laurence Oliphant and Mrs. Oliphant,

both nineteenth-century writers, and note even more significantly that James's recollections of Mrs. Oliphant were included by him in *Notes on Novelists* (1914), which also contains gentle patronizing comments on Hugh Walpole's novels. But the name leads us in a very straight line to letters written by James to Walpole early in their friendship. Here, as we read, we are suddenly confronted by one of James's characteristic flourishes: he begins one letter with an allusion to himself as "poor ponderous superannuated," and follows this in a second (of October 1909) with a direct allusion to himself as a jungle beast—"Beautiful and admirable of you to have threshed through the tropic jungle of your 30 waiting letters to get at *this* elephant—who accordingly winds round you, in a structure of gratitude and affection all *but* fatal, his well-meaning old trunk."

This is a striking image of an all-embracing ponderous old father, almost too possessive, clutching to him (in a grasp "all but fatal") his young son, waving his old trunk in a way to fix the image permanently in Walpole's mind. But James did not leave it at that; there were reiterations and further gambols which would make the memory unforgettable. A few days later James recalls himself as "the faithful elephant." Two weeks later "your old elephant." And two weeks later "your poor old ponderous elephant."

Now the choice of James as name for Tunstall acquires singular relevance. The older Hugh Walpole, the Walpole of 1940, dredges out of the young Hugh Walpole's memory of 1909 the name James Oliphant Tunstall, or James-the-old-elephant—a portmanteau name that would have delighted the author of *Finnegans Wake.* And we have proof that the elephant image was fixed permanently in Walpole's mind: the image of the stout novelist's ponderous figure, bloated by ill health and age. In 1915, H. G. Wells poked fun at Henry James, saying his novels reminded him of "a magnificent but painful hippopotamus resolved at any cost, even at the cost of its dignity, upon

picking up a pea." Walpole quoted this in a reminiscence sixteen years later but committed a zoological error. "The major-
ity of critics," Walpole wrote of James, "thought that his Pref-
aces were a sheer waste of time, the Elephant pursuing the
pea." In this way the Wellsian hippopotamus merged with the
Jamesian elephant in Walpole's mind. James thus is Tunstall;
and his power and fertility made Hugh feel small and effeminate. Walpole would have been shocked at the idea that he
unconsciously thought of homicide in relation to Henry James,
but Hugh's unconscious was filled with violence, as we shall see:
violence submerged behind the civilized author and art collector.

In the light of these links in a chain of subjective evidence,
we can now summarize our literary-psychological speculation.
The writing of *The Killer and the Slain* coincided with the
beginning of the Second World War. Walpole saw in James the
figure he had wanted to be, and the war revived many memories. For this figure Walpole had feelings of admiration and
worship and at the same time resentment—for James was un-
swervingly critical and demanding. James represented the
strength of creativity, and the young writer was fascinated by
him and feared him at the same time, in the way that Tunstall
fascinates Talbot. In the novel we have thus the classic destruction of a father image. Only by destroying this image could
Walpole feel himself creative, potent, masculine. However, he
identified masculinity with evil. He accordingly sketched a
character whose manliness is aggressively macho.

Writing this in the form of a tale of terror and with "The Turn
of the Screw" in his memory, he finally dedicated his novel to
the author of the celebrated story. In the dedication Walpole
puts himself, under the disguise of his act of homage, on the
same level as the Master. Talbot-Walpole kills James-Old Ele-
phant-Turnscrew and then is able to be James. Killer becomes
slain. But then there is guilt. It is eerie to learn that Walpole

died at the age of fifty-seven, six months after completing his novel. Those who knew him said that the war seemed to have undermined his will to live.

At his death he had completed the fantasy: his last novel contained the submerged hostilities he had felt toward the author he had loved. He dedicated the novel to the man he had supplanted in his imagination. That would suggest that he in reality dedicated it to himself.

V I

Having written out the foregoing, I sent it to Rupert Hart-Davis as the "diagnosis" he had asked for. He consulted Walpole's diaries and was able to furnish certain validating evidence. Here are the entries he sent me:

30 June 1940	Began *The Killer and the Slain.*
13 July	11,000 words sent to the typist.
September 1940	"It may be awfully good. I can't tell till I come to the hard part, which is the second half. Meanwhile what a lot of nastiness and pity for my own nastiness, I have in me! It's all coming out in this work."
25 October 1940	Read James's [*Notes of a*] *Son and Brother.* "Very happy."
December 1940	*"The Killer* most exciting to do. It's exactly like automatic writing. A very odd book that nobody will like . . . all these months of fear, uncertainty, restlessness are behind it."
7 January 1941	Book finished. "This book I had to write. In all my long literary life I have never known anything so like automatic writing. I simply put down what I had to put down. This doesn't mean of course that it is good. But technically at least it is, I think, the best of my macabre. Very difficult, but the difficulties, I fancy, are not evident."

| 12 May 1941 | He read through the typescript and decided that it was "certainly a nasty book." |
| 1 June 1941 | Hugh died. |

These entries show the extent to which Walpole identified himself with Talbot—"what a lot of nastiness and pity for my own nastiness, I have in me! It's all coming out in this work." We see the compulsive writing—he calls it "automatic." The connection between the two wars is made. But perhaps the most significant revelation is his reading in *Notes of a Son and Brother* about Henry James's relation with his father. Walpole's rereading of this work at this moment shows the extent to which his old friend was in his mind as he was writing a macabre in which he was killing him. James was there in the exact role of Tunstall —and Walpole is made happy with the renewed acquaintance with his old generous but critical friend. He almost feels as if he were writing "notes of a son" and a father—but the notes are filled with conflict and violence. He then placates the Master by dedicating the work and praising "The Turn of the Screw" and expressing his humble admiration. But the fantasy includes the death of Talbot—and so, by this token, Walpole closed the book of his own life.

An Afterword

After rereading and revising this paper written thirty years ago, it occurs to me that I may have created an impression that Hugh Walpole was given a cruel upbringing by his religious parents. The Hart-Davis biography makes clear that Walpole suffered not so much from parental strictness as from neglect. In his need to be loved, he searched for a benign father, since Bishop Walpole was taken up with major clerical duties. Life refused to give reality to Hugh's fantasies. There was no ideal father figure. And father figures like Talbot and Tunstall were "doubles," a mix of good and bad. Sent early to school in England, when his father was teaching theology in New York, Hugh Walpole suffered much abuse from the older boys and some of his sadistic masters. His escape into fantasy—fantasies of good and evil inculcated in him by his father and confirmed by his school experience—was continuous. He remained, as one who knew him in his boyhood said, "a misunderstood and lonely and unhappy little boy," a solitary child, eager to be loved, and eager to express his young enthusiasms. He was a young romantic who admired women but also feared them; and he was driven into the loves and cruelties of his own sex. "A nice boy," said A. C. Benson at a later stage, "full of anxiety and good feeling." The anxiety was not of the free-floating kind. He was possessed by genuine unconscious terror. All his life Hugh Walpole dreamed terrible nightmares in which he was whipped, strangled, beaten.

He learned to convey this nightmare world in his stories. Life was ambivalence: he could accept his homosexuality, but he also regarded it as sinful and carried constant guilt at "my own nastiness." Henry James gave him love; but he was as demanding as the bishop father. "I am defenseless and naked in a world of hostile enemies," Walpole once said. That bit of redundancy —*hostile* enemies, as if enemies could be friendly—suggests that he divided the world into two kinds of enmity: and this was the way he drew his characters. John Talbot's dilemma is that Tunstall is both hostile and friendly. How defend oneself against such enemies? The answer had been discovered when he was a boy: identify with the strong, become strong, and then one is assured of strength and power. Henry James was a powerful law-giving artist. So in the end Hugh, in his fantasy, *became* Henry James, and to be James was to write his own version of "The Turn of the Screw." Aggression, power, strength, obtained on such terms, bring enormous feelings of remorse.

Some such interpretation might be made of all our data. The

fantasy is as primitive as cannibals who eat their enemies in order to gain their strength. The dedication of *The Killer and the Slain* ambiguously invokes Walpole's long-dead friend—the friendly enemy of his youth. The slip of the pen speaks for the chronic condition of his life—there had always been a turning of the screw for Hugh, a continual conflict of competition and identification that was never resolved. It could never be resolved, for it was both the source of Hugh Walpole's strength as a storyteller and the source of his recurrent nightmares. So he wrote *The Killer and the Slain* and, like James's little Miles, died dispossessed—dispossessed of his demons and finding in death in his fifties the calm his inner self could no longer find in life.

KIPLING'S AMERICAN DOUBLE

Charles Wolcott Balestier, an enterprising young man—he was then twenty-seven—genial, versatile, accommodating, arrived in London in December 1888 to serve as agent for a New York publisher. In the three ensuing years he made a distinctive place for himself in a courageous and businesslike attempt to overcome the pirating of English writers in America, obtaining at the same time a stable of famous authors for his firm. There was a touch of genius in this proceeding; and then he was not afraid to beard British literary lions in their dens. He arrived in London without knowing a single Englishman, and he died— quite suddenly of typhoid at the end of the three years—leaving behind him a wider circle of friends there (so said Edmund Gosse) "than, probably, any other living American." Balestier's compatriot Henry James said, "it never occurred to him that there was not a way round an obstacle," and he referred to his "Napoleonic propensities." Rudyard Kipling, who knew him best, remained silent, nursing a profound grief. He spoke years later of Balestier's having died "so suddenly and so far away: we had so much to say to each other; and now I have got to wait so long before I can say it." Indeed, on the subject of his dead friend he was never able to say what he wanted. Balestier is not mentioned in Kipling's fragmentary autobiography, although many less important acquaintances are.

A darkening photograph shows the features of this American who touched so swiftly and so deeply such eminent lives. Within its dimness we discern a high forehead, the hair neatly

parted and combed down; we glimpse an oversize and floppy
ear (Gosse called his ears "sensitive") and a prominent nose, the
line of which is continued in a long pencil Balestier is holding
to his mouth as if he were chewing on it while pondering a
sentence. Looking out of the shadows are large uncertain eyes.
The figure slouches uncomfortably, awkwardly, its right elbow
on the table, the left hand pressed with great emphasis on the
left thigh. Frozen in time and chiaroscuro, the long, lean,
slouching shape suggests little of the "charisma" and the nervous energy with which Balestier addressed himself to enter-
prise, charm, conquest. We must turn again to the words of
Gosse, who had his living image—"a carefully-dressed young-
old man" and again "an elderly youth." His mouth, said Gosse,
was mobile and whimsical; he carried himself in a stooping way
as in the photograph; his physique seemed ill-matched to the
vigor he demonstrated, "the protean variety and charm of intellectual vitality." On this all the witnesses agree. Henry James
said he had an exotic and curious influence on those around
him, and he added that he possessed a peculiar genius. *Exotic,
curious, peculiar*—these special words in James's lexicon point
to Balestier's flexible spirit, a gift of artless enthusiasm, an ability
to put himself in the place of those he encountered—in sum a
young man, extrovert and self-assured. There remained always
something boyish about him, in his exuberance, his elasticity,
his manner of reaching for reality in the midst of daydreams.

The way in which he established himself in London suggests
his curious American romanticism. He selected his rooms,
which served also as his office, not in the Strand, nor in Bloomsbury. Nothing would do but chambers in Dean's Yard, right
beside Westminster Abbey. The bells chimed; the shouts of
Westminster School boys, playing association football, mingled
with the chimes. It was ancient, it was picturesque, it was literature; it was a young American's dream of London and of England, and a way of combining the picturesque with the commercial. Arthur Waugh (future father of novelists) has told in his

memoirs how Balestier recruited and trained him to handle proofs and authors. Balestier had smelled the advent of international copyright, which would end the pirating of English works in America. With his sound business sense he urged writers to let him have their works before they were published in England so that they could appear promptly in America in legitimate form. To this end he signed contracts and paid royalties. English writers understandably greeted this bearer of bounty from overseas with open arms, especially since he brought a largeness of spirit, good humor, and a kind of elderly fatherliness, housed in his young frame, that made him a recipient of confidences. Moreover, he was tactful and discreet. "He was not merely one of our conquerors," said Gosse (who in reality thought Balestier in some ways a rather pushing fellow), "but the most successful of them all."

Another young man from the provinces, from India, who had known England in boyhood, arrived in the capital eight or nine months after Balestier. It would never have occurred to Rudyard Kipling to seek rooms beside the Thames, under the towers of the Abbey. He had been accustomed from childhood to the sound of distant temple bells and to the spectacle of teeming multitudes. He liked to be in the midst of things, and in his rooms in the Strand, in Embankment Chambers (in Villiers Street) he could hear the rumble of the Charing Cross trains. He would always like trains, machines, vastness. He liked the life that swarmed around him. His windows looked into the entrance of a music hall; strange characters, all manner of females in particular, drifted in and out. An aroma of sausage from the sausage maker's just below his rooms mingled with other odors as he sat and wrote. (Sausage scraps were often his sole item of food, for he had little money.) Kipling would always be masculine-gregarious. He liked soldierly fellows. But there was something aloof in him, for his unhappy childhood had sown seeds of distrust and distanced him from humans, especially women.

It was Edmund Gosse who advised Balestier to read Kipling,

the genius of the hour from India. "Rudyard Kipling?" retorted
Balestier with simulated indifference. "Is it a man or a woman?
What's its real name?" Gosse was somewhat ruffled. "You won't
be allowed to go on asking such questions," he said, and he
predicted Kipling would be one of the greatest writers of the
day. "Pooh, pooh," said Balestier, sustaining his pose, "now you
are shouting." But when Gosse came to Dean's Yard three days
later, he noted that a pile of the blue pamphlets in which Kipling had been published in India was lying on Balestier's desk.

We know that when Balestier hunted out Kipling, the latter
was in no mood for American overtures. Americans were pi-
rates. Moreover, Balestier pushed him hard. Arthur Waugh has
described how he was sent to Villiers Street to ask for a certain
work of Kipling's not yet completed. He remembered the dark
room and the bard from India sitting on a bed with sheets of
manuscript surrounding him. "Extraordinarily importunate
person, this Mr. Balestier," muttered Kipling to Waugh. "Tell
him *The Book of a Hundred Mornings* is all over my bed and
may never get finished. Tell him to inquire again in six months."

But Waugh remembered "my chief's importunity was to be
satisfied in less time than that." Presently, of all the authors who
came and went in the house beside the Abbey, there was none
more frequent—or more welcomed—than the author of "The
Ballad of East and West."

Charles Wolcott Balestier was born in Rochester, New York,
in 1861. His family was from New England, but there had been
Huguenot ancestors who owned plantations in Martinique.
Wolcott grew up surrounded by an admiring mother and two
devoted sisters; the father seems to have died when his son was
quite young. Balestier met the world with the assurance that he
was the beloved male object in his family; there was no faltering
of identity, no misgiving about his capacities. He attended Cor-
nell; he wrote sketches for the *Atlantic* and was patted on the
back by William Dean Howells. For a while he was a reporter

and a library assistant in New York, and then, at ease with the world, he set out to explore the American West. He camped in mining towns in Colorado; he made his way southward to Mexico. Frail in health, he seems nevertheless to have found enough energy to be ceaselessly active. Returning to New York in his mid-twenties, he joined the publishing firm of John Lovell and in due course, as we have seen, was dispatched to London to carry out his plans for more amicable—and lucrative—relations between American publishers and English writers. What he carried with him also was a vision of the American heartland and of the railroad, then making its way across the continent.

As the expanse of America was in Balestier's mind, so the expanse of India was in the mind of Kipling: his inward vision harbored a sense of the spacious colonial life, servants, people, animals, ancient rites, and the great tracts of desert, although his boyhood had been less fortunate than Balestier's, and he was melancholy and distrustful where Balestier reached out to people, objects, experiences. Both, on the other hand, shared in common a love for the male world of the Victorians. Woman's place in that era was distinctly in the home. This was an unchallenged fact. The barroom, soldiering, the sea—the pistol, the galloping horse—West or East—both knew this kind of camaraderie intimately, in the actual and in fancy. Kipling had lately written his famous ballad in which West and East were never supposed to meet, but one must not overlook the lines in which he made such a meeting possible:

> . . . there is neither East nor West, Border, nor Breed, nor Birth
> When two strong men stand face to face, though they come
>   from the ends of the earth.

In retrospect we can read this as a prophecy of his friendship with Wolcott Balestier. "No man," says Kipling's biographer, Charles Carrington, "ever exercised so dominating an influence over Rudyard Kipling as did Wolcott Balestier during the months of their intimacy."

The record of this intimacy must be deduced from scraps of information. We know that it was brief, less than a year, but the friendship had a strange and powerful intensity. After their first aloof meetings, Balestier's winning ways, his assurance, his four years of seniority, established him as counselor and comrade in the eyes of the young man from India. Moreover, Balestier's mother and sisters, who had come to England to bask in their son's success and take care of him, made Kipling feel thoroughly at home. Once the publisher had organized his affairs and established his good faith, he was able to take London in an easier stride; he found a small cottage retreat on the Isle of Wight, on the south shore, where his sister Caroline was often hostess. Henry James remembered a couple of August days there, a drive with Balestier to Freshwater over the great downs, a lunch in the open, and "a rambling lazy lounge on the high cliffs." Balestier loved this temporary refuge where the great autumn windstorms ministered to his sense of romance and drama. Kipling was with him more often than James. Not only had the two become bosom friends, but they were working together. "I have been seeing even more of Kipling, with whom I am writing a story in collaboration," Balestier announced to the benignant Howells. Henry James remembered that "an intimate personal alliance with Mr. Rudyard Kipling had led to his working in concert with that extraordinary genius, a lesson precious, doubtless, and wasted, like so many of his irrepressible young experiments—wasted, I mean, in the sense of its being a morning without a morrow."

That Kipling, so powerful in his craft, should accept as collaborator an amateur, even though in some ways a skillful journalist, may seem curious if we judge the collaboration with professional eyes. But such collaboration—unless it relates to hackwork—is usually an act of friendship, a partnership of the spirit, an act of love. There was also its practical side. Balestier had convinced Kipling that what the author of "The Ballad of East and West" needed to do was to write—with him—a novel of East and West. He knew the American plains and the infant towns; he knew the men of the frontier; what more charming than to transplant a full-blooded American into exotic Anglo-India. Henry James might move Americans of the eastern seaboard into the titled houses of England, but what a reach one might give the "international" novel to have an American on horseback involved with the magic and intrigue of the East! So there they were, whether in Dean's Yard or in the cottage on the Isle of Wight: Wolcott at one of those early big clumsy typewriters, Kipling pacing the floor, "each composing, suggesting, or criticising in turn, and the mind of each stimulating the other to its best work."

The story announced to Howells was the novel *The Naulahka,* and some years later Kipling included it in his collected works, as if Balestier's part of it belonged in the corpus of his own writings. It was a tribute to this magical moment, to memories that haunted him for a lifetime. If Balestier had neither the verbal endowment nor the required imagination, he had his own concretions of experience and he made the collaboration work. Reading the American's clumsily written newspaperish tales, we sense a Kiplingesque temperament which does not possess Kipling's literary power. In another incarnation the two probably would not have bothered with something as effete as literature; they might have been a couple of happy cowboys, pals of the plains, so great was their love of movement and courage and the sense of mastery of ground and sky from a galloping horse. They might also have been railwaymen feeling the power of their engine as they ran, say, the No. 14 over the range on one day and brought back the No. 3 the next. They would have played with real trains with the same delight and attention that boys play with models. Every signal, every stop, every sidetrack, every hint of danger would have been an adventure—not least the conquest of space and time.

The Naulahka makes strange reading today. It embodies all the qualities of what we have come to call the Western. Its

general burden is that woman's world is marriage and domes-
ticity and that men belong wherever high adventure is to be
lived. The opening scenes, written by Balestier, set in an American town which awaits the coming of the railroad, consist of a
long-drawn-out argument between the town's leading politi-
cian and the girl he wants to marry. She wants to be a missionary nurse in India; she is a very "manly" woman. The American
hero has no alternative but to follow her. The two Americans,
male and female, thus arrive in the world of Rudyard Kipling
—and here that master of the Anglo-Indian scene takes over.
Among the rash commitments of the hero is the promise of a
bribe to a woman who can influence a railroad president to
bring the railroad to his western town: he is certain he can
obtain a rare temple necklace, the Naulahka. The American
gallops his way through the best-written parts of the story—
Kipling's parts—in India. He is the hero of a thousand deaths.
Bullets always miss him; his own aim is deadly. Daggers are
thrown; there are plots of poison and kidnap. He is the future
Owen Wister cowboy dressed in Kipling's prose with the sensual qualities of the Indian landscape and Indian heat and smells
and long night rides rendered for us with the vividness of a
modern movie, long before the coming of the cinema. There
they were, the two collaborators, like a couple of literary Teddy
Roosevelts, "from the ends of the earth," sharing daydreams
and entering one another's fantasies, fantasies of masculine
prowess, with the glee of boys just out of school. In that sense,
Balestier was Kipling's double. Kipling looked up to him, as if
his four years' seniority gave him particular authority. Balestier
in turn looked up to Kipling, because he was a literary genius.
All this we can discern in the fruit of their collaboration. Late
in 1891, their tale done and beginning to appear in the magazines, Kipling set out on a long trip to reimmerse himself in his
India. He parted from Balestier in the full confidence that they
would meet again. Balestier was busy then with a new dream
of empire. He and Heinemann would form the firm of Heine-

mann and Balestier; they would publish continental editions. Baron Tauchnitz, who had had the field to himself, would be challenged.

In the interest of the new firm, Balestier journeyed to Dresden in November of 1891. Almost immediately Heinemann received a message from the American consul reporting that his partner had come down with typhoid. Mrs. Balestier, Caroline, and Josephine went to the bedside of the son and brother. He lingered for three weeks. Henry James and William Heinemann set out early in December, but it was no longer to attend the living. Alice James, the novelist's sister, recorded in her diary, "The young Balestier, the effective and the indispensable, dead! swept away like a cobweb, of which gossamer substance he seems to have been himself compounded, simply spirit and energy, with the slightest of fleshly wrappings."

It was a dismal moment—the mourning women, the alien cemetery in Dresden, the baroque German funeral equipage— and it all seemed strange and macabre to Henry James, with his thoughts of the "yesterday-much-living-boy." The services were read by a local chaplain. James handed to Balestier's younger sister a pot of English flowers he had brought across the channel; Mrs. Gosse had given him this bit of English earth and fragrance, and the sister let it fall into the foreign grave. As James came away, the older sister, Caroline, beckoned to him to ride with her in her carriage. They were alone in it; she wanted to talk to him. "Poor little concentrated Carrie" sat and talked in the big black and silver coach, with its black and silver footmen perched behind, dressed in her deep mourning. James found her "remarkable in her force, acuteness, capacity and courage—and in the intense—almost manly—nature of her emotion. She is worthy sister of poor dear big-spirited, only-by-death-quenchable Wolcott." James would always remember "her little vivid, clear-talking, clear-*seeing* black robed image." And he added, in a letter to Gosse, "she can do and face, and more than face and do, for all three of them, anything and

everything that they will have to meet now." He never revealed what she said to him, but an enigmatic sentence to Gosse
suggests that she may have hinted at the possibility of a marriage to Rudyard Kipling. "One thing, I believe the poor girl
would *not* meet—but God grant (and the complexity of "genius" grant), that she may not have to meet it—as there is
reason to suppose that she will. What this tribulation is—or
would be, rather, I can indicate better when I see you." We may
believe this was James's way of saying he could not believe in
such a marriage and that he hoped it might be averted. One can
believe the only "tribulation" Caroline might have had at this
moment would have been a negative word from the celebrated
storyteller to whom she had sent a cable bearing the terrible
news.

Kipling received word of Balestier's death in Lahore, to
which he had just returned. We have no record of his grief, but
we know that it was long and profound. He left promptly for
London and made the journey—difficult as it was then—in a
fortnight. Henry James wrote a long tribute; Gosse memorial-
ized Wolcott; other authors in London had elegant praise. Kipling remained silent, he who could be so articulate. What indeed could he say that would measure his grief? It is clear,
however, and so his biographer assumes, that Wolcott's death
determined him to marry Caroline. There had been some
courtship during the previous year; but there also were rumors
that its course had not been smooth. Kipling was not at ease
with women. Moreover Kipling's mother opposed the match.
She had from the first had an intuition that *"that* woman is
going to marry our Rudyard." Another plain-spoken Kipling
relative called Caroline Balestier "a good man spoiled." But
perhaps this "manliness" enabled her to become a kind of permanent stand-in for her dead brother in Kipling's life; it was
almost as if the extinguished friendship could be revived, within
the intimacy of marriage, a permanent anodyne for grief. At

any rate, Henry James, performing his role with becoming gravity, played the father and gave Caroline Balestier in marriage to Rudyard Kipling at All Souls, Langham Place, on 18 January 1892, scarcely five weeks after Wolcott's burial in Dresden. The bride was in mourning; Mrs. Balestier and the younger daughter were home with influenza. Heinemann, James, the Gosses, and one of Kipling's Poynter relatives, made up the congregation at this strange nuptial over which hung so profound a shadow. Henry James said he couldn't understand Kipling's marrying Caroline; it was "an odd little marriage." A few days later the newly married couple sailed for America.

Was it Wolcott's personal magic that gave to this particular friendship such depths and intensities? Who can say? Years later, Henry James, brooding on this, and writing every year in remembrance to Mrs. Balestier (on the anniversary of the Dresden pilgrimage), wondered what "Wolcott would have made of some of Rudyard's actualities—and what complications *that* friendship might have had to reckon with: but the mystery swallows up the question." As we review our meagre records, the memorials, the gossip, the newspaper paragraphs, we discern above all that the two men were singularly matched. It had been a meeting of Anglo-American West with Anglo-Indian East: the two "strong" men could enter into each other's lives and dreams and had a common sense of grandeur. Both had found themselves in the thick human scene of London at the very dawn of the 1890s. Both could share the memories of their lives on continents. Balestier had large plans of business empires and wealth, great coalitions of art and prosperity. Kipling had a night-dream—recorded late in life—that somehow matches. He was leading an enormous force of cavalry mounted on red horses with new leather saddles under the glare of a green moon across steppes "so vast that they revealed the circle of the earth." Kipling's imagination, we can see, was no less Napoleonic than Balestier's. They invented adventures as they invented difficulties to challenge their courage and their manliness. Kipling would say that what he liked in Americans was not only their "English instincts" but the fact that they were trained "from youth to believe that nothing was impossible." Balestier was Kipling's kind of American.

He was more. Behind a façade of exaggerated masculinity and cowboy swagger, was the attachment of the two in an age when the world of men was well-defined. Over drinks, in bars or in their clubs, men could exchange intimate feelings and stories, know, possess, a profound sense of brotherhood and union. It was the love of man for man, the hearty kind that swaps tall tales and can use language prohibited in the drawing room. Between Balestier and Kipling it was a case of camaraderie and of love, almost at first sight. Platonic, quite clearly. Both would have been terrified at any other suggestion.

NOTES

The epigraph from Coleridge is from his *Notebooks,* I (1957), edited by Kathleen Coburn. The lines from Yeats are in his poem "Among School Children," *Collected Poems* (1951), pages 212–14.

A Journey to Vienna

My recollections of this journey have been refreshed by a reading of some of my old travelogues written when I was a correspondent-at-large for the *Montreal Star,* 1928–32. For Alfred Adler, see his biography by Phyllis Bottome (1939); Lewis Way, *Adler's Place in Psychology* (1950); and Heinz L. and Rowena R. Ansbacher, *The Individual Psychology of Alfred Adler* (1956). I was indebted for my introduction to Adler to Shula Doniach, the English pianist and musicologist who was then studying in Vienna.

Stuff of Sleep and Dreams

Aside from *Biographia Literaria* I used I. A. Richards, *Coleridge on Imagination* (1935), and Kathleen Coburn, *Experience into Thought: Perspectives in the Coleridge Notebooks* (Toronto, 1979). These were Professor Coburn's Alexander Lectures, delivered at the University of Toronto the preceding year. See also Kathleen Coburn, *In Pursuit of Coleridge* (1977). Dickens's letter on dreams can be found in F. W. Dupee, *The Selected Letters of Charles Dickens* (1960), pages 177–80. For the details of hypnotism of Mrs. De la Rue, see Edgar Johnson, *Charles Dickens* (1952).

The Nature of Psychological Evidence

This paper, published in the *Journal of the American Psychoanalytic Association* (Vol. 29, No. 2 (1981), pages 447–67), under the title "The Nature of Literary Psychology," has undergone many transformations during the past ten years. The portion dealing with Conan Doyle and Rex Stout is expanded from a review of Ronald Pearsall's *Conan Doyle* (1977) and John McAleer's *Rex Stout* (1977) in *The American Scholar* (Summer 1978), pages 418–21. I used to meet Rex Stout and sat with him on committees of the Authors' Guild. See also Phyllis Greenacre, *The Quest for the Father* (1963), pages 10–12; Robertson Davies, *World of Wonders* (Penguin, 1977), page 115. I met Edith Wharton in 1931 and had several visits with her in 1936, the year before she died. My "bald statement of doctrine" at the end of this essay is derived from an earlier paper entitled "Toward a Theory of Literary Psychology," in Earl G. Witenberg, ed., *Interpersonal Explorations in Psychoanalysis* (1973), pages 343–54.

The Mystery of Walden Pond

This paper derives from my pamphlet on Thoreau originally published by the University of Minnesota Press as No. 90 of its series of Pamphlets on American Writers (1970). I extracted from this my lecture inaugurating the Citizens Chair of English and the Humanities at the University of Hawaii, 12 May 1971; the lecture was published by the University of Hawaii during that year. A revised version of the lecture appeared in *The American Scholar* (Spring 1975), pages 272–81, entitled "Walden: The Myth and the Mystery." My material was drawn from Thoreau himself and the standard works on him—Sanborn, Whicher, Canby, Krutch, Bode, and Walter Harding's *The Days of Henry Thoreau* (1965).

James Joyce

The first four sections were published in *The American Scholar* (Autumn 1980), pages 467–87, entitled "The Genius and the Injustice Collector: A Memoir of James Joyce." The section dealing with Joyce at the opera was originally a talk to the James Joyce Society in New York. The Zurich portion of this paper appeared in part as *James Joyce: The Last Journey* (1947), in the form of a small book published by the Gotham Book Mart. Other portions subsumed my reviews of the Joyce letters. I drew also on many personal observations of Joyce in Paris 1928–32, Richard Ellmann's *James Joyce* (1959), and Professor Ellmann's edition of *Joyce: Selected Letters* (1975). The fifth section was written for this book and contains material first sketched by me in "James and Joyce: The Future of the Novel," *Tomorrow* (August 1950), pages 53–56, notably my analysis of the Abin caricature.

The Madness of Art

This paper was delivered as the Benjamin Rush Lecture at the 128th annual meeting of the American Psychiatric Association, Anaheim, California, May 5–9, 1975. The lecture was published in the *American Journal of Psychiatry* (132:10 [October 1975], 1005–12). My principal sources were Benjamin Rush's *Medical Inquiries and Observations Upon Diseases of the Mind* (1812), the first book on psychiatry ever published in America. Here I found his use of the word "tristimania" to describe what we today call manic-depressive. Other works included *Letters of Benjamin Rush*, Vol. II, 1793–1813, edited by L. H. Butterfield (1951); Henry James, "The Middle Years," in Leon Edel, ed., *The Complete Tales of Henry James,* IX (1964), pages 53–76; A. Alvarez, *The Savage God: A Study of Suicide* (1972); Edward K. Brown, *Willa Cather,* completed by Edel (1953); Franz Kafka, *Dearest Father (Brief on den Vater,* 1954), pages 138–96; Quentin Bell, *Virginia Woolf* (1972), pages 40–45; Tolstoy, *Anna Karenin,* translated by Rosemary Edmonds (Penguin, 1954); R.W.B. Lewis, *Edith Wharton* (1975); Edmund Wilson, *The Wound and the Bow* (1947), and *The Twenties,* edited by Edel (1975); Marcel Proust, *Time Regained* (London: Chatto &

Windus, 1951), pages 433–34. Readers of this volume may note that this lecture consists (in part) of a summary of some of the other papers published here.

Portrait of the Artist as an Old Man

An early version of this paper was first delivered at a gerontological conference on "Human Values and Aging—New Challenges to Research in the Humanities" held in November 1975 on the campus of Case Western Reserve University. The conference was funded by the National Endowment for the Humanities. Further revised, this paper became the 1976 Helen Ross Lecture at the Chicago Institute for Psychoanalysis. The paper appeared in *The American Scholar,* Winter 1977–1978, pages 52–68, and in David Van Tassel's edition of all the papers delivered at the Case Western Reserve Conference on *Aging, Death, and the Completion of Being* (1979), pages 193–214. It has been further expanded and revised for publication in the present volume. My principal sources were Henri Troyat, *Tolstoi* (Paris: Fayard, 1965); Ernest Simmons, *Leo Tolstoy* (1946), pages 452–54; Edmund Wilson, "Notes on Tolstoy," in *A Window on Russia* (1972); Leon Edel, *Henry James: The Treacherous Years* (1969), the fourth volume of the *Life of Henry James;* Henry James, *French Poets and Novelists* (1964), pages 250–51; Leon Edel, ed., *Selected Letters of Henry James* (1955), pages 173–74; W. B. Yeats, *The Tower* (1928), page 4; Richard Ellmann, *Yeats: The Man and the Masks* (1948), pages 181–82; Edmund Wilson, *Axel's Castle* (1931), pages 57–60; Yeats, *Collected Poems* (1951), pages 281, 309, 222; Yeats, "The Bounty of Sweden," in *Autobiographies* (1955), page 541. See also Johann Peter Eckermann, *Gespracht mit Goethe in den letzten Jahren seines Leben 1823–1832,* 3 vols., 1836–48, and *Conversations with Goethe* (Everyman's Library, 1930), pages 192–93. Yeats was in Montreal for a lecture, 27–28 November 1932, and I had an opportunity for an hour's chat with him at his hotel.

Abulia and the Journey to Lausanne

This essay was written during 1980–81 for the present volume. I am indebted to Valerie Eliot's illuminating preface to the facsimile edition of *The Waste Land* (1971), which first gave me insight into the life of Eliot during the years leading to the writing of his poem. I have used also *Metamorphosis* by Ernest Schachtel (1959); Stephen Spender, *T. S. Eliot* (1976); Herbert Howarth, *Notes on Some Figures Behind T. S. Eliot* (1976); Robert Gathorne-Hardy, ed., *Ottoline at Garsington* (1974); Bernard Bergonzi, *T. S. Eliot* (1972); and Richard Ellmann, *Golden Codgers* (1973), pages 154–68. Of particular value is Dr. Harry Trosman's "T. S. Eliot and *The Waste Land:* Psychopathological Antecedents and Transformations," in *The Archives of General Psychiatry*, vol. 30 (May 1974), 709–17. The Virginia Woolf material on Eliot comes from Anne Olivier Bell, *The Diaries of Virginia Woolf*, I (1977) and II (1978). See also Louis Simpson, *Three on the Tower* (1975); Hugh Kenner, *The Invisible Poet: T. S. Eliot* (1959); and Grover Smith, ed., *The Letters of Aldous Huxley* (1969).

The Madness of Virginia Woolf

I have excerpted this section from my book *Bloomsbury: A House of Lions* (1979), the chapter entitled "The Other Face" which sorts out the different strands of Virginia Woolf's recurrent tristimania. The materials I used are drawn from Woolf's posthumous *Moments of Being* (ed. Jeanne Schulkind, 1976); Quentin Bell's life of Woolf (1972); *Sir Leslie Stephen's Mausoleum Book* (ed. Alan Bell, 1977); Mrs. Woolf's *Letters* I (Nicolson and Trautmann, 1975); and the Woolf diaries edited by Anne Olivier Bell, I and II (1977, 1978).

Wystan Auden and the Scissors Man

This essay is derived from an imaginary conversation originally used by me as an address delivered before the English

Association of Great Britain in Cambridge University in 1973. It was subsequently published in its original form in *Contemporary Approaches to English Studies* (1977), pages 38–58, and appears in its essay-form here for the first time.

A Cave of One's Own

This was originally the fourth section of my book *Literary Biography* (1957), where it was entitled "Psychoanalysis." I have rewritten the chapter for this volume and was able to use material I had originally set aside out of deference to the wishes of the late Edith Lewis, Cather's executor. My principal sources among others are the Brown-Edel life of Cather (1953); Edith Lewis's memoir, *Willa Cather Living* (1953); and E. K. Brown's *Rhythm in the Novel* (1950).

The Critic as Wound-Dresser

This portrait of Wilson was written originally after he had named me in his will as editor of his papers. I used it as introduction to the first volume of his journals, *The Twenties* (1975). I have revised portions of the essay and inserted material relevant to this book. My material is drawn from Wilson's writings, his posthumous papers, and my conversations with him during his middle years.

The James Family

The three papers dealing with members of the James family were written at different times during my work on the life of Henry James. The first, "Father and Children," was my address at Union College, Schenectady, when it conferred an honorary degree on me. Henry James, Sr., was an alumnus of this college, class of 1830; most of the materials are drawn from his writings and the letters of his children. My address on this occasion was published in the college series *Union Worthies* (No. 18) in 1963.

"The Anguish of Alice" was originally titled "Portrait of Alice James" and appeared as introduction to my edition of Alice

James's diary (1964). My revisions have been made for this volume and for the Penguin edition of the diary and have benefited from Jean Strouse's recent biography of Alice James (1980).

"The Terror of the Usual" is reprinted from my anthology of Henry James's *Stories of the Supernatural* (1970), where it served as introduction (v–xiv).

The Killer and the Slain

This experiment was called originally "Hugh Walpole and Henry James: The Fantasy of the Killer and the Slain," when it was published in *American Imago,* vol. 8, no. 4 (December 1951), pages 3–21. It has been entirely rewritten in the light of the materials on Walpole and James which I used in my life of James, Vol. 5, *The Master* (1972), in the chapter entitled "Hugh" (pages 397–409), and the letters to Walpole now in the Humanities Research Center at the University of Texas at Austin. I also, in the intervening years, was able to consult the manuscript of the novel in the possession of Sir Rupert Hart-Davis and to read portions of Walpole's diaries.

Kipling's American Double

This biographical excursion was written originally at the invitation of John Gross for his anthology of essays on Kipling published in London and New York in 1972. In that book it carries the title "A Young Man from the Provinces." My material is drawn from the obituary articles on Wolcott Balestier, particularly those of Henry James and Edmund Gosse—James's appeared as preface to Balestier's posthumous volume *The Average Woman* (1892); Gosse's in *Portraits and Sketches* (1912), pages 213–25—also Charles Carrington, *Rudyard Kipling* (1955); Arthur Waugh, *One Man's Road* (1931); and various letters of James's describing Balestier's funeral, some published in Henry James, *Letters,* III (ed. Edel, 1980).

INDEX

NOTE: The principal figures in this book, Wystan Auden, Willa Cather, Thomas Stearns Eliot, Sigmund Freud, the Jameses, James Joyce, Edmund Wilson, Virginia Woolf and Hugh Walpole are at times designated in this index by their initials.

Joyce, James *(cont.)*
97, 101–03; 107, 109, 140; *Ulysses,*
66, 73–74, 78, 87, 90, 92, 96, 97, 98,
102, 104–07, 112, 114, 122; *Finnegans Wake* (Work in Progress), 67,
74, 76–81, 86, 90, 92–94, 97, 100,
105–06, 108, 112, 114–15, 217–18,
318; "Anna Livia Plurabelle," 76–
78; "From a Banned Writer to a
Banned Singer," 67
Joyce, Nora described, 83–85; 109
Joyce, Stanislaus, 92, 108
Jung, Carl Gustav, 81, 104–05, 134,
184, 189, 218

Kafka, Franz, describes writing as
form of prayer, 127; irrational "arrest" and abulia in *The Trial,* 128–
29, 183
Kallman, Chester, 215
Keats, John, "Ode to Melancholy," xii,
136–37; 82, 217
Kemble, Frances Anne, 293
Keynes, John Maynard, 4
Kipling, Caroline Balestier, 329, 332;
described by HJ, 332–33
Kipling, Rudyard, 257, and Wolcott
Balestier, 324–35; arrives in England, 326; Balestier seeks out, K.,
327; intensity of friendship, 327–29;
collaboration with Balestier on
Naulakha, 330–32; marries B's sister Caroline, 333–34; dream of
power, 334
Knopf, Alfred, 219
Krafft-Ebing, Richard, Baron von, 92,
109, 111

Laing, Dr. R. D., 183
Lamb, Charles, 217
Landor, Walter Savage, 142
Lang, Alois, Christus at Oberammer-
gau, 5
Larbaud, Valéry, 114
Lawrence, D. H., 160; *Lady Chatter-
ley's Lover,* 213
Lauri-Volpi, Giacomo, 67, 69
LeFanu, Sheridan, 37
Léon, Paul, 74, 85
Leonardo da Vinci, 139

Levin, Harry, 78
Lewis, Edith, 232, 234
Lombroso, Césare, 127
Loring, Katharine Peabody, meets AJ,
289; relations with her, 290 *et seq;*
reinforces AJ's dependency, 291
Lowell, James Russell, 55, 59, 293

MacCarthy, Desmond, 263
Manuel, Frank, 43
Mather, Cotton, 281
Maugham, W. Somerset, *Cakes and
Ale,* 316
Maupassant, Guy de, 131, 281
Maurras, Charles, 171
Marmor, Dr. Judd, *Modern Psychoa-
nalysis,* xii
Martinelli, Giovanni, 70
McAlmon, Robert 103, 114
McClung, Isabelle: invites WC to live
in her home in Pittsburgh, 233;
marries Jan Hambourg, 233–37
McClure's Magazine, 233
Meyerbeer, Giacomo, 67, 69–71
Michelangelo, 137
Michelet, Jules, 245, 265
Millay, Edna St. Vincent, 136, and
EW, 249, 257
Milton, John, 122, 166, 190
Moissi, Alexander, 8
Monnier, Adrienne, "La Maison des
Amis des Livres," 72–77, 83, 92
Montaigne, Miguel de, 163
Moore, George, 90
Morrell, Lady Ottoline, 170, 179, 183–
85, 303
Mozart, Wolfgang Amadeus, Salzburg
Festival, 4–7, *Don Giovanni,* 4; 140
Muir, Edwin, psychoanalysis releases
poetry, 134

Napoléon, 324, 334
Navire d'Argent, Le, 77–78
New Masses, 30
Nixon, President Richard M., 23
Norton, Grace, 23

Oedipus complex, 129, 207, 218, 243–
44, 314
O'Neill, Eugene, 218

Sullivan, John, Irish tenor, at Paris Opera, 66–71
Swedenborg, Emmanuel, 271, 281, 301
Swinburne, Algernon Charles, 252

Taine, Hyppolite, 245, 265
Talmud, 20
Tecumseh, a Shawnee and his imperial ambitions, 27
Tennyson, Alfred Lord, 136–37, 201, 276
Thackeray, W. M., 201, 281–282
Thomas, Dylan, 138
Thoreau, Henry David, 1817–1862, xi, 47–65, 90, 144–46, 263, 274; on dreams, 18, 35; relations with townsfolk, 50–55; life with Emersons, 55–56; sets fire to Concord woods, 56–57; sets up hut at Walden Pond, 258; allegory of loneliness, 60–62; *A Week on the Concord and Merrimac Rivers*, 60; *Walden*, 47–49, 51, 58–62, 65
Thurber, James, 27
Tintoretto, 139
Titian, 139
Tolstoy, Count Leo, 1828–1910, xi, 96, 143–49, 156, 158, 161–62, 274; *Anna Karenin*, 130–33, 144, 241, 294; *The Kreutzer Sonata*, 146; *War and Peace*, 13, 144, 146, 280; his chronic melancholy, 146–48; "The Death of Ivan Ilytch," 133, 147; and HJ Sr., 273
transition, 77, 80, 87, 112
Tristimania. See Rush, Dr. Benjamin
Trollope, Anthony, 131
Trosman, Dr. Harry, 166, 184
Tuckey, Dr. Lloyd, uses hypnosis on AJ, 294
Turner, J. M. W., 122
Twain, Mark (Samuel L. Clemens), *Huckleberry Finn*, 4; 263

Valéry, Paul, 72
Vaux, Mary James, 287
Verdenal, Jean, TSE dedicates "Prufrock" to him, 171

Victoria, Queen, 30
Virgil, 190
Vittoz, Roger, 1863–1925: Swiss psychiatrist recommended to TSE for his abulia, 182–83; goes to Lausanne for treatment, 184–87; Vittoz's methods, 183–86; 188
Vogüé, E. Melchior de, on Tolstoy, 162
Voltaire, 97

Walpole, Hugh Seymour, 1884–1941: *The Killer and the Slain*, 109–33; ambiguous dedication of macabre novel to HJ, 309–10; love-hate situation, 315–17; problems of macho-homosexuality, 319–20; diaries of HW, 320; violence and loneliness, 322; drive to power and conflict, 322–23
Walsh, Catherine (Aunt Kate) and the Jameses, 282, 284–86, 288–89, 292
Walter, Bruno, 5
Ward, Mrs. Humphrey, 293
Warren, Austin, *The Elder Henry James*, 274–75
Watts, George Frederick, 200
Waugh, Arthur, 325–27
Weaver, Harriet Shaw, 90, 92, 98
Wells, Herbert George, 318–19
West, Rebecca, 257
Westermann, William Lynn, 232
Wharton, Edith, 1862–1937: Tale of "All Souls," 36–40; impending death, 39; loneliness as child, 40; "facilitated" life, 38; at Pavillon Colombe, 40; *The House of Mirth, The Age of Innocence, Ethan Frone*, 134; writes self out of depression, 134; 257
Whitman, Walt, 55, 176, 257, 262–63, 267
Wilde, Oscar, 97, 131, 253
Wilder, Thornton, 78
Wilson, Edmund Sr., attorney general of N.J., 242; depressive state, 242; career, 245–46
Wilson, Edmund, 1895–1972, 78, 82, 148, 241–67; meets Joyce, 100–01;

Wilson, Edmund *(cont.)*
 on Tolstoy, 148; childhood, 241;
 difficulties with parents and personal relations, 241–44; influence of
 father, 245–46; conversational style,
 247; amateur magician, 243, 247;
 sphinx-like mother, 247–48; homoeroticism, 249, 262; sexual preference for lower class women, 249; at
 Princeton, 252; reporter on *Sun*,
 254; medic in war, 253–57; Greenwich Village and Edna Millay, 257–
 59; breakdown, 259; *Philoctetes*
 seen as allegory not only of artist
 and his wound but critic as wound-
 dresser, 266–67; reportage, 264; *A
 Prelude*, 241–42, 247, 251, 255–56;
 Axel's Castle, 253, 259, 265; *I
 Thought of Daisy*, 249, 257–58; *Memoirs of Hecate County*, 241; *Patriotic Gore*, 262; *The Triple Thinkers*,
 251; *The Wound and the Bow*, 262–
 63; *The Cold War and the Income
 Tax*, 256
Wilson, Helen Mather Kimball, EW's
 mother: her deafness, 242–43, her
 practicality and gardening, 248; a
 sphinx, 248

Wilson, President Woodrow, 246
Woolf, Leonard, 189
Woolf, Virginia, 1882–1941, xii, 93,
 99, 127–29, 131, 182, 192–203, 217;
 describes TSE, 176, 179–80; dream
 of "other face," and fear of mirrors,
 192; childhood, 193; mourning and
 melancholy, 194–95; guilt and
 shame, 193–97; dissociation and
 inability to experience grief, 194–
 97; and half brothers, 198–99; love-
 hate of father, 199–202; *Mrs. Dalloway*, 195, 202; *To the Lighthouse*,
 201

Yeats, John Butler, 161
Yeats, William Butler, 1865–1939,
 xii, 12–13, 92, 93, 97, 137, 142, 150–
 63, 178, 187, 217; rage and depression at aging, 157–62; *The Tower*,
 157, *The Winding Stair*, 157, *A
 Vision*, 159; "Among School Children," 12; "Sailing to Byzantium,"
 158

Zen, 20, 185
Zola, Émile, 258

Copyright Acknowledgments

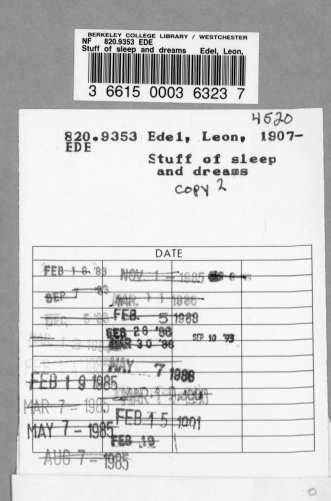